Mash
To Albert
Centre Way
Chalk Pit
Contalmaison Wood
Black Watch Alley
Contalmaison Villa
Sausage Valley
Bailiff Wood
Contalmaison
Front Line-British July 22 Sept 5
Front Line-German
Trenches dug between July 22 and Sept 5 British German
Scale of Yards
0
500
1000

On the Western Front

Eyewitness Accounts from Australians in the Great War

MICHAEL ENRIGHT

Schiffer Publishing Ltd
4880 Lower Valley Road • Atglen, PA 19310

Other Schiffer Books by the Author:
Flyers Far Away
978-0-7643-4270-7

Other Schiffer Books on Related Subjects:
WWI German Aviators
978-0-7643-1879-5
Uniforms, Equipment and Weapons of the American Expeditionary Forces in World War I
978-0-7643-2431-4

Library of Congress Control Number: 2015941288

Designed by Molly Shields
Cover designed by John Cheek
Type set in Garamond Premier Pro/Times New Roman

ISBN: 978-0-7643-4828-0
Printed in China

Published by Schiffer Publishing, Ltd.
4880 Lower Valley Road
Atglen, PA 19310
Phone: (610) 593-1777; Fax: (610) 593-2002
E-mail: Info@schifferbooks.com

For our complete selection of fine books on this and related subjects, please visit our website at www.schifferbooks.com. You may also write for a free catalog.

This book may be purchased from the publisher. Please try your bookstore first.

We are always looking for people to write books on new and related subjects. If you have an idea for a book, please contact us at proposals@schifferbooks.com.

Schiffer Publishing's titles are available at special discounts for bulk purchases for sales promotions or premiums. Special editions, including personalized covers, corporate imprints, and excerpts can be created in large quantities for special needs. For more information, contact the publisher.

Contents

ACKNOWLEDGMENTS

I am grateful to the following people:

The staff in the archives section of the Australian War Memorial, Canberra. Ian Carroll, on behalf of the Trustees of the Estate of Charles Bean, for permission to publish from Charles Bean's personal diaries, papers, and records. John Dark and the Mitchell Library, New South Wales, for permission to use the papers of Eric Dark. The late Joan Bayford and her grandson, John Bayford. Those former members of the Royal Australian Air Force who served in Europe during WWII and, who as custodians of their father's and uncles' diaries, correspondence, and memoirs from that first war, kindly granted permission for the inclusion of these hitherto unpublished materials.

Unless credited otherwise, all photographs reproduced in this book are of Australian origin and are now in the public domain. Every effort has been made to trace and secure permission from copyright holders for all material under copyright that is quoted in this book. If I have infringed upon such rights, I offer sincere apologies.

My personal thanks to John Osborne for reading the manuscript and adding his critical comments. The final work remains my responsibility and is probably the poorer for not heeding all his advice. Jemima Mills for production of the maps. Given the need to balance available space with detail, the scales given for the maps are approximate. Most of all, my thanks to Janine for the tea, sympathy, and terra firma.

INTRODUCTION

The centenary of the Great War has brought renewed interest to this first of the world wars. Although fought on a variety of fronts, it is the land war that developed in Belgium and France—on what became known as the Western Front—that has been instrumental in fashioning our thinking about this most terrible conflict.

The actions, thoughts, and reflections of these men are now consigned to history. They are beyond living memory. Because they can no longer make their point of view, much free use of their attitudes and actions has been made in recent years. The shaping of the popular image of the Great War Australian soldier in this century is beyond their control. Their passing has seen even more liberal and, at times, opportunistic political and commercial use made of their deeds.

This book contributes fresh streams of thought about those Australian soldiers who participated. It draws heavily from their personal diaries and memoirs, the vast majority never published.

Enriching their stories are the personal accounts of Charles Bean, the official Australian historian of the Great War. He was at Gallipoli, Egypt, and the Western Front. He mixed freely with the soldiers and all levels of command. His vivid accounts, drawn from his personal diaries and papers, often contrast sharply with the much more tempered official history that he oversaw and his personal diaries, papers, and correspondence for the preparation of the official history reveal a much sharper and often cutting perspective of war. As such, they are essential to this work.

Where quotations are given, two types of parentheses are sometimes included in the text. Those (thus) are parentheses used by the diarist himself. Those [thus] contain an explanation to assist the reader with idiomatic terms and any syntactical anomalies. For the most accurate maps, the reader is encouraged to refer to one of the commercially available digital trench map collections and to the excellent IGN Blue Series (Institut Géographique National: Série bleue, 1:25,000) maps.

To place the Western Front experience in perspective, the book commences with a review of Australia (and those who saw themselves as Australians) from the opening of the war in 1914. Events on Gallipoli and the subsequent expansion of the AIF in Egypt follow. These are included for they constitute key reference points to the soldiers' ultimate experiences on the Western Front.

Gallipoli deserves inclusion in this story. To have been at Gallipoli was to accord that soldier a status no other war service could achieve. April 25, 1916—the first anniversary of the Anzac landing—was already a solemn occasion. The battalions that served on Gallipoli were subsequently sent to Egypt, where they were used to strengthen new units in the rapid expansion of the Australian forces preparing for the Western Front. Egypt was where Anzac veterans met and intermingled with raw recruits fresh from Australia.

What had gone on at Gallipoli during 1915 was, for the Australians, a new standard for bravery and suffering. The Gallipoli experience would become a reference point for unimaginably cruel experiences. Yet those who survived Gallipoli and went on to France saw the Western Front as a much more horrible experience; more deadly, more frightening, more deafening, and certainly more protracted.

There is a prevailing view of the Australians during the Great War. It encompasses Gallipoli; it evokes "Anzac" as a peculiarly Australian identity. This book invites the reader to take a look through the eyes of soldiers who served in the AIF. Here is fresh ground. Given the dominant narratives and conventional wisdoms that frame views of the Western Front, combined with a substantial drift in remembrance and commemoration from that first Anzac Day in 1916, it is useful to reflect on the extent to which Australians have stayed true or strayed from the founding concepts and indeed, the primary experiences of those who were there.

Some accounts of the Great War are prone to uncritical embellishment. These tend to focus on Gallipoli, with only a recent renewal in public interest in the Western Front prompted by the 2010 recovery and reinterment of 250 of the British and Australian soldiers who died at Fromelles in July 1916.

There was much more Australian involvement in the Great War than Gallipoli, and there was much more to Australian involvement on the Western Front than just Fromelles.

In keeping with their perspective, the attribution "Great War" rather than "First World War" is used. Those who served on the Western Front had little if any idea of the wider strategic shifts, let alone the ultimate consequences, of the war. They rarely had a perspective beyond the confines of their own battalion, let alone at brigade or divisional levels. They certainly did not anticipate a repeat of war in Europe as soon as 1939. To them, this was not the first war, it was the Great War. They did not know how it would end, let alone whether they would survive.

The Great War was a century ago. The uses made of it today seem quite different from its intent at the time. Let the experiences of these soldiers take you back to its unvarnished state.

Chapter One

Europe's Road to War

How did a war of such terrible consequence—this first truly global conflict—come about?

Prewar Europe was riven with schismatic tendencies. Presiding over this were some crumbling but still potent monarchical dynasties. There had been a proliferation of secret and not-so-secret treaties and alliances. Since the eighteenth century, some European powers had also found an outlet for their ambitions beyond the European continent. They competed for colonial possessions, particularly in Africa and Asia. By the second half of the nineteenth century, the race for colonial possessions was led by the British and French, with the Dutch, Belgians, Portuguese, and Italians following. Also amongst this trailing group, and something of a late starter, were the Germans.

The British and French empires led the race for trade, profit, and prestige. To each power, the three factors seemed inextricably intertwined. The British would refer to their development of parts of Asia and Africa as "the white man's burden"; the French, perhaps more pointedly, as "*la gloire*." Each power possessed the naval strength to undertake it. By comparison, the new Germany, set as it was between the French to their west and the Russians to their east, tended toward a more continental emphasis in their attempts to make sense of their place in the world. There was tension in this sense of compression between such powerful neighbors. It manifested as an aggressive survival imperative. It was their *Sonderweg*, that "special path" between the perceived vulgarity of Western democracy and the autocratic superciliousness of the tzars that Germany would follow into 1914.

One state had been created just to ease such continental tensions. In 1830, the Belgian states had claimed independence from the Netherlands. Belgium's independence and neutrality had been guaranteed by the British, French, and Prussians in 1839. The place had seen so many battles for so long that it was known as "the cockpit of Europe." This creation of a neutral state between the French and the Germans seemed a good idea. At least the Germans had avoided trespassing on Belgian soil during the Franco-Prussian War of 1870-1871.

Europe nevertheless remained entangled in a maze of older dynastic alliances. Compounding this situation was an efflorescence of even newer treaties. Treaties perform two equally significant functions: they define who is let into an alliance, and they announce who is kept out. Just who was in and who was out with each country was becoming increasingly difficult to assess.

Great Britain and Australia

Great Britain was the pre-eminent empire. It had the largest navy and a small but very well trained professional army. This reflected its maritime orientation. It sought freedom of maneuver from the continent. Only when its empire or the sea lanes that supported it were threatened did it engage in continental affairs. Britain either ran its colonies or held a strong association with them in the more egalitarian form of dominions.

Australia had enjoyed such dominion status since Federation in 1901. Australians had committed to war with their mother country on two previous occasions: the 1899-1902 Second Boer War and the Boxer Rebellion of 1900-1901. These were not, however, profoundly defining influences on the broader Australian community. Many in Australia were dubious about participating in either action. In the case of the Boer War, there were Australians fighting on both sides. The outbreak of war with Germany in 1914 meant much more. Australians volunteered in droves.

Germany

There had been a German Confederation of nearly forty central European states and principalities since the Congress of Vienna in 1815. In a final series of Prussian-dominated skirmishes with lesser members, the German state officially came into being in 1871. That year, the Prussians gained ascendancy in the Franco-Prussian war of 1870-71. It was also the era of Otto von Bismark, Germany's first chancellor. He had employed the concept of *realpolitik*, a sort of hyper-practical if sometimes amoral default position to an extreme pragmatism, one that saw the justification of any means toward a nationally desirable end. The Germans were not the only ones to see merit in the pragmatism of *realpolitik*, but they did refine and practice it with unparalleled zeal. Since the middle of the nineteenth century, Prussian belief in the desirability of the unification of German-speaking people had manifested in strong pan-Germanic sentiments that reached as far north as Scandinavia and south to Austria and Hungary. There were ethnic as well as linguistic themes in the pan-Germanic philosophy. During the nineteenth century, Germany had become the center of much interest in extending the development of Charles Darwin's theories of evolution into "social Darwinism" and concepts of racial hygiene. Using Darwin's theories in such a way was something of an irrelevant transfer of logic.

This German extrapolation of Darwinian thought, accompanied with the appropriation of the works of philosophers such as Hegel and Nietzsche, along with the music of Wagner, would set the new German state on its special path to war. The new Germany now pursued the British and French in the imperial race. By the beginning of the twentieth century, they had established a territorial presence in parts of Africa and the Pacific. Among these was the colony of German New Guinea, just north of the Australian coastline.

The initial German experiences of colonial rule in southwest Africa had seen their first application of a frighteningly cruel response to any form of resistance: the Herero and Nama revolts of 1904-1907. The Germans were not alone in exercising colonial repression: witness the Belgians in the Congo, the French in Indochina, the Dutch in the Netherlands East Indies, and the British in India. However, the Germans had committed to something beyond just victory in an uprising or a war. They were committed to annihilation, to an "absolute destruction."[1]

Austria-Hungary

Although the Germans had failed to integrate Austria in their program of unification, the two had become close allies. Austria had also emerged as a strong state from the 1815 Congress of Vienna. In a compromise with the Hungarians in 1867, the Austro-

Hungarian Empire was created with Franz Joseph I as emperor. It was not as homogeneous as the German state. Perhaps under different circumstances the Germans could have absorbed Austria, or Austria might have absorbed Germany. By 1914, it mattered little. They were guarantors of each other's political and military excesses and adventurism. They were allies.

By the Austro-German Treaty of 7 October 1879—also known as the Dual Alliance—the two countries developed mutual obligations in the event that Russia attacked either or both. On 20 May 1882, the Austro-Hungarians, Germans, and Italians came to a secret agreement known as the Triple Alliance. This Triple Alliance was followed by an Austro-Romanian Alliance on 30 October 1883. Romania was aggrieved at the loss of southern Bessarabia to an expansive Russia in 1878. Such were the bases for so many alliances and treaties.

Italy

The Italians had been a member of the powerful Triple Alliance since its conception in 1882. This arrangement between Germany, Austria-Hungary, and Italy was renewed on 28 June 1902. Two days later, on 30 June 1902, the Italians proceeded to sign a secret treaty with the French. Eventually, Italian interest in the Triple Alliance unraveled. These arrangements would become central to what happened in August 1914. In 1915, the Italians joined the *entente*.[2]

France and Germany

The French suffered a humiliating defeat in the Franco-Prussian War of 1870-1871. Prussian soldiers briefly occupied Paris. France lost territory: the provinces of Alsace and Lorraine were occupied by the new German state. Like the Russians, the French too felt isolated. Neither country was on the best of terms with Britain. Despite historical differences that peaked in 1812 under Napoleon, the Franco-Russian Alliance of 4 January 1894 drew these two relatively distant nations closer together.

It was another alliance signalling who was in and who was out. Germany had reason to feel pressure. It saw the problem of these potential enemies to its west and its east and responded with a master plan. Within its Imperial Staff, under the guidance of Alfred Graf von Schlieffen, the Germans applied themselves to an extreme and absolute response. The Schlieffen Plan called for a lightning knockout of France through Belgium before then turning attention to the Russian front. Work on the Schlieffen Plan commenced in 1897, just three years after the Franco-Russian Alliance had been concluded.

The British Response

Now, with the realization that a combined French and Russian fleet was more powerful than their own, especially in defense of any possible threat to Asian and African interests, the British in turn responded with the Anglo-Japanese Alliance of 30 January 1902. This was designed to bring a substantial part of the Royal Navy from patrolling Asian waters back to establishing naval primacy in home waters and the Atlantic.

The intent of the British in the Anglo-Japanese Treaty was for the Japanese fleet to fill the Pacific gap. It proved an unpopular arrangement not only to the French and the Russians, but to the Australians as well, who by now were used to a reliance on the British fleet in their waters and had no desire to see an increased Japanese presence.

Subsequently, wiser heads prevailed in Paris and a cessation to the more strident colonial rivalries of the French and the British was achieved by the Anglo-French *entente cordiale* of 8 April 1904. This was significant for the new, additional pressure—real or otherwise—brought to bear on the Germans about the intentions of the British, French, and the Russians. German rumblings only served to convince Britain that Germany would one day constitute a real threat on the continent. These British fears of German intentions hastened them to conclude yet another treaty, the Anglo-Russian Agreement of 31 August 1907.

Many of these alliances and treaties were proclaimed by their signatories to be free of martial intent. This was not the case. The Anglo-French Naval Agreement of November 1912, like most of the other treaties, served a military purpose. German expansion of its fleet, which developed into an Anglo-German naval arms race, worried both France and Britain.

There were many more treaties and alliances. Those mentioned above were the most significant. Of themselves, they were not the cause of war as much as they were a manifestation of anxiety about national sovereignty and imperial ambition. The treaties were not just about mutual continental protection. They often concerned themselves more with the maintenance of spheres of influence in Africa and Asia. The Franco-Italian Agreement is an example. It referred as much to a careful subdivision of a part of North Africa as it referred to matters on the continent. France agreed to keep Morocco, and the Italians confined themselves to Libya.

By 1914, the situation had achieved considerable clarification. There was the entente, led by Britain, France, and Russia. Then there was the Central Powers: Germany and Austria-Hungary. Those nations yet to be convinced were left to waver between these two camps.

To War

Whilst it has been found convenient to attribute one simplistic cause for the war, it is more realistic to see several. They lie in a mixture of militarism, nationalism, colonialism, and increasing tension throughout Europe about the growing pan-Germanic sentiment. The assassination of Archduke Franz Ferdinand—the heir to one of Europe's "iron thrones," the Habsburgs—by a Bosnian Serb in Sarajevo on 28 June 1914 may have been seen as the cause of the war, but matters ran much deeper than the death of an archduke.[3]

Several little wars preceded that of 1914. Between 1905 and 1914, there had already been much belligerence and localized fighting: two Moroccan Crises (1905-06 and 1911), the Turkish-Italian War (1911-12), the Anglo-German race for naval supremacy (1889-1913), two Balkan wars (1912-early 1913 and again in mid-1913), two Albanian crises (both in 1913), and the Liman von Sanders Affair of 1913-1914, by which a German general was appointed to the Turkish War Council and given command of the Turkish 1st Army in Constantinople when Turkey was still officially a neutral country.

On 1 August 1914, Germany declared war on Russia. On 3 August, it declared war on France. The next day, Germany invaded neutral Luxembourg and Belgium in its drive toward Paris. On that day, 4 August 1914, Britain declared war on Germany.

Chapter Two

AUSTRALIA

On Being Australian

Australia is in the unusual position of having undergone a federation of its individual colonies without a war. In 1901—the year it became a federation—a census was taken. It counted a population of around 3.7 million. The next census, in 1911, is the closest we have to the commencement of the Great War. Australia's population was now 4.45 million.[4] Much of that considerable increase was due to migration from Britain.

How "Australian" was this population? Whatever being Australian meant appears to have been in development. It still is today. In 1911, nearly 600,000 were British-born.[5] A further estimated 2.6 million were the sons and daughters of British migrants. That means over seventy-seven percent of the population were British-born or born of British parents.[6] Most of the remaining thirteen percent of the population were of British descent.

Unlike their convict predecessors, these British-Australians were here by choice. They were colonials and they were—as were all Australians—not only Australians, but also British subjects. Just when Australia became self-governing is debatable, but it was not at federation in 1901.[7] That only permitted the population to exist as a "self-governing colonial federation." Her membership in the British Empire had not expired and, like other members of the empire—India, Canada, and New Zealand, for example—Australia was at war when Britain was at war. Real nationhood, depending on how it is defined, was probably no earlier than 1931.[8] All passports held by Australians were marked as British passports. It would be 1949 before the first Australian passports were issued to Australians.

At the beginning of the twentieth century, these Australians were generally healthier and more robust than their counterparts in Britain. Perhaps they had to be to make the trip. Perhaps a land at the other end of the world attracted those of a particular disposition. The demand for labor in Australia attracted many Britons from the dimmer prospects they faced at home. They were better fed, more likely to be employed, and enjoyed a longer life expectancy than in Great Britain. Collectively, they were also in search of cultural and experiential markers for a brand new national identity. To the majority, Britain was nevertheless "home," real or imagined. Correspondence with relatives and talk of home towns flourished and for some, a chance to visit relatives was the ultimate pilgrimage.

In 1914, on the eve of war, Australia was economically dependent on Britain, more concerned about Japanese movement in the Pacific than Germans on the European continent, still using British bank notes and coins along with the new local currency, firmly of the belief in their fundamental egalitarianism and an emerging cult of "mateship," and ensconced in a rigid immigration system.[9]

It was not just the Germans who were influenced by social Darwinism. Newspapers and books of the time commented openly of the "British race" or the "Anglo-Saxon race," which was a broader term designed to include the United States. One of the first acts of the new Australian parliament was to pass the Immigration Restriction Act of 1901. It was a "White Australia" policy.

The Australian Military Situation

There was a militia raised in each of the colonies. After federation, a more centralized approach was undertaken. The first national army came into being on 1 March 1901, and was known as the Commonwealth Military Forces (CMF). It comprised a subsidized militia (for which members received pay), a series of volunteer forces, and a cadre of permanent, full-time soldiers. At the outbreak of war in 1914, the call to arms created a new group of volunteers, adding yet another layer to this complex organization. They were known as the Australian Imperial Force (AIF) and they had a remit to serve abroad.

The AIF certainly had representations from the other, earlier forces, but it overwhelmingly comprised civilians who, but for the outbreak of war, would not have considered a career in the military. This is central to understanding some of the characteristics for which the Australians became well known on the Western Front in particular. This AIF name, and the characteristics it displayed, seems to have gained primacy over all others. Even after 1916, when another government committee changed the title to the "Australian Military Forces," it was the "AIF" by which they were commonly known.[10]

There was anxiety over the withdrawal of the British Fleet and recurring fears of invasion by Japan and further meddling (or worse) from a growing German naval and colonial presence in the Pacific. In 1909, the Australian government invited Field Marshall Lord Kitchener to consult on the military situation. During his visit to Australia, Kitchener pressed for a Royal military college and appears to have been instrumental in coalescing various political and pressure group parties into the drafting—on a national basis—of youths into a compulsory period of military training.

The system got underway on 1 January 1911. Three groups were involved. Boys turning twelve went to the junior cadets. Those turning fourteen to eighteen went to senior cadets and those between eighteen and twenty-six went to the Citizen Military Forces. All three categories were for part-time training. Exemptions were granted to the ill, unfit, and theology students, those inhabiting designated isolated areas, and those in a very few other sundry occupations. The only other way out was evasion. Fines were imposed on those who were caught (or their parents). Such avoidance was not, however, as popular as doing your service. In this way were civilians at least conversant with military doctrine.[11]

By 1914, the vast majority of Australians were attuned to the notions of race, war, and loyalty to the mother country. It was, however, a position involving contradictions. Australia was a world away from Britain, but the mother country was everywhere: from framed rural prints over the fireside, to good Sheffield cutlery, letters, relatives, and a common language. As the Australian historian Bill Gammage so eloquently put it:

> They vaunted their sunlit land, and drew snowmen on Christmas cards. They proclaimed their achievements in sport, and feared whether the British race degenerated in the Antipodes. They heralded a new society, and venerated the English King. They were "independent Australian Britons," defenders of the white race in the Pacific, volunteers to die in the defence of the ideals they had chosen.[12]

Charles Bean

Because this book makes extensive reference to the writings of Charles Bean, some background to the man is given here. Bean was born in Bathurst, New South Wales, in 1879. His family moved to England ten years later. During his time abroad, he developed a fascination with reliquary, possibly initiated by a visit to the Waterloo battlefield. In 1904, Bean returned to Australia. Bean worked as a lawyer in the rural circuits of New South Wales. After several minor publications, Bean joined the *Sydney Morning Herald* as a reporter in 1908. In August 1914, he was chosen by fellow journalists to be Australia's official war correspondent. He was in Egypt, then Gallipoli, then the Western Front.

As the official war correspondent, he had access to nearly every level of the AIF and he used this opportunity to maintain a daily account of events. He amassed over 286 personal diaries, folders, and notebooks. It was intimated to Bean that he might be appointed after the war to write the official history of Australia's involvement. In 1919, his dual proposals that he write the official history and that a memorial museum be established were realized.

Between 1921 and 1942, he oversaw the publication of the twelve volumes of the Australian official history. He was the series editor and the author of six of the volumes; those dealing with Gallipoli and the Western Front.

Although Bean appears to have seen himself as a "British" Australian, as did so many Australians, he never displayed any class consciousness from his time in the smaller geopolitical orbits of life in England. He would more than once decline a knighthood—a most unusual decision for a man of his background and time.

Bean can be read at different levels and from different perspectives. His twelve-volume official history is just one of these. His diaries are much more personal and they stand as a remarkable eyewitness record of events alongside the personal accounts from the soldiers themselves. Whilst accessible in the archives of the Australian War Memorial in Canberra, there is very little published material using these sources. They are writings made on the spot and are often very difficult to decipher, especially as Bean occasionally used two forms of shorthand: one is the old Pittman reporter code and the other is personal shorthand that gradually reveals its meaning after repeated readings and deciphering.[13] Reference is made to these personal diaries in later chapters.

Whilst Bean saw Australia as a place in quest of identity, he was not the only writer to feel confronted with an Australia coming to terms with nationhood at a time when it was still bound up in the ambivalence of being part of Britain. The bush poet and writer Andrews "Banjo" Patterson did as much in his reportage of the Boer War.[14] Like Henry Lawson—another famous Australian literary figure—Patterson guided his thoughts through the presumably distinctive characteristics of rural values, cynicism of authority, and an omnipresent and yet-to-be answered question: just what is "Australia" in the 1900s and how should Australians make sense of their universe?

These were not themes owned or generated by Bean, Lawson, or Patterson, any more than they were those that resonated amongst Australians themselves.[15] The imagined community of Australians as resourceful, egalitarian, mentally and physically robust, and possessed of a sense of initiative predates federation and the outbreak of the Great War. It certainly predates Bean's writings. This point is important, given the treatment of Bean in recent scholarship.

In reviewing Bean's twelve volumes of the official history, one author has described them as detailed to the point of being almost boring, but unerringly accurate.[16] They were, after all, official histories, and Bean's postwar correspondence with survivors of various actions is testament to the forensic style he employed getting the stories accurately recorded.[17] By contrast, Bean's personal diaries are far more fluid, much more personal and, in these ways, very much in the style of the other firsthand accounts used here.

War in history was by no means as popular a subject during the 1930s and 1940s as it has become today. Bean himself reminds us of this in the foreword to *Anzac to Amiens*—a sort of synopsis of the official history—which was published in 1946, after yet another world war. He wrote:

> There is little fear that a short history, written largely for teachers and school libraries, will meet today among teachers the disapproval which it would have met for many years after the First World War. Not that the detestation of war was then greater than now; but there was a widespread feeling, not merely that military operations had bulked too largely in history—which is true, despite the immense influence of wars on almost every phase of human development—but that, by sustaining a pride in the military efforts of our countrymen, the history of war encouraged war.[18]

It is from Charles Bean's personal diaries, folders, and notebooks that we turn for occasional reference. In conjunction with the firsthand diaries and memoirs of Australians at war that shape this book, along with some extracts from the original divisional and battalion war diaries, a richer context of war on the Western Front is found.[19]

August 1914

On 1 August 1914, Germany declared war on Russia. The following day, the Germans issued an ultimatum to the Belgian king, demanding free passage of German troops. This was also the day the Germans invaded Luxembourg. The next day, Germany declared war on France. Early in the morning of 4 August, the first advance parties of German troops crossed into Belgium. An hour before midnight on 4 August, Britain responded with a declaration of war with Germany. At about that time, it was already mid-morning of 5 August in Australia's capital, Melbourne. The city is situated at the northern end of a bay forming a rough circle of water before giving onto the southern oceans through a narrow opening between two headlands at its southern end. At 7:45 a.m., the German ship *Pfalz* left her moorings by the city at Victoria Dock, heading south down the bay in the company of a pilot who would guide the ship through the treacherous waters between the headlands. News of Britain's declaration of war seems to have been confirmed around midday. By this time, the *Pfalz* was just beyond the headlands. A radio message was received, ordering the ship to return to port. A short struggle between the pilot and the German captain was followed by a shot across her bow from the neighboring fort at Point Nepean. The ship returned to moorings inside the bay.

The British were not yet in a shooting war with Germany. It is highly likely that this shot—the first and only shot in the Great War fired on Australian soil—was also the first to be fired by British forces in the Great War.

The AIF

The recruitment for the AIF began in early August 1914. A division was raised in quick order. The 1st Division was composed of 12,000 troops in three brigades, with each brigade made up of four battalions. Also included in this new 1st Division was a light horse brigade. A full-strength Australian infantry battalion comprised around 1,000 men. The men identified with the battalion level; it was the battalion one served more than the AIF and it was the battalion's reputation that meant the most. There were good and bad battalions. Reputations could be earned unfairly.

On 1 November 1914, a convoy of twenty-six ships carrying the Australian contingent and fourteen carrying the New Zealanders assembled off the Western Australian coast and departed for England via the Suez Canal.[20] Whilst at sea, they received news that Turkey had joined the war on the side of the Central Powers. The convoy never reached its destination. The troops disembarked in Egypt and set up camp outside Cairo. It is unclear whether Turkey's entry into the war or the parlous state of the facilities in England—already crowded with Canadian troops—was the real reason for the change in plan. It probably had something to do with both.

The Australian experience of training in Egypt forms an important part of this story. Because it covers a period that both precedes and follows Australian participation in the Dardanelles campaign, it has been reserved for chapter four. We now move directly to the Dardanelles Campaign. How did the Australians who were being shipped to France become involved on the eastern shores of the Mediterranean?

Station Pier, Melbourne, sometime during 1915 or 1916. Soldiers board the troopship A 40 HMAT *Ceramic*. Officers in peaked caps file forward to the gangplank. Enlisted men crowd the end of the pier. Others, nearly all officers, relax in the foreground with their kit, waiting to be called. [*Australian War Memorial*, hereafter, *AWM*]

Chapter Three

The Dardanelles Campaign

Events on the Western Front and the Rationale for the Dardanelles Campaign

The decision to attack the Dardanelles is directly linked to the developing situation on the Western Front. There the war had ground to a halt. The Germans' Schlieffen Plan had proved to be what it always really was: an ideological doctrine rather than an actionable plan. Its inherent flaws had seen a rapid war of movement bog down to such an extent that the Germans had actually retreated in some places. They consolidated on a line that represented the most they could hold. That line came to be known as the Western Front.

That Western Front line also represented the most that the French—and the much smaller British and Belgian forces—could defend, and in some rare instances, such as the Battle of the Marne east of Paris and small sections of the Ypres salient to the north in Belgium, could re-take.[21] The thrust of the initial sweeping battles had quickly diverted into a kind of lateral race to secure positions stretching from the English Channel to the Swiss border.

This stalemate was well established by late 1914. The war of movement had lasted perhaps twelve weeks. The Entente powers argued over what to do. The Germans were by now also engaged in a war to the east with the Russians. The failure of the Germans to quickly remove the French from the war saw the emergence of the dreaded double front that the Schlieffen Plan had promised to avoid. Chronically short of food and materiel, the Germans nevertheless kept a war going on each front.

The Russians were suffering heavy losses in the east. They appealed for help from the other Allied powers.[22] This came in the form of a diversionary plan to take the entrance to the Black Sea, which was separated from the eastern end of the Mediterranean by a narrow stretch of water known as the Dardanelles. This was Turkish territory. It was hoped the opening of the Black Sea would permit supplies to reach the beleaguered Russians, divert German strength away from the Western Front, force their eastern adventures to falter, and stop the Turks from expanding toward the east bank of the Suez Canal.

Winston Churchill, then First Lord of the Admiralty, has attracted much of the blame for the disastrous Dardanelles campaign. Although not without misgivings, Lord Kitchener—a confirmed "westerner" who wanted little to do with resource-sapping "easterner" plans for the Mediterranean—approved the idea.[23] Kitchener also found tentative agreement with a man who reported to Churchill, the First Sea Lord, Admiral John "Jackie" Fisher. Kitchener favored a purely naval assault, as did Fisher.[24] A naval bombardment of Turkish fortifications at the entrance to the Dardanelles failed to open the straits to the Black Sea. Subsequently, Churchill pressed for an amphibious landing.[25] An army was committed to securing beach heads, then moving inland and securing a strategically significant part of the Dardanelles—the Gallipoli Peninsula—in a land battle.[26] The Australian and New Zealand forces in Egypt were sent to join the campaign.

Gallipoli

An initial expeditionary force of 70,000 men was raised for the land campaign at the Dardanelles. Kitchener appointed Sir Ian Hamilton to command this hastily prepared force, which by the last week of April 1915 was positioned off the entrance to the Dardanelles. Kitchener had provided Hamilton with military intelligence, but it was sketchy and outdated. The interval between the failure of the naval bombardment during the preceding weeks and the main force landings of 25 April 1915 had seen the repair and strengthening of Turkish positions by the resident German Gen. Liman von Sanders. The Turks were well aware of the Allies' poorly concealed intentions.

British raiding parties had actually set foot on either side of the Dardanelles to complete destruction of some gun emplacements and forts during February and March, but they had withdrawn quickly. Hamilton—apparently unaware and uninformed of the strengthening of the defenses—was about to commit to an amphibious assault. The majority of the soldiers were British and French. The Australians and New Zealanders, commanded by the British Indian Army Gen. Sir William Birdwood, were aggregated into the new Australian and New Zealand Army Corps (Anzac) for the operation. Numbering over 16,000, they constituted a small portion of the Allied force.

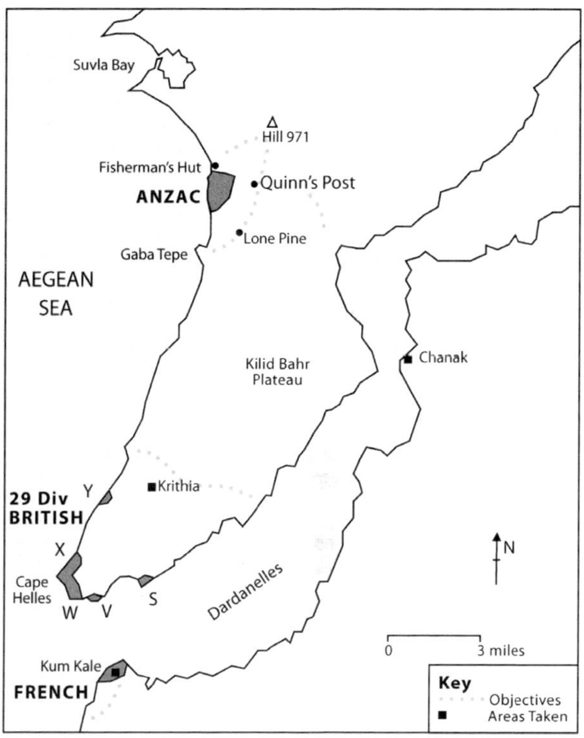

The Dardanelles Campaign

The 25 April Landings

There were three main landings on 25 April, one of which involved the Anzac contingent. Whilst the British set their 29th Division ashore at Helles, on the southern tip of the peninsula, the French made landings on the other side of the Dardanelles on

Gaba Tepe, just south of the Anzac landing area on Gallipoli. This is the remains of D Company, 1st Battalion, at morning roll call on 30 April 1915, five days after the landing. They had gone ashore at Anzac Cove on 25 April and into action with a strength of six officers and 213 other ranks. By 29 April, the muster was one officer and eighty-eight other ranks. *AWM*

Asia Minor proper, at Kum Kale. The Anzac wave landed about halfway up the west coast of the Gallipoli peninsula at first light. They had been put ashore in the wrong place—about a mile north of the intended beach that would have given on to low hinterland.

Instead, they found themselves in a small cove with a very narrow beach bordered with high cliffs and ravines. This was hardly the ideal place for a landing.[27] By 8:39 a.m. there were 8,000 men ashore, and by 4:30 p.m. this had risen to 13,000.[28] By the end of the day, at least 1,800 wounded Anzacs had been evacuated to the larger ships that had brought them to the peninsula. Perhaps another 1,000 or more were dead. The figures on that chaotic day have never been satisfactorily reconciled. The most accurate official estimate is for the period 25 April to 3 May: 8,500 casualties. This includes 600 from the Royal Naval Division involved in getting the boats to shore and the wounded out. More wounded remained on duty and are not included in this figure. Within those 8,500 casualties in those first nine days at Gallipoli were 2,300 dead Australians and New Zealanders.[29]

As the weeks wore on, more troops were landed, crowding the beach and the steep slopes in the unbearably hot sun. Water had to be transported from offshore. Aside from the battle casualties, thousands fell ill with dysentery. Hordes of flies covered everything, including the thousands of unburied, rotting corpses of both sides. An occasional truce would be called so that some of the dead could be buried, but even they could be exhumed in the process of subsequent trench digging. Pvt. Apcar de Vine—a British-born soldier now living in Sydney—was serving with the Australian 4th Battalion. He wrote in his diary during May:

Gallipoli. A cross section of Australian soldiers. Some are well into their thirties, a couple barely in their twenties. They are on water carrying duties. There is more variety of attire amongst these six men than would be found in a regiment of British soldiers. Headgear ranges from a pith helmet to a cap, to two styles of broad-brimmed issue hat and, at rear, what appears to be a civilian item. They rest in a relatively level part of the track surrounded by steep terrain that characterized the topography of the peninsula. *AWM*

The Nek, Gallipoli, 24 May 1915. With barely a month's fighting underway, both sides recognize the need to bury the dead. Bodies rapidly decompose in the hot conditions and the stench at this place would be unbearable. A cease-fire has been arranged. Both Australian and Turkish soldiers tend to their dead, burying them as quickly as possible in shallow graves. *AWM*

> Our new firing line ..... is a most gruesome sight ..... as they have made it under where all the Light Horse bodies are lying, and just on the parapet of the trench may be seen legs, heads, and bodies of our men.[30]

Reinforcements

The battle dragged on. More reinforcements were landed. In the early hours of Sunday, 5 September, Australian farmer Captain William James was amongst those hurriedly

Gallipoli Peninsula, 1915. An Australian trench at Lone Pine. The parapet is lined with the decomposing bodies of at least two Australian and possibly one Turkish dead. Webbing and a pannikin can be seen hanging from a bayonet driven into the trench wall. The officer is Capt. Leslie Morshead, who subsequently served with distinction on the Western Front. The standing soldier looking directly at the camera is Pvt. James Bryant of the 8th Battalion. He would reenlist as a lieutenant in 1939 and spend three years as a prisoner of the Japanese at Changi in Singapore. *AWM*

transported to the shores of Anzac Cove as part of the 24th Battalion. That day he wrote in his diary:

> …ship's people very anxious to get us off as they are mortally afraid of shelling commencing at daybreak ….. [I] wonder if I will be a coward under fire. Got away on lighters at about 4.45am ….. We marvel at the [original] landing, many of the hills are as steep as it is possible for hills to be and would appear impregnable.[31]

They were quickly moved to a hotly contested area the next day:

> Orders to move up to Quinn's Post. Move the battalion at 10a.m. C Coy [Company] on Quinn's Post. A & B Coys on Street's Post. The men of the old regiments appeared completely worn out ….. We occupy trenches seven feet deep about 100 to 200 yards from the Turkish Trenches ….. Several of our fellows were lying out in front. The form of fighting is a surprise. Find that the trenches are held by sniping from selected posts by snipers, and by throwing bombs at night. Not a head can be seen in front.

In the absence of the battalion's commanding officer, who was still offshore, James had been given responsibility for the bulk of the battalion. This was by no means the open warfare James had been trained for in the militia before the war. It told on the troops' nerves:

> Three men wounded, two of them self-inflicted. These men will have to be court-martialed when they return, as these wounds have been too numerous.

They had been there for all of four days. On Friday, 10 September, he recorded in his diary:

> Ordered to Lone Pine to take instruction from old hands, as this position was only won on August 6th at great cost and is a forward salient. We have to relieve

> the old 7th Battn [Battalion], who are to leave for a spell. The Trenches are only five yards apart in places, and necessitate constant bombing and sniping from both sides. Out in front bodies of our men and also the Turks lie unburied just as they fell. It is astonishing how cheap is life in Wars. No one takes any notice of the fact except that burying parties are occasionally sent out at night to try and recover our own bodies. These are buried after the identity discs are recovered. What were previously saps [communication trenches generally running from a previous front line to the current front line] are sandbagged up at the mouth and are full, in many instances, of the bodies of our men and the Turks.

Battle Temperament

The 24th Battalion stayed at Lone Pine for most of the second half of September. It was exhausting and distressing. Capt. James' diary entries for the period graphically portray the horror of being shelled and shot:

> Getting used to the smells and the dead bodies which protrude at various points. ..... Tippett of B Coy died from result of shell yesterday morning. Poor little Tippett. He was a good fellow. Poor old Usher was hit in the afternoon and died gamely. Mick Sunderland also hit on Snipers' Post. Three good men in one day ..... Heavy bombardment. Walker's arms cut off by piece of iron plate which was struck by shell. He walked out to the dressing station. Webb from B Coy had his head blown clean off, the most ghastly sight.

Rarely do diaries reveal such appalling accounts of shattered and dead men. Such experiences affected the minds of others:

> Jack _______ cracked up, could see Webb being killed over again. Poor old Jack.

James had been ill with dysentery for some time and was eventually taken off the beach at Anzac Cove to recover. He was discharged—apparently still unfit for duty—and was returned home to Australia. He reenlisted and returned to France in 1917.

Just as men could be sickened by the death and general corruption of human bodies, so they could also be aroused to contribute to it. As one soldier recorded:

> We charged three hills that night ..... I bayoneted a Turk who was feigning death ..... He was an oldish man & on the first thrust which did not go right home he tried to get his revolver out at me, but failed ..... a gigantic Turk ..... grabbed me ..... and slowly began to crush the life out of me, I was almost gone when a mate of mine called Tippen came up & bayoneted him ..... We made sure of him and then continued up the hill. Poor Tippen got shot just in front of their trench in the stomach with two bullets, he died groaning horribly. I killed his assailant however by giving him five rounds in the head. I ..... let him have it full in the face. It was unrecognisable.[32]

Reinforcements continued to arrive at Anzac Cove to replace the dead, wounded, and sick. Cpl. Leonard Jones was one of the 3rd Battalion reinforcements landed at

A section of a hill above Anzac Cove during 1915. The Australians have dug sandbag-reinforced revetments into the steep terrain. Clothing dries on a makeshift line while other pieces of kit and equipment are laid out neatly in the sun. *AWM*

Anzac Cove on 3 November. He was born in Coventry, England, in 1893, and as a teenager had spent six months at sea, including a voyage that had taken them through the Dardanelles to Poti, at the far eastern end of the Black Sea. He recalled of those pre-war adventures: "how difficult the ship was to steer up that tortuous channel."[33] Now, by strange circumstance, he was an Australian soldier and back in the Dardanelles, being set down at Anzac Cove:

> There were lights on the hillside and except for some isolated rifle fire that sounded queerly among the gullies, all was quiet. We spoke in whispers, bundled into lighters, shoved on to a pier and sat down on the beach. A guide met us, a gaunt digger dressed in bits of everything and took us to Shrapnel Gully where we camped as we sat in the scrub. Next morning a "ric" [ricocheting shell] bounced over the top and fell among us.

They were quickly set to work on supply duties to the forward trenches. Jones was assigned to D Company:

> In the late afternoon orders came to move and in small parties we made our way to Shell Green where some Indians [troops] with mules were unloading cases of

> S.A.A. [small arms ammunition] up to the Bn [Battalion]. There were many interested onlookers. Up the hill I staggered. Johnnie Turk [the Turkish soldiers] must also have been interested and although I didn't realize it at the time we went through quite a tidy strafe along Artillery Road. I hazily remember a commotion and various explosions. I saw a man come out of a dugout and say something then, half his face and the top of his head seemed to be missing. Thought it time to hurry.

Having reached the battalion lines, they dumped their cases and settled into a support trench immediately behind the firing trench:

> Had some tea, rolled up and slept. The old hands took us quite casually and were mostly interested in details of Home and Cairo. Our officers were rubbing their hands with glee. Here was good digging and fatigue [working party] material.

By this stage in the campaign, the advance had well and truly been halted. Jones again:

> We saw no fighting. It was stalemate, but we were fitting into things well ….. How quickly men deteriorated on Gallip. [slang for Gallipoli]. A wash was not heard of. And the lice. A lot of "old" hands had dysentery. One man I knew had a top coat and a shirt. The remainder of his clothing had had to be discarded as well-soiled linen. I pulled him off the latrine one night dead. He had persistently refused to parade sick.

As a signaller, Jones spent considerable time in the support lines, usually with commanding officers. He was nevertheless witness to the filth and horror experienced by the Australians pinned down in territory over which the enemy had a relatively clear view. Wherever possible trenches were dug, deepened, and extended, making a troglodyte world for the Australians. Those on the harsh slopes and gullies that ran inland from the narrow line of beach scraped out shelters reinforced with discarded tins and packing boxes.

In the absence of adequate supplies, pilfering and thieving were rife. Parcels from home were quickly picked up—in his case by anyone else with the same surname—and consumed. Jones caught a soldier that had taken his parcel. By then all that remained was a pipe. He did not have the heart to "crime" him.[34] The thief had been there much longer and probably needed the food more than him. Unattended packs were ransacked. They picked chalk out of the earth for toothpaste.

There was a considerable compression of the front line, with the support trenches and the rear areas on Gallipoli. The terrain was too steep, too unyielding for anything else. Later, on the Western Front, such compression would relax into much deeper systems, where sometimes miles separated the rear areas from the front line.

There was always a bit more decorum, a bit more civility, in the battalion and brigade headquarters (HQ).Yet casualties could be high. Although not quite as fully developed at Gallipoli as on the Western Front, this was an artillery war. Artillery was killing more men than bullets. As Jones put it:

> The Sig. sec. [Signals section] had been sadly depleted at Lone Pine, in common with the rest of the Bn [battalion], but there were several "dinkum" sigs. left

> and the others quickly were learning the ropes ….. Being near HQ, men had to be reasonably orderly, sober and well – decent.

Writing in November to his family in Adelaide, South Australia, Robert Raws—another English migrant now serving with the 23rd Battalion—observed of his fellow officers:

> Over half of our original officers have either gone away sick or are no more with us. There is considerable feeling against some officers who go away without sufficient reason. An officer, if he cares to pull the strings sufficiently, can usually get away.[35]

These somewhat contrasting views of Australian soldiers can be further complicated by the previously noted concept of "mateship." Mateship is by no means the egalitarian ideal it purports to be. Much has been made of it as a peculiar form of hybridized brotherhood. It is a revered concept in Australia today, just as much if not more than it was at Gallipoli and the Western Front. Mateship, if it can be egalitarian, can also be quite clannish. It is called upon as a firm piece of moral ground far more often than it has been properly defined. It never will be properly defined, for it exists in a variety of forms. An Australian infantry captain explains one of its more enduring meanings:

> Put this flour in your Dixie old man and make my pancakes with yours, will you? Lend us yer fire after you mate. Usin' that bit er fat, I'm short of a piece, let's have it will yer' ….. The trench is no place for a selfish natured man where almost everything is common property, just for the asking.[36]

Here was the Anzac legend in the making. There was certainly something about these troops. Whatever it was exactly has been transmitted down the years and become the stuff of legend and, in turn, become legend's ultimate manifestation: mythology. There are three important points to be made about that mythology. First, it tends toward an uncritical appreciation of the Anzacs, something which this book seeks to balance. They were not gods. Second, there is a pronounced tendency for "Anzac" to mean "Australia." This is certainly the case in Australia. The New Zealanders, through no fault of their own and with no malice intended, are rather left out of the picture. As this story is about Australians, it will concentrate on them, but with the important caveat: that "Anzac" really means New Zealanders as well. Third, the mythologizing of the Anzacs was not, as is often suggested, the sole work of the Australian official historian Charles Bean.[37] Bean was at Gallipoli, where he was wounded. Whilst his writings have been used in the construction of the Anzac legend, he also admonished the Australians for their conduct in Cairo and reported the loitering, as well as the advances on the battlefield at Gallipoli.

The Anzac legend was just as ably constructed by British observers who were noticing the unique style of discipline and courage of these Australians. Watching an Australian 2nd Brigade attack on the Krithia Spur at Helles, a British major wrote:

> The enemy's shelling was shifted onto them in one great concentration of hell. The machine-guns bellowed and poured on them sheets of flame and of ragged

> death, buried them alive. They were disembowelled. Their clothing caught fire, and their flesh hissed and cooked before the burning rags could be torn off or beaten out. But what of it? ..... They were not men but gods, demons infuriated ..... Not for one breath did the great line waver or break.[38]

This military prowess certainly did not come from a British-style top-down rigid rank system. The Australians wore what appeared to others—especially the British—a particularly ill-fitting uniform and often displayed evidence of wearing it less formally or half removed in hot conditions. They were not in the habit of being deferential to superiors in general or the British in particular. They did not polish buttons, nor shine boots or buckles.

Who were these Australians? As was noted earlier, ninety percent of them were either British immigrants, sons of British immigrants, or of British descent. They nevertheless made a point of being noticed for being different. It is ironic. It was they who had left for more adventurous lives in a hot, dry country at the other end of the world, yet on their attestation papers can be seen, almost universally, "natural born British subject."

Stalemate

By November, the hot, dry weather that had parched the battle zone gave way to a once in a lifetime snow blizzard. Men froze at their posts. Trenches and dugouts—always kept scrupulously clean in the heat to reduce the sanitary dangers of heat, excreta, and the piles of dead, which were all thrown out beyond the parapets or became part of them—now wallowed with snow and slime. The decision was made to evacuate the Gallipoli peninsula:

> As far as the Anzac troops were concerned, the only thing to be said for the military operation was that it kept them away from the Western Front for at least a year. Had they arrived in France in early 1915 their casualty list (as operations around Pozieres would subsequently prove) would certainly have been much higher than it was at Gallipoli.[39]

Probably over 66,000 Turks died defending their territory. It is estimated that 410,000 British and Commonwealth troops were landed during the campaign. A further 70,000 French had also landed. Of these 480,000 troops, 252,000 became casualties.[40] Of these casualties, 26,111 were Australian and of these Australians, 8,141 were killed.[41] In the eyes of those at home, only the Australians had played a significant role; a perception that persists today. They represented but a small proportion of the international Allied forces involved.

The failure of the Gallipoli campaign forced Churchill to resign. Adm. Fisher had already resigned in disgust on 15 May 1915. On 5 June 1916, Kitchener perished at sea whilst on a mission to Russia, when the naval vessel he was a passenger on struck a mine. It is unlikely the Gallipoli campaign—for the Australians or for the much larger contingents of troops from other nations—altered the course of the war. It did, however, resound in Australia. Never had so many been killed in battle. Never were so many homes throughout the country involved in grief. The AIF troops who landed at Anzac gave the nation something it would hold and shape forever after: a martial focus in their quest of a sense of identity.

Chapter Four

To Egypt, Then France

The Situation in Egypt, 1915-1916

From late 1914, Australian soldiers were being trained in Egypt. Some were posted just east of the Suez Canal for defense against Turkish forces. For most soldiers, there was only one visit to Egypt. For some there were two. Those troops who had previously trained in Egypt for the 25 April 1915 Gallipoli landings and survived found their way back to Egypt.

Those who returned from the eight-month Gallipoli campaign were a different force. They had seen and survived combat and took great pride in their worn and sometimes quite tattered Australian uniforms. In Australia, the numbers in training had risen from over 16,000 in June to nearly 74,000 in October 1915. These were mostly sent directly to Egypt. Just what to do with these reinforcements was solved by the "doubling": the mixing of the Gallipoli veterans with the increasing flow of raw recruits who had arrived in Egypt after the evacuation of Gallipoli or at a point in late 1915, when it was clear the Dardanelles campaign was failing. The best use of them was to split them up to form cadres for a much-expanded AIF. From late 1915 to mid-1916, these men either remained as a core in their original battalions or became the core of a series of new battalions. In either case, newly arrived recruits were used to bring both the new and old battalions up to establishment. Each of the sixteen oldest battalions was split; thus, the 1st-16th Battalions (1 to 4 brigades) at the Suez Canal created the 45th to 60th Battalions (12 to 15 brigades) at Tel el Kebir.[42]

All trained hard in the extreme conditions of the desert in an area stretching west from around Cairo, on the Nile River, east to around Ismailia, on the Suez Canal. The extremely hard training was matched by some extremely hard play in the urban centers, with or without leave being granted.

We have two detailed accounts of the Egypt training sequence. One is from Leonard Jones—the Gallipoli veteran—who was now seeing the place for the second time. The other is from Henry Hammond, who visited Egypt once as a reinforcement.

Leonard Jones

Leonard Jones sailed from England in July 1914. He learned of the outbreak of war as the ship approached Gibraltar. Unable to jump ship, he continued to Australia. The original intention of his voyage was to join his brother working in Queensland. He thought little of British soldiers back home. To him, they were apparently in the army because they could not find better work. He was even less impressed with the Australian version:

> There were soldiers in the streets – in – to me, queer uniforms, leggings, wide hats etcetera….. I was only just out here and I would be lost with these Australians,

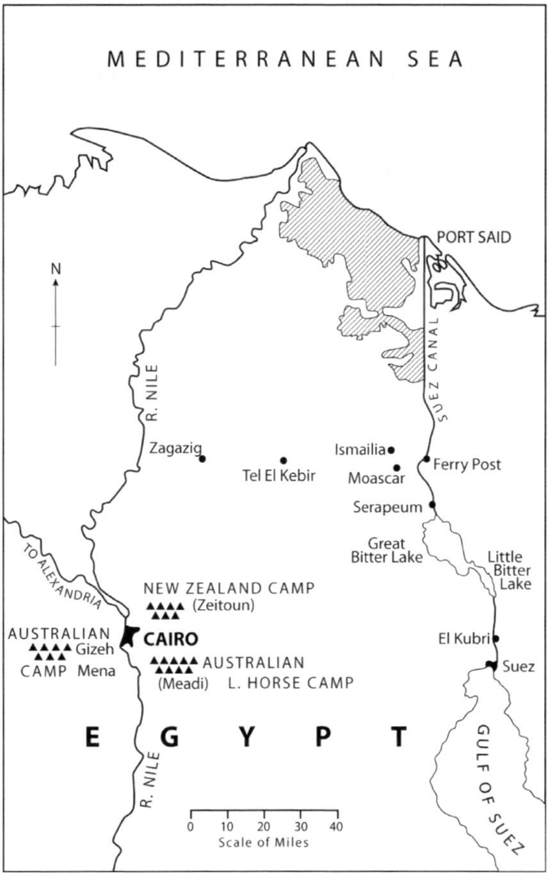

Egypt. The Suez Canal Zone

right out of place ….. these curious Australians. So to Victoria Barracks [in Sydney] I went. Passed through after promising to have a few teeth fixed up ….. Signallers were called for and I and several more stepped out and were then sent to the Sgs. camp close by. I was soon at home and there were many English chaps among them with whom I formed a lasting friendship. Next morning I discovered that all my "issue" of clothing, etc. had gone. Our officer told me that I had either to pay for them or do the obvious. Pinch some….. we were a very happy crowd with very few "boozers."[43]

Jones joined the AIF on 21 May 1915. By September 1915 he was in Egypt:

> We disembarked on the 10th and entrained for Heliopolis Camp. The only man left behind was a Digger sozzled with methylated spirits. The boys seemed to take in everything as if they had been used all their lives to a strange country. The taking included sundry baskets of eggs and oranges off the gyppos [a common but deprecatory descriptor for Egyptians or anyone resembling them].

It was a very brief stay. He embarked for Gallipoli on 22 October 1915 with the 3rd Battalion. He would be amongst the last of the parties evacuated on 19 December 1916:

> The old hands didn't have much to say about the evacuation. Took it quietly. All in the game. Sort of very sorry that all their travail seemed to be for not very much gain. Their mates behind – well – all in the game and anyhow they had proved themselves. Like themselves I was in the soldier's groove of taking things as they came.

How much this young Englishman had changed since his enlistment. Now as a volunteer in time of war and not a peacetime professional, he saw things the soldier's way. Like William James, whom we also met in chapter three, he talked of gameness in death, a sort of sporting metaphor. Men who died doing their best died "game." This is a particularly British concept, but one certainly embraced by many Australian troops. The sporting metaphor was grounded in very strong sentiments of valor and honorable death. Precedents for such thinking were not confined to the British or the Australians. The French were equally capable of expressing such sentiments. Death could be glorious. An English liaison officer with the French Armies in 1914 observed that French officers, even on maneuvers just before the outbreak of war:

> ... were entirely ignorant of the stopping power of modern firearms, and many of them thought it chic to die in white gloves.[44]

By now Jones had an extended vocabulary of distinctly Australian words—"cobbers," "mates," "dinkum," and the like—and upon arrival back in Egypt was treated with reverence by the raw recruits because of his service on Gallipoli. He nevertheless rated himself less a veteran than those he referred to as "the old hands," who would have been anyone on Gallipoli that had arrived before he did. By 29 December 1915, he was back in Egypt, in the middle of nowhere at camp Tel el Kebir.

What was becoming evident was a dilution of his sense of being purely British. Liberal mingling with the British troops in Egypt was putting a distance between them. He, like many Australian soldiers, did not consider the parade ground pomp and spit and polish of the British to be worth the trouble.

As a signaller, Jones endured slightly less of the brutal route marches and training maneuvers and enjoyed the higher and more sedate company of field headquarters. He had the intelligence to apply himself to the highly complex tasks of signalling and the presence of mind to step forward when they were called for. He had nevertheless nearly been killed on several occasions on Gallipoli. The training took them to Serapeum Camp:

> A hell of a place – lots of loose sand, water rationed, and all stuff brought up by light railway. We had sand in our tucker [an Australian term for food] and gear. It was hot and dusty. Route marches and "field" operations were the order of the day and once we marched out, stripped off and were inspected for "chats" [lice].

There were diversions:

> One Sunday we lined up both sides of a track and H.R.H. the Prince of Wales and staff and Birdie [Major General Sir William Birdwood] passed through our ranks – on horseback. There he was [the Prince of Wales] – a slight, rose cheeked boy, horribly embarrassed trotting past us troops followed by hoards of brass hats. I remember one hard bitten dig [digger] yelling "Well I feel sorry for yer Dig, you poor little bastard, come and have a drink and a yarn." Well he did.[45]

Jones witnessed the "doubling" of the AIF:

> On Feb. 13 [1916] they split the [3rd] Bn. up and many of our officers, N.C.Os. and men went to the newly formed 55th Bn. in the new 5th Div. ..... the boys didn't like the idea of going to a new crowd but they soon settled down and still wore the choc. [chocolate] and green bars but vertically.[46]

Leonard Jones of 3rd Battalion embarked at Alexandria Wednesday, 22 March, and disembarked at the southern French port of Marseille Tuesday, 28 March 1916.

Henry Hammond

Henry Hammond kept a meticulous diary of his service with the AIF. He enlisted 17 August 1915 and was assigned to the 13th Battalion. Later in Egypt, he was transferred to the new 54th Battalion on 1 April 1916: a result of the "doubling" of the AIF.

His diary is a catalog of misdemeanors, largely his own. These included a wild stay at Colombo during the voyage and once in Egypt, breaking through British camp lines to purchase food from their better-stocked canteen, deliberately failing to return from leave on time, and being absent without leave in the local bar districts. There had also been plenty of time on the ship bound for Egypt to square matters with misanthropic superiors, in this case one Sgt. Maj. Butter:

> The ship's sergeant major, our old company S.M., being a tremendous roarer on board has caused bad feeling with some of the men. So a sentry on guard in the alley way happened to see Butter with a cigarette in there, against rules, so he reported him to the S.M. All the ship is taking it as a great joke, "the great Butter being crimed!" We've been poking it at him as he's king billy on a transport.[47] We went up onto the boat deck tonight, as seeing a few going up we thought there was to be another lecture on Egypt, but I'm blowed if it wasn't a prayer meeting run by the sky pilot [army chaplain], & we got caught for half an hour, but we survived it and just got back in time for a glass of lime juice at the canteen before closing.[48]

By 22 March 1916, they were marching into camp Zeitoun, just to the north of Cairo:

> There are about 70,000 Australians encamped here. The returned soldiers from Gallip [Gallipoli] have been split up, & new battalions formed with a big mixture of old soldiers & reinforcements thus making a solid army now in training at Tel-El-Kabir [Tel el Kebir]. They expect to be sent to France any time, ... some [1st & 2nd Division] have already gone over. We expect to at no distant date for the big offensive in Flanders.
> Friday 24th Physical drill, breakfast route march, dinner, rifle issue. Visit Cairo evening. Dinner at Restaurante Petrograd.
> March 25th Parade till 12 noon, then, dress & into Cairo evening, visit music halls Kursaal &c.
> Wednesday 30th The drill getting more solid daily, very hot day. I am sergeant for the day of the wet canteen; being a hot day there are a few get drunk & the military

Mena, Egypt. Australian soldiers in informal pose gather round a water cart made by J. Furphy and Sons of Shepparton, Victoria. Rumors and gossip will be dominant topics, giving rise to the Australian term "furphy" for a generally held view that proves to be misleading or without foundation. *AWM*

police give me a hand to keep order. We now hear that the old soldiers from Gallipoli have been split up, also the new reinforcements & the whole formed into our battalion, & we are for the 54th AIF across the other side of the Suez canal.

He detected a change in their nature:

The boys here are very different to when in Australia ... the hardness seems to have hardened them & steadied them down ... all are dressed in light drill tunics, drill trousers & helmets. Our leather equipment is to be changed for webbing, leather having been proved inefficient. We turn in at about 8pm in our new camp with the sky for our covering in tents. The 54th Battalion colours are purple & green worn vertically.
Sunday April 2nd Very cool morning. Our company is duty coy. So we get detailed off for water carrying. The water trouble is very great here ... water being very scarce. Water bottles are to be always kept full in case of having to move off to the trenches at any instant. The enemy is supposed to be close in to our first line about 8 miles out. Aeroplanes are continually buzzing about overhead. We had

> our morning bath in about three spoonfulls of water, a shave & then dressed for church parade. We fell in for swimming parade & marched across the desert to the Suez canal. After a good swim we came back and stood by for lunch consisting of stew. The trouble here is that we are being continuously in the sun on open sand, no tents or shade, not a bit of green in sight. The sand is red hot & a heat vapour rising from the ground like smoke. Nothing to do in the afternoon but lie in the sun and write up my diary, talk & sort out my collection of photos.

One incident had a great impact on those who experienced it and on those who subsequently learned of it. A march across the desert had gone terribly wrong:

> Monday April 3rd The 54th boys tell us about the march from Tel El Kebir across the desert, ... the heat was terrific & one water bottle for three days, on full equipment & rifle & blankets. Ploughing through the sand & heat knocked many over, dropping in the sand, & being left behind. The Arabs came on them with water asking 20 pts [piastres] for a cup full. In some cases the boys being half dead, & mad bayoneted them for this water, & had to use it to keep them away, nine died after the march, the general in charge of the brigade lost his way & they were marching about trying to pick the railway up ….. only fifteen of our company, D coy, arrived in camp. They threw away all gear, & everything they had on the march to lighten their load, all clothes, ammunition, &c.

This occurred during late March 1916, when the newly appointed commander of the 5th Division, Lt. General Sir James M'Cay (also spelt McCay), reluctantly obeyed an order to march II Australian Corps—of which the 5th Division was a part—across the desert to replace I Anzac Corps on the Suez Canal. One of the brigades in that 5th Division (14 Brigade) suffered particularly from the heat and sandy conditions, resulting in the deaths of a number of soldiers from heat exhaustion and thirst. Although M'Cay sacked the 14 Brigade commander, Brig. Gen. Irving, the blame remained with him. M'Cay's subsequent handling of the 5th Division at Fromelles further damaged his reputation.[49]

Citizens As Soldiers

For sustained contempt of authority, there appears no equal to those volunteers in the AIF. Exactly what was at the root of this is not entirely clear. It may have been a tendency for the forces to see themselves still bound by a workplace environment where the privates were workers, the non-commissioned officers the foremen or overseers, and the officers the proprietors or managers. The average age of volunteers was twenty-five. They had been working for years—probably at least ten—and doubtless had been exposed to the very strong influences of the Australian trade union system.[50]

This may make sense for some situations, but it does not account for others. These were not natural born soldiers. That is a myth. However, they may have contained a fair proportion of natural born fighters. They rarely observed strict military discipline. They would refuse to work beyond what they saw as a reasonable limit in the camps and did so in sufficient numbers to resemble what would have been considered mutiny in the British army. They spoke back to officers and argued with them. Offenders whom

Australian soldiers, recognizable in their broad-brimmed hats, stand before the burnt-out remains of a building on Esbekiah Street, in the heart of the Haret el Wasser, the brothel quarter in Cairo. This is after the first or second sackings of the "Wazza" by Australian and New Zealand troops in 1915. *AWM*

others saw as treated harshly were often set free by their fellow soldiers despite and in the face of pistol waving officers.

Perhaps the most significant example of extreme misconduct is what is known as the "Battle of the Wazza" in Cairo in early April 1915. The Wazza was the name given to the Haret Al Wassir district in old Cairo that held a concentration of brothels. These were sacked by the Australians and New Zealanders after tensions flared over prices, tainted alcohol, and possibly antagonism between the resident British forces and the Anzacs. The latter enjoyed much higher rates of pay than their British counterparts and the influx of money had sent prices soaring. Thousands of soldiers held military police and commanders at bay. Of those thousands, perhaps only one in ten were actually sacking the place, whilst the others either tried to intervene or were looking on. Regardless, the Australians got a reputation for alcohol-fueled exuberance. This was reinforced when a second riot broke out in the district in July.[51]

Australian soldiers did not like saluting, nor did they like taking orders. They were, however, capable of doing the job under the right temperament of command. As one Australian officer in Egypt put it:

> After breakfast I put my head outside my hut and rap an order. Do I see men running to obey? No. we are Australians. There are curses and growls everywhere ….. and in about a half-hour the men are on parade. I know all about it so I always call out half an hour before I really want them. Then a job is given them. Do they smartly obey? No. They gather in cliques and finally slouch off, swearing and smoking ….. a dirty black pipe (I have one myself). Parade is over. I look at the work ….. they have done more than I expected. So they go on day after day. A better lot of men could not be found.[52]

From the soldier's perspective—in this case Henry Hammond—such a scene probably played out like this:

> Saturday 15th April Very fine morning ... stand to arms in trenches at 4am for 1 hour, as attack always takes place at that time. Then leaving the day guard, we march back to Ferry Post for breakfast. Detailed off for punt work from 4pm till 8pm.

Anzac Day, Anzac Legend

The first anniversary of the Anzac landings was celebrated 25 April 1916. To be sure, the newspapers at home had been filled with uncritical accounts of the Australians, portraying them as heroes beyond all else. There were several reporters on Gallipoli—including Charles Bean—who at least had official permission to be there as a government accredited war correspondent. But others were there too, including a young Keith Murdoch and Ellis Ashmead-Bartlett. It was Ashmead-Bartlett's reports that were the most stirring and most often confronted the Australian newspaper reader at home.

Right from the first reports of the Anzac operations on Gallipoli that appeared in Australian papers on 9 May 1915, it was Ashmead-Bartlett's accounts that most glorified the Australian soldiers. His reporting played a significant part in laying the foundation for the Anzac legend of determination and bravery under fire, of selfless sacrifice, of that peculiar brand of comradeship that Australians-at-arms displayed. Curiously, Ashmead-Bartlett was a British reporter who had yet to travel to Australia. Just as he was instrumental in the construction of the Anzac legend, he was also instrumental in having the British Gallipoli commander Sir Ian Hamilton relieved of his command.

Regardless of the publicity at home, those in Egypt preparing for the Western Front had already marked the anniversary as a solemn occasion. Henry Hammond:

> Thursday April 25th Anniversary of Anzac landing. Ribbons have been issued to Gallip lads. Red & blue for the landing & blue for any who have who have been on Gallip. Church parade at 9am. Swimming sports in canal in afternoon. We try to slip away to Ismalia but are stopped by military police & sent back again, no luck. Receive 10 letters this evening from Aussy [Australia], very interesting reading them all. Answer a few before turning in under our starry ceiling, as we always sleep out on the sand, the tents are too full being 20 in each.

By May, Hammond had seen the light about being an ordinary infantryman:

> May 13th Saturday After breakfast I strike a good job by knowing a bit about surveying & trig. [trigonometry]. Am out all day with a sergeant, surveying all our trench positions with pole, tape & theodolite. May 14th Sunday My mate returns from Ferry Post & being in the machine gun section, I determine to go in too. So on account of being an engineer I get in. They are nearly all mechanics, & a first class lot of fellows, being only six from each company, it is very select.

He summed up his experience in June:

> Sunday 18th Church parade. 6.30am. After parade we get orders to grease bayonets & rifles, ready for the voyage. My mate & I get some leave in the afternoon to visit Ismalia from 3pm till 9pm. It seems like being out of jail, our first leave from the "sand" for nearly three months. We wander all over the native quarter, very much like Cairo, & at last strike the gardens, which are very fine; we almost imagined we were back in Sydney botanical gardens. At the canal front man-o-war boats & launches ply busily, & Egyptian guards are doing sentry on the main garden entrances. Numbers of French people both civilian & naval are very prominent at this part ….. Tommies [British soldiers] of course are on hand ["everywhere"]. At last we strike, after wandering about, a real English tea room in the best part of the gardens, attended by British girls. We immediately are in & ordered tea & bread & butter, ... by jove if it didn't go, ... it seemed like home again, ... real butter, & after that some English cake, a real treat after Gippo luxuries? ... they [the "Gippo luxuries"] all have the same rotten oily taste, very peculiar. After about 10 courses we left & then went to church ... "British" ... next to the [tea] rooms. It was very nice, ... I never appreciated a church service before; all peaceful inside & a very nice little church, electric light & an English preacher, just like a bit of very old time, after all our trials of the "Heavy" desert life. Meet B. Cox. We return at 9pm. after the most enjoyable evening for three months.

Henry Hammond embarked at Alexandria Wednesday, 27 June, and reached Marseille Friday, 30 June 1916.

To the Western Front

Along with others from the British dominions, the Australians were now arriving in France in force. Most came directly from Egypt and nearly all disembarked at Marseille.[53] Their reputation from Cairo preceded them:

> The local British staff at this juncture was prepared against two contingencies – that the Australians might break out in riot into Marseille, and that disease from Egypt might slip into France with these troops.[54]

After the rigors of the Egyptian desert, the trip north through France from Marseille made a deep impression on the Australians. Henry Hammond:

> Friday 30th June. Reveille 5am, shave & breakfast at 7. Everything a bustle. Form up, on deck, full marching order at 8.30, march off to quay at 10. 54th Battalion lead off at 10.30, the bands striking up the "March of the Allies." We march through Marseille to the entraining yards. A very long train in 1st, 2nd & 3rd class carriages all mixed. We strike a very comfortable car, only seven men to each compartment. The French people are all very enthusiastic & cheer & wave flags as we pass. The train moved out at 11.30, & we immediately pass through some very beautiful country. Seems like looking on a series of

very fine paintings ..... it's like fairyland – bright green fresh fields & cornfields with golden heaps of hay &c., vineyards, & dotted here & there, are bright red roofed cottages. The roads appear perfect, pure white & winding through the hedged fields. All day we pass through magnificent country, a more beautiful country couldn't be imagined.[55]

The trains taking the Australians ran through the beautiful French towns Aix-en-Provence, Arles, and Avignon, bypassed Paris, and in many cases gave the soldiers a view of the English Channel before diverting back to the staging area behind the line near to and just south of Armentières. This section of the front was rated something of a "nursery sector" and stretched roughly westward back to the town of Hazebrouck, some twelve miles away. It was a relatively quiet part of the Western Front considered suitable for final training. Englishman Leonard Jones wrote:

Spring was unfolding herself, a revelation to many men used to the evergreen gums. Great walks we had round the country lanes.

There was a kind of mutual understanding at that time between the British and Germans. The British would avoid shelling the German headquarters in adjacent Lille, just as the Germans kept the shelling of Armentières to a minimum. In the Armentières sector, the Australians freely mixed with British soldiers, where they displayed some contempt for their more tailored and button-polished brethren. They made little effort to "dress up" to the British standard, which they perceived as unmanly. They also continued their tradition of saluting as few officers of any army as infrequently as possible.[56]

There was nevertheless the constant "crump" of artillery from both sides into the rear areas. By May, the Australians were occupying the front line at the Bois-Grenier sector known to the Australians as the Fleurbaix sector. Together with the New Zealand Division, the Australian 1st and 2nd Divisions occupied some ten miles of the front running south from Armentières to a German salient near the village of Fromelles. In front of this village, the German forces held the rise to a plateau known as the Sugarloaf. The Australians made their first trench raid the night of 5 June. By now, hundreds of Australians had already been killed in both the forward and rear areas, nearly all by artillery. Henry Hammond:

Wednesday 5th July 2am, I wake up, & a tremendous bombardment is going on something terrific, but I soon go to sleep again. Gas helmets are worn again, & I write some letters while getting about with it on, ... the stink is rotten after an hour. Sunday 16th [July] Haven't fired the Lewis Gun yet at the enemy. Glasso our gas helmets as windows dim over.[57] Find out that a large number of casualties last night took place in our trenches.

The Australians had arrived.

Chapter Five

THE SITUATION ON THE WESTERN FRONT: 1914 TO MID-1916

The German Plan, The French Plan

Prior to 1914, German military minds were concentrated on the problem of having to fight a war on two fronts at the same time. Who should be knocked out first: the French or the Russians? German Field Marshal Alfred Graf von Schlieffen had convinced himself and Kaiser Wilhelm II that a quick neutralization of French forces and then a war against Russia would be the preferred sequence. By 1905, Schlieffen's plan for swift destruction of the French Army by a grand sweep through Belgium was complete. This would be the blueprint for events in August 1914. There were problems with the Schlieffen Plan. Foremost were its assumptions about the logistical contingencies for a broad but disciplined and rigidly time-tabled sweep through Belgium into France, then south, to the west of Paris, and back into the French armies.

The French had their Plan XVII, which called for a thrust east of Paris to immediately reclaim the lost provinces of Alsace and Lorraine. Such an advance had the advantage of obviating any potential British response to a French preemptive attack on the Germans through neutral Belgium. For their part, the Germans had no such qualms over Belgian neutrality. Plan XVII reflected two key themes in French thinking: first, the lost provinces of Alsace and Lorraine—now under German control—could be returned to France. This was something of a sacred mission. Second, it was a bold advance, one that reflected French commander Gen Joffre's convictions that an *offensive à outrance*—the belief that the only defense was a profound offensive to the end and the sole means to repel yet another German attack on French soil.

For the Germans, it all went wrong in the first week of war. The Schlieffen Plan proved to be a doctrine more than an actionable plan. Helmuth von Moltke, who had succeeded Schlieffen upon his retirement in 1906, made some adjustments to the original plan, but these were minor. Schlieffen died in January 1913, but his revered plan was enshrined in German military thinking. The plan did not anticipate the strength of Belgian resistance.[58] The German Army's expectation they could live off the land to sustain their advance proved problematic. The timetable Schlieffen had developed and von Moltke was now trying to follow was quickly unraveling.[59] The German war aims "to reduce France to a second-class power, Belgium into a protectorate and to create a *Mitteleuropa*,

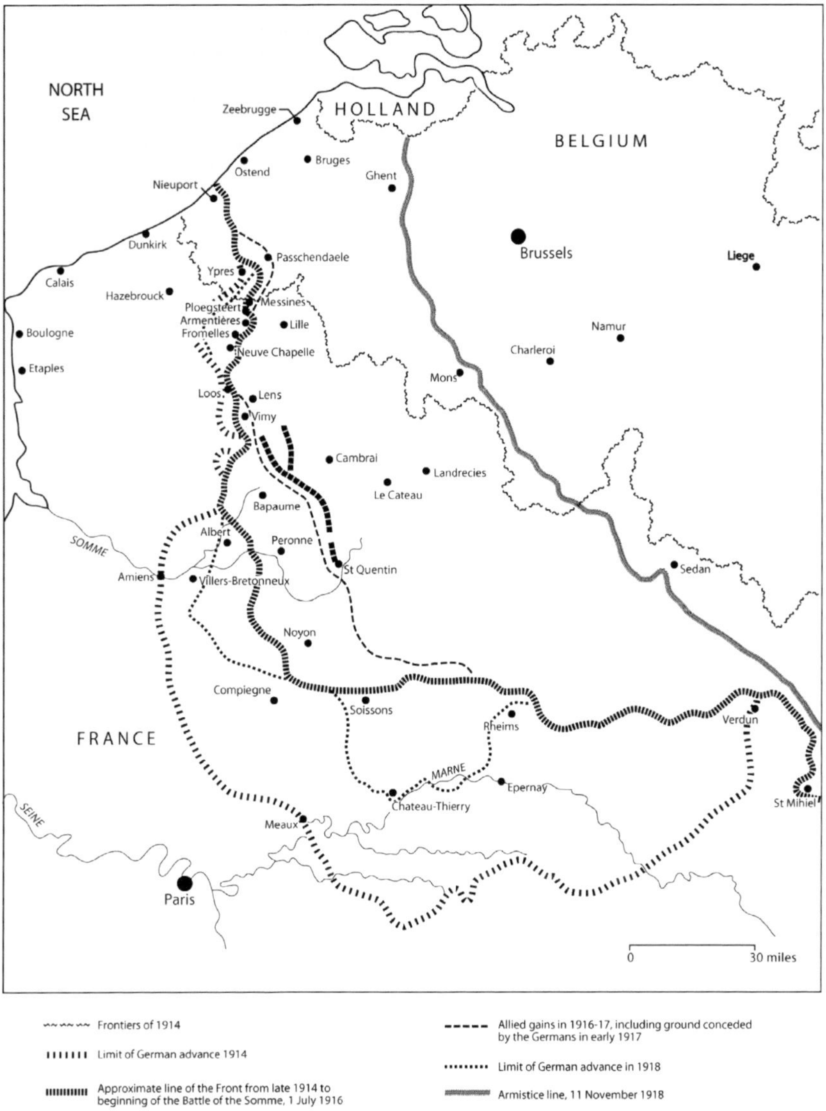

The Western Front 1914-1918

a German-dominated economic zone in the center of Europe"[60] had failed. The war was barely seven weeks old.

The advance was characterized by appalling conduct on the part of the German Army in the occupied zones of Belgium and France. It reflected their practices in 1871 during the Franco-Prussian War and in their African colonies in the 1900s. Hard-pressed troops commandeered everything they needed for themselves and their horses and to replace lost equipment. Belgian civilian resistance was met with German reprisals as early as 5 August 1914. Burning buildings—in some cases whole villages—along with mass executions and deportation of civilians for the German home front labor force were accompanied by stripping all and any capital equipment that could be shipped back to Germany and used for the war effort.

It was systematic violence.[61] During August-September 1914, more than 6,000 civilians were killed and between 15,000-20,000 buildings destroyed in occupied Belgium alone. At the time, these atrocities were potent propaganda for the Allies, who certainly took maximum advantage of them to encourage enthusiasm (and enlistments). Interestingly, these allegations of atrocities were laid to rest after the war and largely forgotten or deemed just propaganda. It would not be until the end of the twentieth century that renewed scholarship verified them. For the Germans, it was as if victory could not be perceived, measured, or realized without a process of annihilation.[62]

The German assault had petered out by the time the great Schlieffen swing to the west of Paris failed to materialize. Instead, the Germans met British and French forces to the east of Paris on the Marne River and the heights to its north, the Chemin des Dames.[63] From here, the war turned from one of open maneuver to a static war of extensive entrenchment by both sides. The Western Front, running from the Channel to the Swiss border, was created.

Developments on the Western Front: October 1914 to Mid-1916

The original, small British regular army—the British Expeditionary Force—had arrived in Belgium and France on 12 August 1914. By the end of the First Battle of Ypres in the northern sector of the Western Front during October-November 1914, they had lost so many men that it effectively ceased to exist. This original force was now being replaced by volunteers in what came to be popularly known as "Kitchener's Army." Most had no prior military service and all were hastily trained and sent to the front.

It was the Dardanelles Campaign that dominated Allied thinking during the first half of 1915. This caused something of a rift in the British command in particular. The "easterners" sought the opening of a new front against the Ottoman Empire. They were bitterly criticized by the "westerners," especially Field Marshal Sir John French and his second in command Sir Douglas Haig. They believed that their efforts on the Western Front were being compromised by the diversion of resources.

Just as with the Eastern Front efforts at Gallipoli, the allied Western Front campaigns proved costly and ultimately disappointing. The British took Neuve Chapelle in the north during March 1915 at great cost. The Germans failed to eliminate the Ypres salient (even farther north) at tremendous cost to both sides.

The Nature of Trench Warfare

Warfare along a continuous trench system had resulted in something of a deadlock. The value of artillery was now more apparent than ever. In the northern sector at Festubert in mid-May 1915, the British First Army, under Sir Douglas Haig, made another attempt to secure a section of the Aubers Ridge (the earlier attempt had been at Neuve Chapelle the previous March). It highlights the problems confronting such attacks at the time. Whilst there was an appreciation of the need for artillery support as part of any advance, there was a shortage of high explosive shells.

High explosive shells did more damage than shrapnel shells to emplacements, fortifications, barbed wire, and trenches. Shrapnel—small lead balls around half an inch in diameter packed into a shell—were an ideal anti-personnel measure for open warfare, but not for the static kind. They did little or no harm to those under cover and were even less effective breaking through barbed wire, which now dominated all forward positions. It has been estimated that ninety-two percent of the approximately 100,000 British shells fired using 433 pieces of artillery over sixty hours at the start of the attack on Festubert were shrapnel. What was left of Festubert was finally taken on 25 March 1915: an advance of less than a mile at a cost of 16,000 casualties.[64]

Subsequent British and French attacks during the remainder of 1915 were just as costly and ultimately indecisive. Worse, the Gallipoli campaign was a complete failure. German airship raids on England across the Channel had begun in January and continued intermittently during the year. Now, frustration on the Western Front was being compounded with the terror of the first ever air raids on civilians at home. The last "Big Push" by the British at Loos in August-September 1915 failed miserably.[65]

A discernible pattern developed with these actions. An attack would be preceded by congestion in the trenches, with as many soldiers as possible compressed into the front lines just prior to going over the top. Enemy shelling would claim many; not only in these front trench systems, but also those on their way to them before the attack. Once over the top and in no-man's land, soldiers were immediately out of contact with those commanding the battle. Those officers leading their men into no-man's land suffered disproportionately high loss rates. Smoke, broken earth, terrific explosions, and often a featureless terrain would disorient and hinder the advance. According to the situation and the disposition of the officers and men and their battle characteristics, sections of an advance would often lose step with those to their left and right. Confusion over whether to press the advance, hold, or even return to the start line would see to this.

Those who survived and reached the enemy line might well be confronted with unbroken wire, the most concentrated of fire and, should they actually reach the German trenches, an often still well armed and determined enemy. If the number who reached the enemy trench was sufficient to take it, they would—perhaps over the next few hours—be subjected to counterattack. Enemy reinforcements would attempt to drive them from their newly won positions, forcing them to retire as German fire was brought to bear on them. It was German military policy to always attempt to retake any lost ground as quickly as possible and do so with utter determination. Despite the limitations of shrapnel shells, artillery would nevertheless be the main killer. It usually accounted for about sixty percent of those injured or dead on the battlefield. The dogged British pursuit of the principle of the offensive was costly.

Just as historians see the turning point in World War II emerging as early as the decision to invade Russia in 1941, or even the German failure in the Battle of Britain in 1940, so some historians of the Great War see the turning point as the German decision to bleed France dry at Verdun in February 1916. An even earlier date—the failure of the Schlieffen Plan after the first few weeks of 1914—has gained currency. They may have a point, but this was not how matters were viewed at the time. For the first seven weeks of the war—a mere fifty days during August-September 1914—French casualties were estimated at a staggering 390,000. As total French casualties for the entire war are estimated at 1,700,000, the French suffered nearly twenty percent of their losses in the first eight weeks of war.[66] During the period August-December 1914, the British suffered nearly 90,000 casualties. During 1915, they would lose another 273,000. By the end of 1915, total German losses stood at nearly 2,600,000.[67] If either side discerned a turning point, it was not showing up in the casualty lists. At the end of 1915, the British commander Sir John French was replaced by Sir Douglas Haig.

War Industrialized

By now the scale of destruction had taken on a momentum of its own, seemingly beyond the control of the opposing high commands. This was in consequence of the rapid industrialization of warfare on the Western Front. Yet aspects of the industrialization were out of synchrony. Whilst artillery had come to dominate the battlefield, the primitive state of field communications made for a less than scientific application.[68] The development of aerial reconnaissance helped, but lagged behind tactical developments on the battlefield. Similarly, soldiers were now equipped with high velocity rifles, far ranging machine guns, chemical weapons, and flamethrowers. Yet the course of an advance could be compromised by the smoke, dust, the weather, and the haze. Contested terrain was often so devastated by artillery that it simply lost its features. No buildings, trenches, woods, or roadways were left recognizable. Because troops climbing from their trenches were effectively beyond the control of their commanders, the best way to provide and receive information on the battlefield remained the runner. Any telephone lines that were laid were constantly being cut. There were as yet no effective, portable communications systems. Commanders resorted to runners to send messages. Being a runner was one of the most deadly occupations.

In these ways the science of war constantly found itself entangled with the frailty of communication systems and indeed, the frailty of those involved. Momentous decisions —or perhaps worse, no decisions at all—were made or left to chance for want of current, actionable information.

This industrialization, combined with the existing primitive means to apply it, was a new experience of war and a frustrating one. There were no military precedents to guide the commanders for this kind of war and little inclination to acknowledge that this war—that so many had expected to be over by Christmas 1914—had no foreseeable end by mid-1916. This was not a war won in a single one or two days' battle. There was no sweep of infantry, no swift cavalry movement, no immediate gain, no rolling up of flanks, and no real winning to be seen. The static line of trenches, the opposing armies facing each other, and the depersonalization of death and injury by artillery, machine gun, and bullet against human flesh had turned the whole thing into a nightmare.

Developments at Verdun and on the Somme

Now, in early 1916, French and British plans for a new offensive were interrupted by Erich von Falkenhayn, an imaginative yet strangely insecure and mercurial German general. He made a preemptive strike well south of the Somme and the British lines against the French at Verdun on 21 February 1916.

For the French, Verdun was a place of great military and almost spiritual significance. It lies to the east of Paris on the River Meuse, a sacred salient guarding the capital, yet still close to the Luxembourg and German borders. It does not appear to have been Falkenhayn's desire to take Verdun, so much as destroy the French Army in a battle of terrible attrition.[69]

By early May 1916, the French forces were in a parlous state. They called on the British High Command to relieve the pressure on Verdun with an offensive farther north. The French part of the line ended just south of the River Somme at a point to the northeast of Paris. Here, the line was picked up and held by the British all the way north, with a small Belgian contingent in the far north.

With spring giving way to summer, the British agreed to undertake some sort of action, but what? It seems the Somme—the place where the British southern and French northern lines met—became an administrative convenience. The British commander, Field Marshall Sir Douglas Haig, decided to launch a major offensive there that commenced 1 July 1916. He would subsequently state a threefold rationale:

> to "relieve the pressure on Verdun"; to "assist our Allies in the other theatres of war by stopping any further transfer of German troops from the Western front"; to "wear down the strength of forces opposed to us."[70]

This was Haig's summation long after the Battle of the Somme had commenced on 1 July. It appeared on 29 December 1916 in his dispatch on the battle in the *London Gazette* almost six months later.

Why had the Somme been chosen as the place to take the offensive? The events of 1 July 1916 are still fiercely debated amongst historians. It is possible it was more a matter of events overtaking the situation than a conscious decision. Whether the Somme Offensive was a success or a failure is still debated.[71]

For their part, the French—particularly Gen. Joffre and his High Command—had formed the view that the British were not entirely capable of conducting a successful offensive, a view reinforced by some of the less than satisfactory attacks in 1915: Neuve Chapelle in March, at Festubert in May, and at Loos in September, and a matter acknowledged in the British official history.[72]

1916

Haig's three-fold justification does not accord with some readings of the events of the first half of 1916. As early as February 1915, Lord Kitchener had visited the front and emphasized the impossibility of any kind of breakthrough offensive. Rather, he counselled placing pressure on the German lines over time. Haig harbored thoughts of a major breakthrough followed by a sweeping cavalry advance to rout the Germans. He was known to hold such designs and was advised against them by senior staff officers, yet his predisposition for the grand breakthrough remained. That it would occur on the Somme and not elsewhere seemed almost incidental to Haig's desire to see a breakthrough —somewhere—along the western Front.

With his originally preferred options for a breakthrough around Ypres displaced by apparent Belgian reluctance and ever-increasing casualties at Verdun, Haig took the opportunity to resolve a by-then confusing and probably exasperating series of alternative schemes at a variety of locations along the Western Front with his own catastrophically ill-conceived attempt on the Somme. If it was not Haig's decision to fight there, it was his indecision that led to the place being the Somme. Either way, it involved inadequate artillery, insufficient forces, and no clear rationale. Haig seemed able to act in this way despite home cabinets and committees urging him not to. As one summation has it:

> One of the most remarkable things about Haig in the latter half of 1916 was the degree to which he would operate without effective control from London.

> In truth Britain's leading statesmen were at least as much out of their depth in the grand strategic direction of a war as he was in its operational conduct.[73]

In February 1916, the number of infantry divisions of the British Command stood at forty-four, plus a further five cavalry divisions. With these they held some eighty miles of the Western Front, from Ypres in the north to Amiens in the south. North of them—for twenty miles of the front extending from north of Ypres to the Channel coast—the line was held by the Belgians and one French division. To the south of Amiens, where the British part of the line ended, the French—with 111 divisions—held by far the greatest part of the line: 370 miles all the way south to the Swiss border. Facing them along the entire Western front were 120 German divisions.

The date of the attack eventually came to be set for the beginning of July. The French originally planned to use nearly forty of their divisions on a thirty-mile front south of the Somme River in conjunction with some twenty-five British divisions north of the river, but these plans went awry when Falkenhayn's offensive on Verdun much farther south in February 1916 began to take its toll on the French.

The French diverted many of their divisions south to Verdun, leaving only sixteen available for the July Somme Offensive. Through Joffre, the French held a nominal supreme command over all forces and, in insisting on some cooperation from the British, appears to have prevailed upon Haig to carry the major burden on the Somme.

Matters got worse. By the eve of the Somme Offensive, only six French divisions (of the original thirty-nine) and thirteen front-line British divisions were available for the offensive, now to be conducted on a rather lengthy twenty-three mile front on the Somme.

Haig's post-battle claim—and the main one he gave—of relieving pressure on the French at Verdun is difficult to understand. Although not immediately apparent to the French or the British, the German assaults on Verdun had begun to wane by 12 July—less than two weeks after the Somme Offensive had commenced. By 18 December 1916—eleven days before Haig's dispatch appeared in the *London Gazette*—the French line at Verdun had been reestablished to where it was before Falkenhayn's attacks.[74]

The British had committed too few resources and no replenishment, no real communication between those in the field and higher command, and for no real profit for the outlay. That this was all the resources they had suggests that too big an offensive was undertaken. The Somme was not industrialized land. It was not closely connected by established, complex road or rail networks. There were no major cities of extreme commercial significance, no places of spiritual or sacred depth or meaning. Those places were Ypres, Paris, or Verdun. They were miles away. There is less evidence of care and more of uncritical optimism. Alternative plans were not fully assessed, debated, and hammered out before a final decision was taken. There was no consultation with those in the field at a battalion level, or even a brigade level. Nobody really asked serious questions beforehand because they were apparently too confident, too afraid, or perhaps too stupid. If there were men in Haig's command of industrial or commercial experience, men with insights into the logistical exigencies of planning, they were silent.

It was well known that on the Somme, the Germans had prepared defense in depth, with several successive lines to be taken. This proved an impossible task for the British.[75] These defenses were well built, well maintained, and carefully planned affairs relying on bunkers thirty to forty feet underground, with many interconnected. Very few German soldiers were manning their equally well prepared surface trenches during the week-long artillery bombardment that preceded the 1 July attack. On the surface were the few who were required to watch for signs of British troops emerging from their trenches. Also on the surface were some Germans who found the confines of the bunkers in the midst of that terrible bombardment too terrifying to bear.

Vast numbers of rifle-equipped German troops were not really necessary to defend the front line anyway. Their plentiful supply of machine guns—always in the bunkers and only brought out after a bombardment or when advancing troops were sighted—was sufficient to lay most of the British down dead, dying, or injured. One observer described the casualties as relatively neat rows spaced apart, just as they had been trained to advance at walking pace after what they had been assured would be a barrage so destructive that all they needed to do was reach the German line and occupy it.

On 1 July 1916, the Somme was the scene of the most severe conditions. On that single day, the British alone suffered 57,470 casualties. Of these 19,240 were dead and over 2,000 missing. It is most likely that actual British deaths that day exceeded 20,000.[76]

It was a place of hitherto unimaginable ferocity, horrific new ways of killing, and new forms of industrialized, total destruction. The war was quite clearly in a zone of its own, what French military minds would term "the zone of the armies." The civilians had fled, permanently. The zone of the armies was devoid of any relationship with tillable land, liveable townships, habitable dwellings, sanitation, peace of mind, or clear sense of purpose. The zone smelt of excrement and rotten flesh, cordite, chloride, lime, gas, fumes, and fear.

There are three significant aspects to the war on the Western Front during 1915 and into 1916. The first was the development of indirect artillery using aerial reconnaissance. The second was the growing intensity of the fighting; the failure by the Allies to gain a strategic advantage with the opening of a new front at the Dardanelles contributed directly to this. Third, there was the emergence of static warfare. The primacy of concealment in trenches and bunkers reflected this. It no longer seemed possible to turn the enemy's flanks. There emerged the problem of attempting to form a salient into the enemy's front. These were perilous enough to create, let alone consolidate. Then, enemy fire would come not just from the front, but from the flanks such a salient created.

The Arrival of the Australians

By July 1916, 90,000 Australians were on the Western Front, with a further 90,000 in England. This was but a very small part of the British forces, which by that time numbered 1,263,000 and were growing by around 100,000 a month.[77] The Australians had seen the effects of artillery and machine guns on Gallipoli, but never killing on a scale such as this.

It was into the Somme that the bulk of Australian divisions were committed in July 1916. After their dark departure from Gallipoli, it fell to the Australians to enter the grind against the German war machine. For this the 1st, 2nd, and 4th Australian Divisions were sent south to that sector of the Somme controlled by the British. The 5th Australian Division was in reserve in the north. Ironically, the attempt to "relieve pressure on the French at Verdun" with an attack on the Somme was deemed by the British High Command to require yet another diversionary attack of its own at a point even farther north than the Somme. That place was the Fleurbaix-Bois Grenier sector, now better known as Fromelles.

Chapter Six

FROMELLES

The Buildup

Upon their arrival in France, Gen. Haig inspected the Australians and New Zealanders in the northern sector. On 9 May, in a letter to King George V, he wrote:

> They are undoubtedly a fine body of men, but their officers and leaders as a whole have a good deal to learn ... A portion of their front was shelled last Thursday night and a small party of Germans entered their trenches. I understand that the severity and accuracy of enemy's artillery fire was a revelation to them![78]

According to the Formation Headquarters war diary for the 1st and 2nd Australian Divisions, that "revelation" resulted in over 200 casualties.[79] During April and June 1916, Australian casualties in the supposedly quiet "nursery sector" had reached 2,384; the result of trench raids, sniping, and artillery.[80]

Meanwhile, the offensive on the Somme had commenced on 1 July 1916. It was going badly. Three Australian divisions (the 1st, 2nd, and 4th) were moved south to the Somme. By mid-July, only the Australian 5th Division—the most recent one to arrive in France—was occupying the front line of the sector in the north, about four miles south of Armentières. Their front line faced a low salient known as the Sugarloaf, on which sat the small village of Fromelles. That salient is no more than eighty feet above sea level. This is flat, low lying land. Bisecting the fields, between the opposing front lines flows the River Layes. Here, it was little more than a wide ditch.

In charge of the 5th Division was the Irish-born Australian Maj. Gen. James M'Cay. M'Cay's reputation had taken something of a beating after the disastrous desert march back in Egypt. Now, M'Cay and his 5th Division were placed at the disposal of British Lt. Gen. Sir Richard Haking.

Haking had earlier put forward a plan to take further sections of Aubers Ridge and develop a salient through Fromelles, well into the German lines. This accorded with a general desire amongst the British staff to take pressure off their line farther south on the Somme, where the great offensive of 1 July—now approaching its third week—continued to meet disastrous consequences. It was known the Germans had diverted some reinforcements from the Fromelles area down to the Somme and it was deemed an appropriate place for a diversion, a feint that might limit German troop movements.

It is worth emphasizing again the strange sense of diminishing returns of effort in this. The Battle of Verdun (south of the Somme) was supposedly being aided by this Somme Offensive. In turn, the Somme Offensive itself was now going to be aided by a third, subsidiary attack at Fromelles. Only three weeks earlier, on 29 June, Haking had committed British troops to a similar undertaking at the Boar's Head Salient some two and a quarter miles southwest of the Sugarloaf Salient. This had failed completely. Whilst some of the British soldiers reached and held part of the German front line, they were repulsed and forced to return to their own lines shortly after. It was not for want of experience that this most optimistic plan for an assault near Fromelles was being considered. Indeed, in May and again in September 1915, similar assaults in the same area had also met with failure.[81]

Haking nevertheless continued to push the idea. Whilst inspecting the line of proposed attack at its widest point in front of Fromelles with a British staff officer a few days before the assault, the commander of 15 Brigade, Australian Brig. Gen. Harold "Pompey" Elliott, expressed grave concern over troops advancing 400 yards toward such an elevated position:

> I said to him "Major, you have read my plan of attack and the orders thereon and have approved of them. I want you now to tell me as man to man in view of the fact that you have had nearly two years' experience in this fighting as against my ten days whether this attack can succeed" ….. He hesitated ….. and said very earnestly ….. "I expect the result to be a bloody holocaust.[82]

In the end, Haking got his way. Haig gave approval to commit two divisions to the attack: the British 61st Division and the Australian 5th Division.[83]

Henry Hammond was in the 54th Battalion. It was one of the four battalions that made up 14 Brigade, which in turn was one of the three brigades comprising the 5th Division. He wrote in his diary:

> Monday 17th [July] move off, & at 1am. arrive at our saphead, shells & machine gun fire busy across the road, fair number of casualties before arriving in sap. Here we pick up our guns, & carry them through innumerable saps till 7am, when we find ourselves in the support trenches, dog tired. The 58th Battalion [15 Bde] are coming out, & look terribly weary, & muddy. We coil down & try for a sleep, but soon, a heavy bombardment on both sides takes place, & old Fritz sweeps our lines with shrapnel, which is flying almost like rain, none in our dugout, not so far. There is to be a charge tomorrow so there'll be something doing for cert. [certain]. At this minute about noon, all artillery is giving hell, the shells flying across the parapet in strings, some shrapnel, some high explosive. A chap is very lucky who comes through much of this without a casualty. The steel helmets are very heavy & uncomfortable, but would stop more than [would] a chap's head. We have dressed them with sacking so as not to show against the clayey [clayish] ground & appear like a sandbag above the parapet. Heavy shelling & bombing continue from the German guns. Stretcher bearers are kept moving. One high explosive shell blows up some German bodies that had been buried. We get gas attacks during the evening, & we don our gas helmets. Snipers causing trouble, have many close shaves with shrapnel.[84]
> Tuesday 18th 1 am. Get orders to move, & leave guns. The charge is postponed. We head up through the saps up to the main road about an hours walk through

winding saps, many close shaves from machine gun bullets. Get a shine [bruise] in several places. After march of two hours arrive at billet dog tired, covered with mud, & whiskers. Sleep till 8am. breakfast. Charge is to take place later.

The Battle

The attack on Fromelles commenced on 19 July 1916. It was a bright, sunny day. The attack was set for 6:00 p.m., with more than two hours of daylight remaining. British artillery had been shelling the salient for two days and would continue throughout the day. The Germans were shelling the Australians, too. Lt. Col. Cass, in charge of the 54th Battalion, would report:

> The enemy ….. shelled the position incessantly right up to the moment of the assault, causing heavy casualties ….. No Man's Land was about 150 yards wide in front of the 14th Brigade, traversed by ditches and wire, and covered with long grass and dank growth of vegetation. About ten minutes to six the first wave went "over the top" in extended order, ready to assault at the instant of 6 o'clock – the time fixed for our barrage to lift off the enemy's front line ….. heavy machine gun fire from the SUGAR LOAF on the right assailed the 14th Brigade ….. there was a constant shortage of grenades and ammunition.[85]

Henry Hammond recorded his own experiences this way:

> Wednesday 19th Wake up at 1am to see that all are issued with iron rations. Give each other our names & addresses, in case any get killed, another can write home. Move off at 1pm for the battle ... suppressed excitement. Waiting for the charge is the strain. At 6 pm over the parapet & away in the face of a tremendous shell fire, shrapnel & high explosive shells. Off we go with the gun & the remainder of the team following with the magazines. The ground is covered with fresh wire & ditches with 2 feet of mud in the bottom, a terrific position to capture. Men are falling in hundreds ... all of a sudden a flash & I knew no more till I woke up with 4 wounds under an old dugout. Bandage myself up. Tremendous explosions all round, dead everywhere; Captain Tuck crawls in with a shot through his leg; shelling is too terrific to crawl back to our trenches ... certain death. So we lie there all night, in wind, shells hitting all round, & expecting every minute, the dugout to go up in the air. At 7 am, the German fire eases up & we crawl along a sap with, in some places, 3 feet of slush, dead everywhere ... awful. The stretcher bearers are working for all they are worth. Tremendous casualties, ... 54th Batt roll call is 20 – Out of [the 5th] division, only about a few battalions left ….. We drive back in ambulances ... get our wounds dressed to hear on all sides [both left and right flanks] all [our] mates killed. A terrible casualty list ….. Have two wounds in leg, one on head, & several in arm.[86]

In perhaps little more than an hour, Henry Hammond's military service was over. He was returned to England and, because of the severity of his wounds, repatriated to Australia.

Others were more or less fortunate than Hammond. Sapper Sidney Donnan of the 14th Field Company Engineers was somewhere out in no man's land that night digging saps and marking the way for those to follow with white tape:

> We hopped over the parapet at a given signal from Lieutenant Ferguson, our section commander and made a dash for the [enemy] front line. With the tape drum and other tools and battle order kit, I think a pick-axe, the run was too far for me, and I decided to walk the last quarter and hang the consequences. Arrived in front line. I could see Lieutenant Ferguson had been hit in the neck and Sapper Saunders staunching the blood which spurted out of the wound at great pressure. The bleeding actually stopped and at that moment some German prisoners (about four) seemed to come from nowhere.[87]

Ferguson died shortly after. Sapper Donnan survived and later transferred to the Australian Flying Corps as a mechanic.

The battle was effectively over by 8:00 a.m. the next morning, 20 July. The 5th Division had taken 5,533 casualties. Of these 400 had survived the murderous enfilade and advanced so far that they became prisoners of war. Thousands lay dead or wounded in no man's land. Many had been killed either in their own front line or on their way to it, so heavy was the German barrage. In a single night, 1,917 Australians had died. Of these 1,299 have no known grave. The Germans' total casualties stood at 1,582. The 5th Division ceased to exist as an effective fighting unit and would not return to the front lines until October 1916.

Charles Bean was present. The night of the 19/20th he wrote in his diary:

> As Mackay [M'Cay] was busy I went round all three Bde H.Qs. Poor old Tivey ….. the one thing he seemed anxious to assure himself of was that his Bde had been tried as hard & had done as well as the brigades in Gallipoli ….. another 8th Bde man told me that a Gallipoli officer who was in action at Lone Pine told him that even they never had shelling like this ….. Pope of the 14th Bde rather disgusted me by the boastful way he talked – I think he had been refreshing himself after the strain. "Well, we were the only Bde who didn't come back till we were told to," he said with meaning. He was rather contemptuous of Elliott and the 15th Bde. Old Elliott was ….. clearly terribly depressed and overwrought. M'Cay was also.[88]

Maj. Gen. Edwin Tivey was then temporary Brig. Gen. in the 5th Division. The reference to Colonel Harold Pope—then temporary colonel in command of 14 Brigade—reflects on the withdrawal of the other brigades in the 5th Division without being ordered to do so. Only 14 Brigade was to receive orders. It appears Pope had indeed been refreshing himself. Later on the twentieth, at about 4:30 p.m., M'Cay tried to rouse Pope, who had fallen into a deep slumber. M'Cay dismissed Pope on the grounds that he had been drunk, and he immediately lost his rank and brigade command. He returned to Australia and was dismissed from the army on 1 October 1916.[89]

Within a day after the battle Charles Bean had returned south to the Somme. Of the disaster of Fromelles, he noted in his personal diary:

> I wrote a cable calling it an "attack" and saying that the losses were "severe." I took this to Amiens arriving there at 8.15 pm & I believe the Censor passed it. He wouldn't have if the bombardment [was] described as "intense" as 1st [British] Army objected that there never was an intense bombardment ….. They say that the official communique calls it "an important series of trench raids" – What is the good of deliberate lying like that?[90]

The effect on 5th Division commander M'Cay was to have yet another stain on his reputation. Often regarded as arrogant as he was intelligent, Bean nevertheless rails against misinformed public opinion in Australia about the man, arguing that he was not responsible for an earlier disaster at Helles during the Gallipoli campaign, had protested the order to march the division through the desert at Egypt earlier in the year and, now, was for a third time being used as a scapegoat for Fromelles. Bean closes the account of Fromelles by observing two things: that M'Cay had been dealt a "gross injustice" and that as far as the troops were concerned:

Fromelles, 19 July 1916. Australians photographed just before the 6:00 p.m. attack. They are from the 53rd Battalion. Of the eight men in this scene, five would be killed. The three survivors were wounded. The trench construction is typical of the northern battlefields. Because of the high water table, a substantial proportion of the "depth" of the trench is made of sandbags. Wooden posts and beams reinforce the excavated section. Sandbags extend from ground level to give height. This is technically as much a breastwork as it is a sunken trench. *AWM*

> The impression already created in the AIF, that the new British armies lacked something in fighting capacity, was noticeably strengthened by this episode.[91]

It was as if the army could not organize itself or be brought to at least some understanding of assessment of risk against profit in the matter of men's lives. We will leave Sapper Donnan—who in peacetime was a country surveyor in New South Wales—with the last word on Fromelles, or as he describes the place, Fleurbaix. It was by this name the Fromelles action was commonly known amongst the Australians until rectified by the British Battles Nomenclature Committee after the war. Here is his cogent summary about armies, command, decision making, and a special form of fool:

As a youngster who had served a good time among engineers and surveyors on practical work on the plains I was struck by the absolute lack of knowledge and even appreciation of the technical side of things in the Army. Any undertaking like this attack at Fleurbaix should have been in the hands of a man who in civil life had been in charge of big undertakings preferably of a big civil engineering character; a man who in his daily life had encountered difficulties in simple looking tasks and had to make decisions on how to overcome them. Such a man would know and foresee difficulties in tasks that the routine office man and amateur soldier would not appreciate. But it was too late. Too many men when war breaks out are given jobs on the strength of parade ground peace time advancement. I would say without knowing who was in command at Fleurbaix that the action was the result of a mug soldier's fond dream.

Chapter Seven

Pozières

Events on the Somme in 1916 dominate literature on the Western Front. It is difficult to find a work that does not draw on the most detailed account of Australian participation, Charles Bean's third volume of the official history.[92] It remains the most comprehensive record. Yet it is evident from Bean's personal diaries written on the battlefield that he initially experienced difficulty accounting for all the events during the battle.

Bean's official history is the result of extensive postwar background research and correspondence with surviving commanders well into the 1930s. These are held in 130 notebooks and a further sixty folders. In addition, the events were recorded at the time in 112 field diaries. These are handwritten—sometimes completed in darkness—curving across the pages as he struggles to commit the next line as legibly as possible. On occasion he employs various forms of shorthand. These diaries can be excruciatingly difficult to decipher. They nevertheless make for compelling reading, containing details, accounts, and impressions not included in his official history.

For Pozières, his personal diary entries move back and forth, intermingling the events of 21 July through 4 August. At one point, he rewrites his notes to clarify their chronological order.[93] No single commander or soldier was in complete possession of the facts. From the battles for Pozières and Mouquet Farm emerge persistent and pervasive confusion. It is not intended here to recount the sequence in detail. Rather, the emphasis remains with the experiences of the individuals who were present.

The action involving the 5th Division at Fromelles took place the evening of 19/20 July. This coincided with the involvement of the 1st and 2nd Divisions some seventy miles to the south, at the southern end of the British line on the Somme. They too entered the line on 19 July. The broader Somme Offensive had commenced three weeks earlier.

The Somme Offensive Falters

The Germans had created very strong defenses on the Somme. British planners sought to neutralize these with a very heavy artillery bombardment. In the five days leading up to the attack, British artillery fired 1.7 million shells on twelve miles of the enemy's front; about 150 pounds per yard. As impressive as this seems, and as terrifying as it must have been for the German troops, it was ineffective. Most of the shells were of the shrapnel variety; ideal for open ground, but hardly effective against the extensive underground bunkers and fortified posts. As many as a third of the shells failed to explode due to hurried manufacture at hitherto unprecedented rates in British munitions factories.[94] On 1 July 1916—the first day of the offensive—the British Army lost over 20,000 killed and 41,000 wounded; for this they gained just three square miles.[95]

There was little to show for the subsequent eighteen days' fighting except in the south, where some advances were made.[96] The high ground nevertheless remained in German possession, particularly on a roughly semicircular ridge running from Thiepval south to Pozières. These are not mountaintop retreats. The ridge is perhaps fifty feet higher than the surrounding countryside—at most 100 in a few places—all with gradual rises. Thiepval and Pozières nevertheless represented two key, strongly fortified sites. Whilst known by their village names, it was the areas in which the villages were rather than the villages themselves that were strategically significant.

The uneven nature of the British advance on the Somme is revealed in the taking of Thiepval and Pozières. Both were listed in Haig's plans as objectives to be taken the first day. Toward the northern end of the advance lay Thiepval. On 1 July, the British front trench line that snaked in front of the Thiepval fortification was, in places, as little as 100 yards distant. Yet it would not fall until late September, some thirteen weeks after it was due to be taken. By contrast, at the southern end, Pozières lay well behind the 1 July start line, some two miles away. Like Thiepval, it was supposed to be taken the first day of the offensive. It would not be taken until 4/5 August, five weeks after it was due to be taken, but still two months ahead of the much closer Thiepval. These two places were the most important fortifications that had to be reduced by the British offensive.

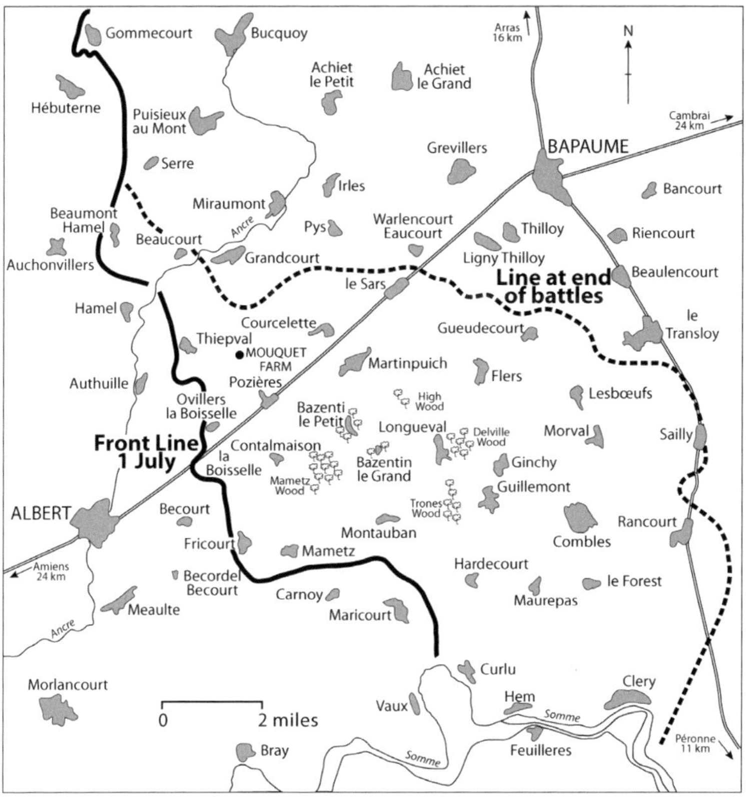

Area of Operations, Somme Campaign, 1916

Pozières

On 18/19 July, the Pozieres front was transferred from Lt. Gen. Sir Henry Rawlinson's British Fourth Army to Lt. Gen. Sir Hubert Gough's Reserve Army (subsequently called the Fifth Army). This transfer was in part due to the wastage of men in the Fourth Army since the beginning of the offensive. To bolster Gough's own dwindling force he also acquired I Anzac, comprising the 1st, 2nd, and 4th Australian Divisions.[97]

With Thiepval's defenses proving difficult to breach and the advances at the southern end of the line more successful, it was to capturing the heights in this area that Haig and Rawlinson turned their attention.[98] By 14 July, Fricourt was in British hands and Delville Wood was being secured. But the Germans still held Pozières, against which between 13 and 17 July the British had made four attacks.[99]

On 19 July, at almost the same time the Australian 5th Division was being cut to pieces at Fromelles, north of the Somme, the 1st Australian Division was marching out of Albert to the front before Pozières. The fourth attack by the British 24th Division had just ended the day before. In the style of his counterpart Gen. Haking at Fromelles to the north, Gen. Gough was keen to make use of the Australians as quickly as possible. He requested the Australians make an attack on Pozières the day after, on the nineteenth.

In contrast to the impatience of Gens. Haking and Gough, there is evidence of competence, care, and stewardship by some British commanders, especially of dominion troops. It may be found in the arguments against Gough's ill-timed and ill-conceived intentions by the British commander of the Australian 1st Division, Maj. Gen. Sir Harold Walker.[100] He resisted Gough's demands and had the attack delayed until the evening of 22/23 July. The 1st Division comprised three brigades: 1, 2, and 3. Within 1 Brigade were four battalions, one of which was the 3rd. Within that 3rd Battalion was Gallipoli veteran Cor. Leonard Jones.

Leonard Jones kept diaries in the field. It appears that after the war, it was suggested by a former senior officer that he commit these to some memoir to alleviate the stress he was still suffering. What Leonard Jones left is a remarkably detailed and ruthlessly frank account of his experiences. A careful analysis of both the official battalion and brigade war diaries show his accounts to be quite consistent —to the day—with the official record.[101] His original diaries no longer exist. His memoir provides the personal, human impact of war that of necessity the official war diaries do not. It constitutes the most comprehensive first person account the author has seen and ranks as probably the best account of war from a personal perspective. It was never published. Here is his account of his battalion's approach to the battlefield:

> At 1700 July 19 we went through Albert with "Annette Kellerman" still holding on at the top of the Basilica.[102] ….. the further we went the more desolate the country. It took us till 11p. m. to get in to support in front of Pozières.[103]

The area they marched through was littered with dead and wounded, full of fresh shell craters, and undergoing further shelling with high explosive, shrapnel, and now gas. Donning gas masks added to the general confusion:

> Passed a machine gun possy [position] with gun cocked up and the crew in bits all over the place. Then the familiar sss --- ssss ----- over, then bang [these were

A finely composed photograph of Australians on the Somme, 28 August 1916. This is behind the lines near the Albert-Bapaume Road before Pozières. By this date that village had been taken by the Australians. A relatively relaxed looking trio of officers gazes at the camera beside their staff car. A considerable number of field cookers are spread along the area, almost certainly somewhere in Sausage Valley. *AWM*

> gas shells]. Just in the gully at back. However we got into our possy, an H.Q. Was in a big ex-German dugout. These were new to us. Splendidly built ….. we got some casualties and a fair bit of shelling – 5.9s [German howitzers]. One salvo lobbed just behind Padre Wilson and I. He was showing me the ridge and the village about half a mile away which the Bn. [Battalion] was to attack. "I hope you come back, Jonno. Keep up the name of the Bn," ….. ….. I had been detailed to hop over with Cpl. Mackenzie with a reel of [telephone] wire with Don [D] Coy. The salvo had lobbed right in the trench killing several including Sergeant Elliot, our Q.M.S.[104] We rushed round but we could only clean up a horrible mess of about four men. Strange to say the dixies [food containers being brought up to the troops by that party] had not been touched ….. Porky Neal and I took the risk, however, and concocted an evil hash of bully and onions.[105]

Men—tired and hungry, and usually terribly thirsty—were driven to salvage a meal from such carnage. There are several accounts from soldiers—including the Australians—describing such behavior as being reduced to animals, including going through the packs and effects of the dead to find food, water, tobacco, and ammunition. Still, there is a difference between looting and survival. When some members of the 3rd Battalion had stolen clothes irons from a back area in the Sailly northern sector before heading south to the Somme, Jones was astonished that troops could or would even find such a useless item worth taking. In the matter of survival on a battlefield, where one could hardly hear anything for the crash and shaken by the concussion of the artillery, the cold, the mutilation, the death, and the unremitting terror, taking food and comforts from the dead—be they yours or the enemy—simply did not count.

Jones continues; it is 22 July, near dusk:

> I carried a reel of wire and a big signal lamp in addition to my kit, rifle, etc. and etc. and then again etc. We were misdirected, passed through a gully with plenty of stiff men about and a lot of m.g. fire …..we were over the top and groping forward paying out the wire ….. After about another hundred yards a bullet whistled just over us. Mac yelled "By Cripes that was one of ours". We knew the sound of a Lee Enfield rifle. He yelled out and we suddenly found ourselves on a crowd of Diggers, facing the wrong way. All was confusion. There was an officer on the ground shot through the stomach, N.C.O.s excitedly arguing, and about thirty men trying to deepen a shallow trench. They were 3rd Brigade chaps. We told them who we were and that they were facing the wrong way and on the wrong track, but nothing would do ….. Well I tried to argue with these chaps. All to no avail ….. No, they were right and I was mad, so away I staggered with rifle and equipment, phone, lamp and reel. In front was a furious, almost incredible Hell. I felt very lonely and very frightened.[106]

Over the course of the night of 22/23 July, Jones' signaller party appears to have stumbled into at least three separate parties of men, as well as twice making and losing contact with the D Company they were attached to.

Here is the confusion of trench war exemplified, with no effective communication or control from higher command. Their telephone wire was being continually cut by the shelling, repaired, then cut again. Like the others, they had experienced the disorientation that beset those leaving trenches. The encounter with the 3 Brigade soldiers showed how extreme the disorientation could be.

As dawn broke, they found themselves at the left edge of the remains of Pozières, just south of the Albert-Bapaume Road that bisects it. Effectively, none of the village remained intact. Jones learned later that his pal Mac had been hit in the neck by shrapnel and another friend hit in the eyes.

The Australian attack on Pozières that night resulted in a foothold gained on the southwestern end of the village. Here, the fortified post known as Gibraltar was taken. Over the next week, the Australians would invest the ruins of the village and threaten the twin defense trench system that ran along the ridge from northwest to southeast. This trench system was known as the OG lines. They were overrun on the south side of the Albert–Bapaume Road by the Australians, who then worked northward while also attacking the OG line frontally from the village ruins. During this time they were subjected to a horrific artillery bombardment.

There are a number of firsthand accounts describing the appalling conditions encountered between 23 July and 31 July. As usual, Charles Bean's personal diaries make for more compelling reading than the subsequent official history. In this entry from his personal diary on 23 July, Bean has reached 2 Brigade Headquarters in Contalmaison and then makes a dash to 3 Brigade Headquarters, perhaps some 200 yards away. He records the time as fifteen minutes after midnight on 22/23 July:

> Arrived at General MacLagan's dugout in Contalmaison. In the scurry of the last 100 yards across shrapnel swept roads in the middle of which I had to put on my gas helmet ….. Felt very sick just before getting in but [gas] helmet is certainly a help. We have had several men lose their way here already. Pioneers sheltering under their own dump. Someone coughing. Helmets on again. Aromatic smell of gas all round.

Shortly after, Bean recorded this surreal account:

> I had had no experience as to when gas was bad enough to put a helmet on and when it was safe to go without. The hill sloped down and as I went down it seemed to me that I got into a soft aromatic smelling air – was this gas? There was a dugout by the road with a man in it in the side of a cutting. Perhaps he knew. I asked him if they had had gas there.
> I couldn't make out his answer but it had to do with a sprained ankle. He had been told to take a pigeon basket back to British Brigade H.Q. in Contalmaison and he had sprained his ankle and wanted to know what to do. The sprain I know was pure funk. He was afraid to go alone in the shelling and the gas. I said: "Here, give me a hand of the basket and I'll help you" and we went together.
> As we got down the hill there was no doubt we were getting into gas – no doubt whatever. Was it bad enough for helmets. For all I knew it might be doing a deadly injury to one's lungs – so I decided to put the helmet on. The man beside me said: "Get into this trench, Sir - ." He evidently knew a trench beside the road. It seemed to me a bad place for gas – a low trench, but perhaps he knew. So I got into the trench and followed him – he knew the way – I had no idea of it.
> In one's helmet it was impossible to see – it was almost deadly dark. I could just make out the lurid flash of shrapnel (or probably gas shell) on the other side of the road – and it made me hurry. I hadn't the ghost of an idea what was ahead or where I was going.
> I knew it was a bad thing to exert oneself in a gas helmet but had forgotten. It brings on acute suffocation. I could hardly take my breath in and out. The only thing was to lie down in the trench and rest till I got it again. I knew I mustn't take the helmet off.
> Really I thought then I was done. I didn't know the way. I seemed to be going into a shrapnel barrage. I didn't know if I should soon get back my breath and I couldn't see and yet did not dare take off my helmet.
> However, as I lay down my breath came back. The road was better than the trench – there seemed to be some transport moving along it. So it must be moderately possible to go along it. The first men that passed me seemed to have masks on like Inquisitors, but presently two came by with no masks. I tore mine off at once. Clearly it was not bad enough for a mask there. My

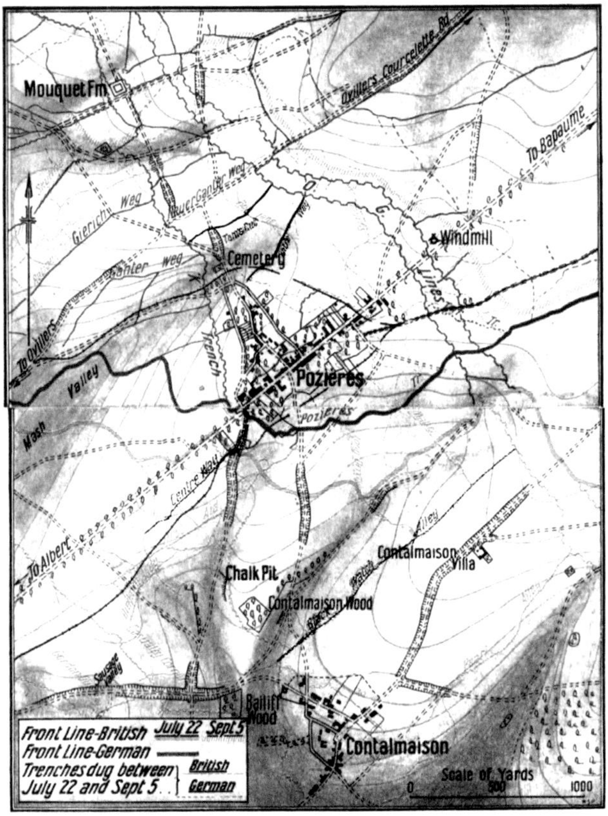

A reproduction of Charles Bean's map of the Pozières and Mouquet Farm area of operations July – September 1916. The original appears in volume III of the official history.

friend with the pigeons came up to me with his pigeon basket thrown away. "That'll be alright," he said.[107]

This from Leonard Jones on 23 July:

No one seemed to know where H.Q. was ….. shelling was hot and sensing one salvo that would surely drop in we fell flat, me full length. It just went over the top. The earth heaved and shook and clods fell on us. Feeling something warm under me I found I was lying on the naked remains of our Sergeant Toc Oates. There was only the trunk left with the "Cawnpore Angels" a relic of his India days tattooed on his back. Along the trench was an arm holding a D.3 phone.[108]

And for 25 July:

Early in the morning of Tuesday our possy [position] got the inevitable ….. I must have been blown into the sap and probably wandered about dazed for some time, for the next I remember I was sitting down in a strange place picking the entrails of a man off my puttees. There I was, just like picking bits of straw as we used to do in the billets, only it was a pal's inside.

Perspectives can differ. Cpl. R. C. Shutler of 7th Battalion was killed in action the same day. Well after the battle a fellow soldier wrote to Shutler's grieving mother. What would she have made of his words?

> I am writing this letter with the hope of giving you a little consolation; for it is a grand thing to know that you were able to help the Empire in some way. The loss is certainly heavy but what a glorious way of dying; and after all, we all have to go. This is the soldier's way of looking at the hard fact and did you ever see a man of service who was not a fatalist. You have the sympathy of the whole platoon or rather those who are left ….. I cannot say exactly where the boy is buried. All that I know is that he was buried on the spot where he was hit and that is a little to the southwest of Pozieres. Buried in company with many other brave lads.[109]

The writer of that letter was Lt. John Gordon, Shutler's company commander. On 26 August—the day after Shutler's death—Gordon himself was severely wounded in both arms and hospitalized in England. He would return to Australia in May 1919.[110]

The "game" or "glorious" death is a recurring theme in such letters. This from George Powell of the 28th Battalion concerning his Italian friend Luigi Rimaldi, who had only been naturalized in September 1915 and died at Pozières on 29 July. He concludes the letter:

> I can only say that if it be God's Will that I must go under I pray that I shall die as gloriously as did my friend.[111]

And this from Sgt. Fred Barbour (9th Battalion) to the father of Sgt. P. G. Browne, who was killed at Pozières on 19 July:

> Deeply as we all regretted his loss there is not one of us but envies him so glorious a death in his country's service.[112]

On 28 July, Bean wrote in his diary:

> We [the Australians] went out in daylight to collect wounded. Germans in most cases stood up and withheld fire. In some cases they said: "Go on collect your wounded and get back!" When somebody started collecting arms [weapons] they fired on him. Another wounded man says that a German took his equipment, water bottle and rations and said: "You're lucky not to get a bomb for breakfast." Lieutenant Flett was killed and Kennedy and Brind and Raws is missing.[113]

Robert Raws was with the 23rd Battalion—part of the 2nd Australian Division—that had by now been drawn into the battle to relieve the weary 1st Division. Another brother, John Alec Raws—also of the 23rd Battalion—had searched in vain for his brother's body. In a letter written during rest behind the lines on 8 August, John advised his sister that Robert—affectionately known as Goldy—had gone missing on 27/28 July:

> First, as to Goldy, though. He is either dead, prisoner or wounded in the head, so that he is more or less blind, but should recover. The confusion of an offensive such as ours is so great that I have been unable to discover just what happened.

He then continues his letter with an unusually candid account of the horrors of the Pozières battlefield at the end of July:

> In the midst of this barrage our line was held up. I went up from the rear and found that we had been cut off – about half of us – from the rest of the Battalion, and we were lost. I would gladly have shot myself, for I had not the slightest idea where our lines or the enemy's were, and the shells were coming at us from, it seemed, three directions ….. We eventually found our way to the right spot, out in No Man's Land. I was so happy that I did not care at all for the danger. Our leader was shot before we arrived, and the strain had sent two officers mad. I and another new officer took charge and dug the trench ….. it was awful but we had to drive the men by every possible means. And dig ourselves. The wounded and killed had to be thrown to one side. I refused to let any sound man help a wounded man. The sound man had to dig. Many went mad ….. We got away as best we could. I was again in the rear going back, and again we were cut off and lost. I was buried twice and thrown down several times – buried with dead and dying. The ground was covered with bodies in all stages of decay and mutilation, and I would, after struggling free from the earth, pick up a body by me to try to lift him out with me, and find him a decayed corpse. I pulled a head off – was covered with blood. The horror was indescribable. We got down to the first Dressing Station. There I met another of our men who was certain his cobber was lying wounded in that barrage of fire. I would have given my immortal soul to get out of it, but I simply had to go back with him and a stretcher bearer. We spent two hours in that devastated village searching for wounded. But all were dead. The sights I saw during that search – and the smell – can I know never be exceeded by anything else the war may show me. I went up the next night and stayed there. We were shelled to hell continuously. My Company Commander went mad and disappeared ….. we hung on, until eventually we were relieved on 6/8/16[6 August 1916]….. I've hardly told you anything. There is so much to say. My nerve lasted alright and my constitution. I had not even a coat and we had no dug-outs. I got water and biscuits from a German body.
> I saw many of my friends die.
> The post is off. Good luck.[114]

In his personal diary, Bean described the scene in and around Pozières on 31 July. He approached from the south, making his way from Casualty Corner through broken trench lines and tracks. He describes what amounts to a field of dead. The way was littered with bodies, often in small groups where a shell had burst. He found his way to the northern edge of Pozières, then:

> I turned back and followed the goat track path to the right. There were only blackened dead and occasionally bits of men – torn bits of limbs unrecognisable along it. I wandered on for 5 minutes without seeing a sign of anyone till I came to a gradually improving trench – quite deserted – peopled only by dead men half buried – some sitting upright with bandaged heads – apparently little

hurt except for the bandaged wound – others lying half covered in the little holes they had scratched in the trench side.[115]

He also noted the salient feature of the Pozières Heights to the east:

I kept as much as possible in the bottom of the craters and presently found the wall of a house in front of me. I climbed over the broken bricks. The Windmill where they say the Germans have observation was always unpleasantly obvious ahead.[116]

The windmill had by now been reduced to a heap of rubble, but logically enough for a windmill, it did mark the highest point just to the rear of the second OG Line.

On 1 August, Bean noted that a chaplain was burying Australians to the south of the road:

He and Sergeant Lang were burying 24 others today on road from Chalk Pit past dressing station in order to have them out of the way of the troops going in. It does not encourage new troops to see a sight like that. They simply turn them into the nearest shell hole and cover them up. No time to get identity disk – it is generally rotted away. So these poor chaps go down as "missing" unless someone has their disk already.[117]

Such graphic accounts never made their way into the official history. In this respect, Bean's personal diaries are a far more potent resource.

The enemy was also suffering. At the same time Bean was writing of the carnage wrought on the Australians, a few hundred yards away on 2 August, a German soldier wrote to console a wounded comrade:

One is no longer a man here, one is worse than a pig, filthy from top to toe ….. for you, the beastly show is at an end. Don't take it too much too heart about the loss of your left arm, the chief thing is to be far, far away from here ….. If the dear ones at home could just see this …..[118]

Bean would devote a full seven chapters in his subsequent official history to the taking of Pozières. As for the village itself, he was sufficiently transfixed by the devastation to describe it in unusually graphic detail. This from his small book *Letters from France*, published during the war in 1917:

Imagine a gigantic ash heap, a place where dust and rubbish have been cast for years outside some dry, derelict, God-forsaken up-country township. Imagine some broken-down creek bed in the driest of our dry central Australian districts, abandoned for a generation to the goats, in which the hens have been scratching as long as men can remember. Then take away the hens and the goats and all traces of any living or moving thing. You must not even leave a spider. Put here, in evidence of some old tumbled roof, a few roof beams and tiles sticking edgeways from the ground, and the low faded ochre stump of

Pozières before the war, looking northwest along the Albert-Bapaume Road. In the distance, the village gives way to a tree-lined section of the road, to the left of which would be the windmill. *Author's collection*

Pozières after its occupation by the Australians in August 1916. Here, the remains of the road are intersected by Centreway Trench. The place from where this photograph was taken is very close to that in the preceding photograph. *AWM*

> the windmill peeping over the top of the hill, and there you have Pozières. I know of nothing approaching that desolation.[119]

This account is more or less repeated in his official history.[120] It is certainly a more sanitized version than the horrors of his diary entries for the same place at the same time. The three versions: the personal diary account, the later version in *Letters From France* and, finally, the official history version illustrate how the retelling of a story can almost immediately induce a philologically challenging "drift." By the third version, Bean enters the village by a slightly different route and cites the source as "An Australian who on July 31st inspected the whole Anzac front."[121]

The attacks of 22/23 July saw the Australians secure the southwest end of Pozières and nearly complete an occupation of the OG lines (the "Old German" Lines) south of the Albert-Bapaume Road. Some occupations of parts of the village north of the road were made, but these were tentative. The OG lines north of the road and substantial sections of another German trench to the immediate west of the village later known as Kay Trench still blocked progress. For the rest of the week the Germans heavily bombarded the village.

The exhausted 1st Division was replaced by the 2nd during 25/26 July. They undertook two costly attacks. The first, on 29 July, was a failure. The second, on 2 August, constituted a very costly and limited success. The 2nd Division completed the slow and dangerous work of putting out jumping-off trenches to the east of the village. By 4/5 August, the Australians had reached and held the first OG line. Those who moved on to the site of the windmill could not at first locate the second OG line. It had been obliterated, but Pozières Heights was theirs.

It had left the 2nd Division in a worse state than the 1st, which it had relieved. It was at this time that the 4th Australian Division was drawn into the battle. Before this, however, the Australians in and around Pozières were subjected to the most intense artillery bombardment yet. It kept them sheltering until, in the early morning light of 7 August, a German counterattack swept through the OG lines and pushed the Australians back toward

An Australian crew loading their heavy trench mortar. This is a scene from behind the lines, as indicated by the casual poses of those in the background. The date is 2 August 1916. They are on the Somme, most probably near Pozières. *AWM*

the village on a front of about 400 yards. In fierce fighting—often at very close quarters and hand-to-hand—the Australians forced the Germans back and regained their positions in and around the remnants of the OG lines and the windmill, seemingly without direction from higher command and of their own initiative.

This was a significant action. It fell to small groups to retake the ground. It was not a case of a consolidated line being re-formed, with men being briefed and then directed back across the lost ground.

The Australians were not necessarily endowed with greater intelligence than their Allied counterparts. Nor were they showing any signs of stricter military discipline. However, they were generally displaying coherence, individuality, and a propensity for well-developed critical faculties. They might not salute officers, but they could work in groups regardless of rank. These elusive and seemingly contradictory traits sprang from deeper sentiments about how to face ordeal. Here was their discipline, seemingly formed amongst those who for a variety of reasons had found Australia a preferable home to Britain. Those who were Australian-born carried these individualistic traits from their English migrant forebears. They were also volunteers for a very distant war, paradoxically not far from the place many still referred to as "home."

The Australian impression of the British command was nevertheless low. Gallipoli, Fromelles, and now Pozières constituted a real test, and it is that test that is perhaps central to the AIF and the legendary status that subsequent generations of Australians have rightly or wrongly crafted into the Anzac tradition. Crafting that legend has on occasion led to some misleading conclusions, even in matters as primary as the salutary names with which they have been endowed. "Digger" is a good example. Its original meaning had nothing to do with Australians. The term arose to describe the Pioneer battalions of the New Zealanders. At forty percent of all eligible males, the New Zealanders had the highest rate of mobilization of the dominions.[122] The Australian fashion of describing all Australian soldiers—then and ever since—as "Anzacs" also has the problematic twist of invariably overlooking the New Zealanders.

Over the twelve days it was in the line, the 2nd Division had suffered the worst of the unprecedented German artillery bombardment, with 6,846 casualties.[123] The 1st Division that preceded them suffered well over 5,000 casualties. The last division in (the 4th) took 1,000 casualties. This amounts to close to 13,000 casualties, of which around nearly 4,000 were killed. There is no place in any war where Australians have suffered such high casualties, ever.

As with those at Fromelles, the soldiers at Pozières had been sorely tried. In their ordeals they seem to have found themselves to be more Australian than anything else. The dynamics of the emerging sense of Australian identity commenced well before this war, but they were at work more forcefully here than before.

It needs to also be acknowledged that an inestimable number of these men were left traumatized and debilitated for the rest of their lives. And of course, the thousands of unknowing horses and mules that hauled the material of war were just as susceptible to bomb and bullet. They tend to be forgotten altogether. The screams of wounded animals and the detritus of the dead, rotting carcases added to the obscenity of war.

The three Australian divisions would almost immediately be sent back into the line for the subsequent push toward the next objective on the ridge: Mouquet Farm, to the north of Pozières. Before covering this action, a brief review of the performance of the High Command—and particularly its Commander, Haig—is given.

Haig's Instructions

In the matter of the July 1916 Somme Offensive, the British High Command under Haig seems to have defaulted. It has been noted that Haig either fell into a decision or was somehow overtaken by events, rather than having made a preparatory analysis leading to an alternatively based decision. Haig preferred an attack farther north in Flanders, probably at the Ypres salient. He saw little to gain in Picardy. Yet it was in Picardy, on the Somme, that he attacked. At best, he appears to have yielded to French pressure for want of a thorough analysis of the situation.[124]

Haig was known for his tendency toward visions of the grand breakthrough, where infantry opened the way for a decisive cavalry sweep. Kitchener knew of it in early 1915 and the Chief of the Imperial General Staff, Sir Ian Robertson, was among those who—like the now-dead Kitchener—had cautioned Haig of this tendency. Robertson advised extreme caution right up to the July offensive.[125] Haig was still anticipating the cavalry sweep of times past in a now very industrial war.[126] What was the impact of Haig's command on the Australians?

Haig had already overseen multiple failed attempts on Aubers Ridge in the north, the latest resulting in the disaster at Fromelles. He had done much the same thing, albeit on a much grander scale, on the Somme on 1 July. On 2 July—the day after the Somme Offensive commenced—he wrote:

> A day of downs and ups! ….. visited two Casualty Clearing Stations ….. The wounded were in wonderful spirits ….. The AG [Adjutant-General] reported today that the total casualties are estimated at over 40,000 to date. This cannot be considered severe.[127]

Now, nearly three weeks into the Somme Offensive, Haig was seeking to exploit what little progress had been made in the southern sector around the Albert-Bapaume Road. This is where the Australians were committed by the impatient Gough to the attack on Pozières. In his diary on 1 August, Haig recorded:

> Our losses in July's fighting totalled about 120,000 more than they would have been, had we not attacked. They cannot be regarded as sufficient to justify any anxiety as to our ability to continue the offensive.[128]

For Haig, this seems to have been a dominant train of thought. In a letter to his wife on 10 July he wrote:

> The battle is being fought out on lines which suit us ….. the Enemy puts his reserves straight into the battle on arrival, to attack us, thereby suffering big losses.[129]

Any plan for a concerted attack to take the ridge on which sat Pozières degenerated into small, set-piece engagements.[130] On this matter Bean, in the official history, is particularly pointed.[131] The effect of Haig's written orders as opposed to his verbal urgings resulted in contradiction and indecision. Added to this was a new note of caution in the written orders themselves. Attacks must now be "suitable to the existing situation," but nevertheless see that the enemy's troops are "worn down during the present phase" and at the same time "secure the whole of the Morval-Thiepval Ridge," but always with "Due regard to economy."[132]

These instructions were sufficiently vague as to constitute a brief more likely to be exceeded or failed rather than met. They were broad to the point of being vague and ambiguous to the point of being incapable of compliance. Haig confided to his diary a much clearer opinion of the performance of the Australians at Pozières:

> 22 July. I visited General Gough after lunch to make sure that the Australians have only been given a simple task.
> 25 July. After lunch I visited HQ Reserve Army and HQ Australian Corps ….. The situation seems all very new and strange to Australian HQ. The fighting here and shell fire is much more severe than anything experienced at Gallipoli! The German too, is a different enemy to the Turk!

We have a subsequent account of the events at that 25 July 1916 meeting. At headquarters that day was Brudenell White, Chief of Staff of I Anzac Corps, and the British Gen. Birdwood, then temporarily but soon to be permanently in command of the AIF. In May 1928, Brudenell White recalled the atmosphere in a letter to Bean:

> The C. in C. [Haig] came to see us ….. He "dressed us down" severely and one of the phrases he used to General Birdwood was "You are not now fighting Bashi-Bazouks [a reference to leaderless Ottoman mercenaries]. This is serious scientific war and you are up against the most scientific and most military leaders in Europe." Had the discussion been on preparation as you suggest there would have been no need for him to have spoken the way he did ….. Moreover I actually remember his saying that he had visited Legge some days previously and thought that he was a "birch-stick" (those were his words) who was quite confident upon no foundation of knowledge or experience. This also is clear in my mind as I did what I could , properly, to defend Legge, pointing out that whatever his mannerisms are he had not undertaken the task in any light hearted spirit.[133]

Haig made a further entry concerning the Australians:

> 29 July. After lunch I visited HQ Reserve Army and impressed on Gough and his SGSO (Neil Malcolm) that they must supervise more closely the plans of the

> Anzac Corps. Some of their Divisional Generals are so ignorant and (like many Colonials) so conceited, that they cannot be trusted ….. Luckily their losses have been fairly small considering the operation and the numbers engaged – about 1000 for the whole 24 hours.[134]

Little wonder that the Australians were forming less than assuring views of the British High Command. The impact of Haig's command on the Australians at Pozières was clear: it was a gross, callous, and unnecessarily exorbitant expenditure of their lives.

In one of his last letters home dated 19 August 1916, Alec Raws provided this summation of the High Command:

> I want to tell you, so that it may be on record, that I honestly believe Goldy and many other officers were murdered on the night you know of, through the incompetence, callousness, and personal vanity of those high in authority. I realise the seriousness of what I say, but I am so bitter, and the facts are so palpable, that it must be said. Please be very discreet with this letter – unless I should go under.[135]

Four days later, on 23 August 1916, Alec Raws was killed in the advance from Pozières Heights on Mouquet Farm.

Chapter Eight

MOUQUET FARM

Just who held the heights was not immediately clear to the Australians. So pulverized was the ground that initially the German OG 2 line and the windmill at first could not be located. They were eventually found. The area was still heavily contested, as this extract from an unnamed soldier of the 5th Field Company Engineers dated 5 August 1916 attests:

> By 7.30 a.m. this morning Fritz had launched two counter attacks. His first at 4 a.m. was repulsed with very heavy losses. He got within a few yards of our trench, and left hundreds of dead or wounded. The second at 7.15 a.m. was a very half hearted go indeed and before they got half way over many of them threw down their rifles and surrendered ..... This is the second charge we have been in in a fortnight and I hope we don't get into any more. One doesn't notice it at the time but it is afterwards.[136]

By 7 August, the Australians were in firm control of the area. The remains of the windmill and the OG lines were occupied and fortified. Further along the road to the northeast, they could now clearly see the village of Courcelette, in the general direction of their originally planned eastward advance, but it was to the northwest that their attention was now directed.[137]

Ever mindful of haste, Gen. Gough set the Australians the task of taking Mouquet Farm, the next fortification on the Thiepval–Morval Ridge. It was a questionable decision. It required the creation of a very narrow salient back into the southern side of the much larger German salient. It constituted a treacherous adventure. The front that the Australians were now being asked to create in their advance to Mouquet Farm was extremely narrow. It could be enfiladed from both sides by German fire. It was as if the whole thrust eastward had, for want of advances farther north, somehow defaulted to the area in the south around Pozières and turned nearly back on itself by getting the Australians to work back along the ridge and take Mouquet Farm, and hopefully more.

Gough's plan was that by this narrow front, the Australians would isolate Thiepval by extending the line behind it. This would make the Thiepval fortifications more open to British assaults. In Haig's plan for the entire Somme Offensive, Thiepval had been a first day objective, to be taken on 1 July. Now, on 6 August, the preparatory artillery barrage on the German lines in and around Mouquet Farm commenced. On the night of 8 August, the Australian 4th Division—with the British 12th Division on its left—commenced the advance along the ridge to Mouquet Farm.

It is indeed ironic that the British High Command could now calculate with precision the time it would take for a division to be worn down based on the experiences of the previous five weeks. For the Australian advance on Mouquet Farm, the least exhausted Division (4th) would bear the weight of the attacks. The 1st and 2nd Divisions, along with the 4th, would then be relieved by changing places with the Canadian Corps presently at Ypres. What the soldiers of the 4th Division did not know as they advanced toward Mouquet Farm on 8 August was that as early as 6 August, arrangements had already been made for their departure north from the Somme after 6 p.m. on 6 September.[138]

The Australian attacks on Mouquet Farm were a repeat of the horrors of Pozières, but on a narrower front. The British II and V Corps on the Australians' left formed a sensible enough looking semicircle of attack on Thiepval on the maps, but it all swung on the Australians taking Mouquet Farm. That such a risky advance along an enfiladed ridge was being undertaken at all was simply because a better way of reducing Thiepval did not occur to the British High Command. More mud, more filth, more corrupted bodies, more shattered minds, and more ill-considered use of men's lives.

Edgar Rule

Perhaps the best personal account of the Battle for Mouquet Farm is from the diary of Edgar Rule of the 14th Battalion, a part of 4 Brigade of the 4th Division.

After the war, Rule's accounts became known to Newton Wanliss, the father of another 14th Battalion man (Harold Wanliss) who was killed in September 1917. Newton Wanliss commenced a history of his late son's battalion. In the course of his research he came into contact with Rule, who made his diary accounts available to Wanliss. Sometime during 1924 or 1925, Wanliss in turn made these available to Charles Bean, who was then writing the official history. So impressed was Bean that he had the material typed up and returned to Rule for final checking. The first typed drafts appear to have been ready by August 1925.[139] Rule's diaries were published in 1933 in memoir form under the title *Jacka's Mob*, a reference to Albert Jacka, VC, MC, who was also with the 14th Battalion. The book sold well and was reprinted.

It was not until 1999 that a limited edition of the 1933 original was published, this time purporting to include the names of some whom Rule had omitted from the 1933 edition for the usual reasons. The text is broadly the same as the 1933 edition but has undergone some editing. Again, we encounter the philological drift that comes with the retelling of the original story.[140]

Within the vast files of Charles Bean's archived materials may be found Edgar Rule's original, unblemished early chapters in their first draft typed form. It is from these unedited accounts that we will draw.[141] Rule entered one of the many German dugouts of the OG Lines on Pozières Heights, somewhere north of the windmill. It is 7 August 1916:

> This lot of dugouts were evidently a Hun H.Q., as the dugouts were fitted up pretty elaborately, but before we could use them we had to shift the dead out of them. In my two sections' dugout a young Aussie boy lay on some straw with his shirt off, and the other had two ripe Huns who fairly stunk the roof off and no one was game enough to get hold of them and drag them away. They were just at the door of the dugout in a sort of outhouse and we finished up by covering them up with dirt. The dugouts further along were just the

The front cover of a second edition of Edgar Rule's *Jacka's Mob*, first published in 1933. The foreword by the English Poet Laureate is awash with uncritical, highly sentimental praise that may have helped sell books at the time, but is entirely at odds with the undiluted horrors Rule records. As with the British reporter Andrew Ashmead-Bartlett at Gallipoli the year before, the almost hagiographic writings of Masefield fueled the Anzac legend and rather misdirected it. By comparison, Bean's accounts, official and unofficial, are highly restrained. *Author's collection*

same. One of them had two Aussies lying side by side in the passage and at the outer end a big Hun sprawled out laying face downward on the floor. Another had an Aussie with his head jammed between two beams which kept him in an upright position ….. Those that we could get at with dirt we covered over, and those we could not reach we kept away from.[142]

The semblance of a front line running roughly east to west was now being established just north of the outskirts of Pozières village:

> The sights we saw were enough to haunt a man for the rest of his days. It was the greatest number of dead I'd ever seen …... every shell hole had one or two dead men in it. The shell holes were very close together ….. No one but those who have endured such conditions can ever realise what a nightmare it was. Practically living among the dead, wherever you went or looked you had dead bodies to look at, let alone the awful stench.

Some survived. Rule writes of a wounded German who was among those who gave themselves up:

> I had a look at him and it looked as if a bayonet had been pushed right through his back and the point just come through above his nipple. As he breathed air bubbles played in the wound in the back, and it was clear that as he breathed air was coming in and going out through it. As our stretcher bearers were overworked in getting our own boys out, the Huns had to take pot luck ….. I wished he'd die and get it over. None of us went near him during the night, and the next morning as several other new Huns were going out down the C.T. [communication trench] I got the shock of my life to see this fellow staggering along with them.

Several attempts were made to seize Mouquet Farm over the next three weeks. The Australians reached the farm and established a front line, but time and again were cut off and forced to retreat as the Germans took maximum advantage of the narrow salient. There was nothing left of the farm above ground; it was the extensive underground system of fortified posts and underground galleries that were being fought over. The bombardments were unbearable and men were breaking under the strain. Rule on the outskirts of Mouquet Farm:

> The shelling never let up at all, and I began to feel that the sooner it was all over the better, because I never expected to see the rise of the sun ..... I felt sick of the whole thing and did not care if a shell blew me to pieces.

These sentiments are very similar to those expressed by Alec Raws. The difference between the two is that Raws was killed thinking that way, and Rule survived to reflect on it; such is chance.

Just on the southern outskirts of Mouquet Farm, Rule was leading a bombing party. On this occasion his party has been "bombed out" by the Germans. He provides interesting insight into a cross section of Australian soldiers at war:

> I went out to the bottom of the bank and lit my red flare and to my disgust I saw my supporting platoon all digging a trench about 100 yards away, and not making an effort to get to us. Just as I was going back up to where the rest were, the Huns were coming back and pelting bombs at us. One almost hit my foot and I only got about a yard from it when it went off. I felt as if someone had stabbed me with a lot of hot pins along my legs, and I felt blood running down my hand. It knocked the breath out of me and I remember staggering around for a while ..... My ears were ringing with the row [noise] of the bombs ..... We all got out about 50 yards and got into shell holes ..... I was sore perplexed what to do because we were under the bank and the Hun could soon bomb us out. As we were waiting here, suddenly out of the smoke and dust two men appeared coming at us with fixed bayonets. I was standing up at the time and managed to see them first. I felt sure that all our men were out that could get out, and without waiting I yelled at the lads to open on them ..... I saw their tin hats and realised who they were. One poor laddie staggered to his feet and limped over to us ..... Just before we bolted I ran over to the man we had shot and he seemed as dead as could be, and after pulling him over I left him. He was face down with his knees under him.

They made their way back to the quarry farther south that formed the only decent shelter for the whole attack on Mouquet Farm:

> I went straight to Captain Hansen. "How did you get on," he said. "No good, chased out," I replied. "Yes and you bloody well ran all the way I suppose," he said. It just knocked me flat ..... Suddenly we heard Lt. Dean's voice outside, "here we are, here we are again," and he staggered in his face covered in blood. A bullet had lifted the top of his skull and he had a wound that he died from some time after.

Rule made his way back to a trench known as Tom's Cut, just near the now-destroyed old civilian cemetery on the northern edge of Pozières. Another section of the 14th Battalion was now attacking the farm. Tom's Cut trench was hardly a good resting place:

> Parts of men were sticking out of the parapet, and they were covered with big green-backed flies until it was impossible to see the flesh at all. The smell was awful.

The Australians never did take Mouquet Farm; that task was completed by the Canadians who relieved them. For a short while, between 2 and 5 September, the Australians and Canadians fought together. Even then, the farm was again retaken by the Germans before finally falling to the Canadians on 26/27 September, and then only after Thiepval—a key, original objective that was meant to be taken on 1 July—finally fell to the British on 26 September. Mouquet Farm itself fell only after it was isolated by the British advance well beyond Thiepval.

The Cost

After the taking of Pozières in July, the Australians subsequently made seven attempts to take Mouquet Farm. The cost of taking Pozières and Mouquet Farm over the six weeks from 19 July to 5 September was a casualty list of 23,000 officers and men. To put this in some perspective, these losses are higher than for the eight months at Gallipoli.[143] The 1st Division had lost 7,700, the 2nd 8,100, and the 4th 7,100.[144] The ground gained for these 23,000 casualties was about two square miles. Among the 23,000 casualties were 6,800 dead.

To this can be added the 5th Division's losses for the 19/20 July feint at Fromelles of 5,533 casualties in one night.[145] The total casualties for Fromelles, Pozières, and Mouquet Farm stand at over 28,000. At Fromelles, of the 5,533 casualties 1,917 were killed. Of these—despite recent recoveries—1,299 have no known grave.[146] Of these 28,000 Australian casualties, nearly 9,000 were killed.

The Australian divisions were depleted and remained that way. There were insufficient reinforcements from Australia. The troops on the Western Front were disillusioned. Birdwood's reputation as a popular leader of the Australians so carefully developed on Gallipoli was severely damaged. Most Australian and British brigade, divisional, and battalion commanders were appalled at the rushed, simplistic direction of the battles Gough's command had inflicted on them at Pozières and Mouquet Farm. How could the attempt to make a narrow salient toward Mouquet Farm back into the much larger German salient have ever been conceived?

In a similar vein, had Haking ordered the Australians into Fromelles. As commander in chief, Haig either condoned these orders or knew of them. Desertion rates amongst the bewildered and battered Australians grew alarmingly. They had had enough of British High Command and they rightly believed they had been squandered.

In the official history, Bean makes the point that by the commencement of the assault on Mouquet Farm, it was evident the Australian divisions were already under-strength.[147] It would be well into 1917 before sufficient reinforcements could be brought up, although it appears the Fromelles-Pozières-Mouquet Farm sequence was one from which they never fully recovered in trained men, quality, or actual numbers. The Australians would fight on, but they had been very nearly broken.

Bean records in the official history "a certain bitterness towards the high command."[148] He is more forthcoming in his less official version of events in *Anzac to Amiens*:

> In those forty-five days Australians had launched nineteen attacks – all except two being on a narrow front, and sixteen at night ….. For the frequent shallow

The site of the windmill outside Pozières today, looking northwest. Somewhere to the immediate left would have been the OG1 and OG2 trenches. The windmill is just a grass-covered mound. On the horizon stands the Thiepval Memorial, its arch showing just above the tree line at left. Somewhere between the two are the remains of Mouquet Farm. It was from this high ground that the Australians commenced their advance on Mouquet Farm during August 1916. *Author's collection*

> thrusts on narrow fronts Haig's policy was largely responsible. He looked on this as a "wearing down" phase of the struggle ….. Haig was certainly wearing down his enemy; but he did not realise that he was even more quickly wearing down the numbers ….. of his own army.[149]

In his personal diary written at the time in the field, Bean is even less restrained. In the entry for 29/30 August at Mouquet Farm, Brudenell White discusses the limited and under-manned nature of the probing patrol attacks they have been ordered to undertake and Bean reflects on the matter. Given the extracts from Haig's diary, it is obvious that the "general" mentioned is Haig:

> The general is apt to push a division at a place like Pozieres and then talk of the "unnecessary loss of life" being due to the Divisional commanders using "a quite unnecessary number of troops … My dear chap, to take one of these lightly held positions you don't want a great depth in the attack – you don't

need a lot of men all swarming over the place to be shelled to hell next day. Quite a light line will do it ...[150]

And two pages later:

We could have been up to Mouquet Farm on July 22/23, I daresay, if the staff of the Army had been prepared for it; and we could certainly have had Courcelette on August 4/5. The imagination of the staff doesn't seem equal to these occasions. They don't realise that when we break through a front there is usually nothing in the trench behind – any more than there is in ours ..... As it is we have to give up the theory that this battle [for Mouquet Farm] is an attempt to push through: it becomes simply a big diversion – a gigantic feint ..... if we did not suffer from such a poverty of brains .....

Writing to Bean in 1923, Colonel Raymond Leane, commander of the 48th Battalion, observed of Mouquet Farm:

Never in my whole experience of the war did I experience such continuous and concentrated shelling ..... We went into the trenches with over 1000 men ..... We returned to the trenches a few days after, but the Battalion strength was then under 300.[151]

The effect of the fighting at Mouquet Farm on Edgar Rule:

As far as I was concerned I never got over this lot for fully six months. During that time the thought of the front line sent me into shivers, and often at night I'd wake up and in a dazed way live some of it all over again. I know lots were the same as I was.[152]

The Australians were relieved by the Canadians in early September 1916. In accordance with the master timetable of the British High Command, they were transferred to the quieter Ypres sector, where they commenced digging in for the winter.

Chapter Nine

INTO WINTER

Battle Periodization and the People Who Were There

It is popular to record a start and finishing date for a battle. Casualties can be tallied, ground won or lost can be measured, and the efforts of all involved—from the trooper to the field marshal—can be given a convenient chronological narrative foundation from which springs notable feats of arms, decisive engagements, and so on. So it is with the Somme Offensive, which officially commenced 1 July 1916 and officially ended 13 November 1916.

This is a convenient administrative device for the war leaders, for those who write the official versions of the events, and for subsequent generations of interested readers. There is sense to the approach. To some extent it is used in this book.

However, this is not necessarily the periodization used by the combatants involved. All these events were unfolding before them in a much more random and relatively incoherent order. It serves our eyewitnesses well if we bear this in mind and permits us a deeper understanding of the stories they have left. Unless he was at the highest level of command—and this of itself was no guarantee—the soldier on the battlefield appears to have had no clear idea that his actions at the time would eventually enjoy such compartmentalization. Rather than the highly formalized nomenclature of battles there are three distinct markers of time and place for soldiers: first, they were present at the time; second, some of them have recalled, often in diaries and memoirs, all that they experienced and chose to set down; and third, they were amongst the ones who were still alive.

In this way the personal accounts often see the nature of war quite differently from those who subsequently give it its official written and visual form, those who embroider the place names on battle standards, and those who seek a linearity and causality for all that took place. These last factors—linearity and causality—are particularly problematic. The search for a cause, an effect, and a result of actions can lead to the construction of stories that overlook the fortunes and misfortunes of war; its discontinuities. These discontinuities and uncertainties are more readily found in the letters, diaries, and memoirs of the soldiers themselves. It is in the official and learned histories where causality is allowed to dominate and provide us with the seeming comforts of a beginning and an end, success and failure, black and white, and chronological coherence. To those on the battlefield, it was a lot more ambiguous and rather grey. No matter how much history is shaped to fit a cause and effect narrative, there remain the personal accounts to remind us of those who were there at the making of the history, not just the subsequent construction of it.

September 1916

Although the Australians were resting in a quiet part of the Ypres sector, this did not mean the end of casualties for the Australians. Patrols and skirmishes continued while the main effort was directed towards consolidating their new position by digging in.

Henry Neaves of the 45th Battalion has put the events on the Somme in a soldier's perspective:

> The people in Australia thought that the Somme battle was everything and because the Germans were pushed back there that it was everything. However when a map is taken and you see what a small area was being battered about and at what a cost, you could realise what a tremendous task was ahead of the Allies. The wastage in an army is enormous and could not be realised by those who saw nothing of the war.[153]

Meanwhile, south on the Somme, the British and New Zealanders were involved in fierce fighting at Flers–Courcelette.[154] This was an attempt to get the armies to the higher ground of the heights around Bapaume. The battles continued for a short while, gradually slowing as the weather deteriorated. Heavy rains made the area even muddier and less favorable to movement. This drive east had stalled. Haig was nevertheless anxious to make further progress before the onset of winter and on 9 October duly ordered the Australians now in the Ypres sector back to the Somme.It had turned out to be a short rest.

The Australians were dismayed to learn of their early return to the Somme. This entry from Haig's diary is dated Saturday, 2 September 1916:

> General Birdwood and the CGS of Australia Corps (General White) came to lunch ….. and thought they were now going to Ypres, I had no intention of leaving them there all winter.[155]

For this return tour to the Somme, the 1st, 2nd, and 4th divisions were joined by the now-replenished 5th division that had been out of the line since its disaster at Fromelles.

The Australians at Flers and Gueudecourt

As the Australian divisions were making their way back to the Somme, the autumn rains so drenched the place that it became a quagmire. As they moved past Pozières, the landscape was a sea of mud and water-filled shell holes corrupted by the incessant artillery and now, the rain. Roads and paths were near impassable or ceased to exist as the wear and tear of transporting materiel to the front lines in the wet weather degraded the whole thing into a stupefying slog. Journeys by foot of five to six miles were now taking as long as twelve hours, so poor was the condition of the terrain.[156]

The first of the Australians arrived at the Flers–Gueudecourt sector on 21 October.[157] Exhausted men—constantly in waterlogged trenches and falling from muddy paths and slimy duckboards into shell holes of freezing water—were suffering trenchfoot and frostbite. The wounded spent hours, even days, confined to stretchers man-handled by relays of exhausted bearers.

Attacks were made on the fortified positions of Flers and Gueudecourt on 5 November in heavy rain without success. A further attack was made on Flers on 14 November.

For each of these three attacks, some Australians had reached and held parts of the enemy line, only to be beaten back by the German forces. These actions cost the Australians another 2,000 casualties. Now, the harshest winter in forty years descended on the battlefield. Maintaining trenches always under bombardment in the freezing conditions and the mud and slime, scattered with the remains of the dead; all these took their toll on the troops' morale. Hot food and supplies were arriving infrequently and irregularly. Men were dying of exposure for want of warmth, shelter, and food.

Leonard Jones describes conditions at Flers on 30 November 1916:

> So commenced what will remain to most of us a nightmare, of a dreary, dead landscape – of mud – shell holes of filthy bloody water and slime with half a black body rotting in it. Men heavily laden hopelessly bogged, mules and horses sinking out of sight. Some shot and left to rot and stink. Sunken roads always under accurate heavy fire of 5.9 and 8". Wounded men kicking and screaming in mud. Parties on fatigue, lost, crawling about trying to do a job. A water-proof sheet propped up on broken rifles against a rotting bank. Wet muddy "blankets." Lice and more lice, rain and more rain. Frost and snow. Rations wet and muddy. The God-sent rum and whale oil. Numb wet feet and legs and body. The skeleton of a village – Flers. The whole terrain ploughed deeply by shell fire. Natural drainage stopped. The "earth" crumbly and denatured. It was a miserable Hell.[158]

Moving about under such conditions was difficult and the matter was compounded when trying to get food to the troops. Lt. Henry Neaves of the 45th Battalion was in charge of getting the food to one section of the line:

> The track from the dump to Longueval was very good, then from the bottom of Delville Wood to Brigade [headquarters] was very poor, but passable. From Brigade, however, the track was terrible. The mules had to plough through mud up to their bellies for a mile and a half. The place was covered in shell holes and these had to be dodged, then trenches and wire were everywhere and some of these were very hard to get across ….. Every bad part you came to you would have a couple of mules down. Difficult parts were everywhere and on an average I would say every 100 yards a mule would be down. This meant that the load (by this time it would be covered in mud) had then to be taken off, the mule dragged out, reloaded and then proceed on your way. To make matters worse too the men at this time that were sent with mules were generally the men who were no good in the line and were sent away to get rid of. Usually they were a lot of duds and they were frightened, windy [panicky] and continually growling [complaining]. The practice of sending these men away on this class of work was a very short sighted one because on the work of these men largely depended the welfare of the men in the line.[159]

Presently, the battlefield became frozen. Pvt. John Bartley of the 30th Battalion was in the trenches near le Transloy in December 1916:

> The trenches were frozen, as was also bread, meat and the water. Water was brought up in petrol tins, but was one solid block of ice. The water in the men's

> bottles was in the same condition, and the corks were frozen hard into the mouths of the bottles. Heavy frosts fell at night, no Man's Land was all snow ….. The bombs had to be turned round every half-hour during the night, or else they would freeze hard and fast into the side of the trench.[160]

We left Edgar Rule of the 14th Battalion dazed and shell-shocked somewhere near Mouquet Farm in late August. Now, after an all too brief rest in the Ypres sector, he was back in the line in the Flers-Gueudecourt sector in mid-November. As usual, he was accompanied by the lice:

> The "chats" attacked in massed formation. They always went straight to the following localities – under the armpits, the crutch, and round the knees and the waistline.[161]

On 15 November, the 14th Battalion was at Bernafay Wood, just east of Montauban. Across to their immediate east lay Trônes Wood. Winter had set in. Edgar Rule:

> We surveyed a scene of desolation. About all there was to look at was blasted tree trunks. Across a little valley Trônes Wood appeared, a place where English troops waded through blood and guts to capture. On the edge of our camp ran the road to Longueval, a quivering mass of slime, slush and mud. In front of us two 6-inch naval guns made day and night hideous by their frightful explosions ….. The cold was so intense that sleep only came in snatches. Our feet were our worst problem. It was utterly impossible to get them warm, because our one pair of boots were continually wet, and the work of getting into them after getting out of our three blankets of a morning was a painful ordeal. The boots were frozen stiff and were like boards ….. It would be impossible to convey to civilians the squalor and misery of the whole thing.

In a similar vein, Leonard Jones—English migrant turned Australian soldier—of the 3rd Battalion described the place:

> Many have tried to describe the Somme 1916-1917. It would be easier for English people to get some idea, but not Australians at Home – ever. How we ever stood up to it I don't know. It does speak wonders for all of us who went through it that we "carried on" day and night under absolutely unspeakable conditions. We plumbed the depths of human and animal misery and discomfort. Contrary to some written stuff, I rarely saw much "humour" up in front.[162]

In the same area was Sapper Adrian Henry Edmonds of the 2nd Division Signal Company. On 4 November—about ten days before Edgar Rule's entry—Edmonds wrote in his own diary:

> The mud is awful. We step out of the billets into mud over our ankles.
>
> 5/11/16. Words won't describe this mud through which we struggled knee-deep. Vehicles are out of the question. Pack animals which have failed to in the quagmire lie along the roads and tracks, having been shot as it is impossible to extricate them.

8/11/16. The trench is full of water (up to our knees), and is flowing into the dugout – wet through, cold feet, no sleep ….. We are drinking water out of shell holes and has a flavour of dead bodies, in fact some of the holes have a mixture of blood and water.
9/11/16. Outside our trenches in No-Man's Land are scores of Australian dead, killed in the last charge. It is pure murder to order a charge over this terrible ground.
17/11/16. Last night extremely cold and only one blanket.Shivering all night.This morning mud frozen hard. The poor horses who are used to dragging their feet through mud cannot make out the hard surface, which is cutting their feet cruelly.
26/12/16. Took a walk in Delville Wood, or rather what was left of it – shattered trees and trenches, shell holes, military gear, and corpses by the score are scattered everywhere ….. If only those who are responsible for this terrible war could see those silent forms![163]

Those "silent forms" were everywhere. Now farther up the line near Gueudecourt, Edgar Rule noted their grotesqueness in the mud:

On the other side of the road, about 20 feet away, was a scene which will forever linger in my mind. Scores of dead Aussies lay in all sorts of unnatural attitudes. Many were bogged up to their knees in mud, and their legs sticking fast propped their weather beaten bodies up in all sorts of postures. The poor wretches had been shot down like rats in a trap, and were never given a sporting chance.[164]

We also have an account from Sgt. Apcar de Vine of the 4th Battalion for the same period. The battalion is undertaking the usual practice of alternating its companies between the front and reserve lines.[165] He records its position as being Delville Wood. De Vine is in the firing trench:

6.11.16. The whole country is a sea of mud. I sank in up to my knees twice and had to be hauled out of the mud.

By 26 November, the 4th Battalion was well out of the line and resting at Flesselles. The 4th Battalion War Diary entry for 26 November 1916 reads:

Very wet morning, church parade abandoned but Padre held small services in billets. Strength – 35 officers, 631 others, 52 horses (2 from remount depot). Fifteen men reported absent without leave. Passes to Amiens are never examined at city entrance. Today 2/Lt. Dutton put under arrest charged with – (1) drunkenness, (2) using unbecoming & abusive language to his Superior Officer.[166]

Flesselles is some eight miles north of Amiens. Sgt. Apcar de Vine did not have a pass, but he did get to Amiens that same day. This from his diary:

26.11.16. Decided to visit Amiens with Sgts. Curran and Mills and Cpls. Palmer and Goldwater. We walked all the way, a distance of 13 kilometres, arriving there about 12.30 after dodging the piquets that are stationed on the road as the town is out of bounds. We all succeeded in having a very good time. I have no idea of

> what happened after 5pm. I woke up during the night while an air raid was on, & found myself with Sgt. Curran in the "clink."

De Vine was among those placed under close arrest, then open arrest back at Flesselles. As such, he and the others were exempt from all duties. The normal regime of backbreaking fatigues that characterized these so-called rest periods did not apply to them:

> 5.12.16. Warned that our F.G. [Field, General] Court Martial is to be held at 10am. Pleaded not guilty. We were only charged with being in Amiens & out of bounds without a pass on the 26 & 27/11/16. Evidence of good character given by Lieut. Hill, Lt. McKewan & Captain Judge, all officers of my Coy.

By the next day, the battalion was marching back into the line. On the next, de Vine wrote in his diary:

> 7.12.16. Verdict of court martial in orders tonight. We are reduced to the rank of corporal, with loss of seniority from March until 5/12/16, also to forfeit one day's pay.

Such lenient treatment characterized discipline amongst the Australians. They saw themselves more as civilians in uniform for a particular war, rather than as spit and polish professional soldiers. Their fighting prowess was recognized. They were just an untidy, casual lot for whom saluting needed to be earned more than expected. Aside from Haig—who had strongly urged stricter discipline, including the death penalty for cowardice and desertion—the general view amongst the Australians was that more would be gained by latitude than traditional military doctrine. No Australian ever suffered the death penalty on the field.

The question arises as to whether such matters were "Australian." Many in the twenty-first century would like to think this was the case and that such disregard for authority was the essence of being Australian, of having and giving a "fair go" to all. As appealing as such a construct is for many Australians, it was possibly equally if not more indicative of being "colonials." It is likely that other "colonials"—especially the Canadians and the New Zealanders—displayed similar traits. To characterize these traits as something purely Australian is potentially misleading. The great majority of Canadians and New Zealanders were themselves British migrants or of migrant stock. Confronting the British Army—the apex of the claustrophobic social confines of the very place so many had left for whatever reason—was unlikely to persuade them to act otherwise.

Leonard Jones provides us with a good example of how being "Australian" could seemingly be a process of osmosis. It will be remembered that Jones was a British migrant who was at sea on his way to Australia when war broke out and had unsuccessfully attempted jumping ship at Gibraltar to get back to England and enlist. Now in the 3rd Battalion AIF and back in the vile, wintry conditions in the Flers–Gueudecourt sector, he confides to his diary about getting used to being called a bastard:

> For myself I was getting Aussiefied. I had a bad time writing a nominal role of the boys with their, queer town names. Like most English born I was maturing a bit later than our Aussie cousins ….. Like most English I at first took exception

> to their endearing term. You could say almost anything to the average Englishmen except cast aspersions on his parents, but I gradually shook down. What a great crowd of cobbers.[167]

Jones also briefly compares the Australians with the British and Canadians, and gives some anecdotal evidence to being a "colonial":

> There was always a big difference between a crowd of Tommies on the march and us fellows. The Tommies seemed to take a shorter stride, and nearly always whistled and sang – I believe they were practically ordered to – but Australians seemed to be just determined to get there and rarely "opened out." Saved their breath. But our remarks were rather lurid. It's generally recognised that Aussies could hold their own at cussing but I reckon the Canadians could lick us any time for length, originality and hardness. I heard language up north [Ypres sector] that made me shudder.[168]

Perhaps the essence of being Australian that was forming at the time was as much to do with this as it was to any conscious claim to be Australian. Being Australian was loaded with ambiguities, and it remains so.

Sgt. Apcar de Vine

Apcar de Vine soon got back his sergeant's stripes and continued the winter war on the Somme. By the end of December, advance by either side was out of the question. The cold, inadequate supplies, and the mud and snow saw to that. The shooting nevertheless continued. On 3 January 1917, he was just outside Flers:

> I was standing with a group of my platoon outside H.Q. We were changing our socks and rubbing our feet with whale oil when a large HE [high explosive] shell fell right in the centre of the group, killing ten men and wounding 12 others. I am wounded for the first time, two pieces of shell pass through my steel helmet, smashing it to pieces and badly cutting my head, also the left hand is badly knocked about.[169]

Badly wounded and suffering from shellshock, de Vine was eventually transferred for further medical treatment and then convalescence in England:

> ….. where I made good progress & a complete recovery, only losing the use of two of my fingers for life.

It is not necessarily particularly Australian to put so positive a light on such stress, injury, and lifelong incapacity, but it was De Vine's way. It was his type that were forming the idyllic, self-appraisal of what it meant to be Australian.

His enlistment papers reveal him to be British-born. He had served a term in the Royal Sussex Regiment before migrating to Australia. He was amongst the first to enlist in the AIF on 14 August 1914, a mere ten days after the commencement of war. Perhaps he could be best described as a British-Australian.

On 14 May 1917, De Vine—still in England at an Australian camp—wrote in his diary:

> In camp all the time. Very easy time, nothing to do, attended no parades. Am fed up with this camp life, so paraded before the doctor yesterday. - To be marked fit, so that I could volunteer to go out to France with the next draft.[170]

By 28 May 1917, De Vine was back on French soil. He rejoined the 4th Battalion. On 14 September, he was severely wounded again. By 17 September 1918, he was back in England, recovering from chest wounds. He would not leave England for Australia until June 1919. In 1968, his widow successfully applied for his Anzac medallion, a commemorative piece produced by the Australian government in 1967 and awarded to all those who had served in the 1915-1916 Gallipoli campaign. As evidenced in his records, this had taken some considerable paperwork. Although married at the time of his enlistment, De Vine had nominated himself a widower on his enlistment papers and given his mother's name as next-of-kin. He had not revealed his whereabouts or circumstances to his wife Edith, nor had the Army, until after repeated correspondence with them during 1917 she forwarded them their marriage certificate as proof.

Stagnation

The November-December 1916 period was marked by stagnation. The towns of Flers, Courcelette, Gueudecourt, and their environs remained heavily contested territory marked by occasional advances and retreats on both sides, accompanied by constant shelling, sleet, rain, snow, and unremitting cold.

It occurred to Haig that for this area of the Somme advance was unlikely, and the best effort would be to maintain pressure on the front with occasional small attacks. Haig was by then attracting dismay and disillusionment from within his own camp. What the Australians, and indeed others, had been ordered to undertake into winter was the reduction of a set of villages that had been fortified by the Germans since September: Martinpuich, Flers, Gueudecourt, Lesboeufs, and Morval. The British Gen. Sir Henry Rawlinson, commander of the Fourth Army, had drawn up plans that fell well short of Haig's overly optimistic and persistent dream of a pre-Christmas breakthrough.

In his personal diary, Haig is highly critical of Rawlinson for:

> not making enough of the situation and the deterioration of the Enemy's troops. I think we should make our attack as strong and as violent as possible, and go as far as possible.[171]

Haig was ignoring the rapidly deteriorating conditions as much as he was constructing his own straw man argument that the Germans were now completely demoralized and irresolute.[172] We have two examples of senior officers arguing the point of continued attacks in such atrocious conditions: one is from a British officer, the other from an Australian.

By late October, matters had deteriorated to the point where Lord Cavan (Rudolph Lambart)—commanding British XIV Corps at the south of the Somme—insisted that if his commander Rawlinson, who had by now capitulated to Haig's demands for a breakthrough attempt, really believed ordering an attack was that worthwhile, he should visit the battlefront himself. Cavan had written to Rawlinson, virtually demanding he visit, making the observation that:

> No one who has not visited the front trenches can really know the state of exhaustion to which the men are reduced.[173]

This was strong language and was probably aimed just as much at Haig himself as Rawlinson. Rawlinson did visit the front line and reported to Haig.

Equally unimpressed with the muddy, freezing conditions was Australian Brig. Gen. Harold "Pompey" Elliott, commanding 15 Brigade of the 5th Division. He wrote in his diary:

> 1st November. Called to see General McCay and told him that proposed attack was madness and impossible in the present state of the ground. Wagstaff backed me up and McCay telephoned to General Birdwood. I had told General McCay that if I was to carry out the attack I would require an order in writing from him stating that I had objected to the attack and had been overruled and carried it out under protest.[174]

Haig initially agreed to cancel a subsequent attack for 5 November but then changed his mind. The attack went ahead, won no ground, and cost 2,000 casualties.[175] Such attacks continued through December 1916.

On 16 November, an inter-Allied conference at Chantilly resolved to recommence the advance in the spring of 1917.[176] This brought the Somme battles to an official end. Between 1 July and mid-November 1916, Haig had indeed overseen an advance—at its maximum no more than six miles and then only in some places—over 141 days. It cost the British around 420,000 casualties, the French over 200,000, and the Germans 500,000.[177] It was a catastrophically limited victory.

For the Australians on the Somme, and despite an official conclusion date, the war did go on well into December with a series of ill-considered and ineffective attacks around Flers–Courcelette: so much for battles—whether in the Ypres sector or the Somme—having neat beginnings and endings.

Chapter Ten

INTO 1917

Winter Continues

By January 1917, the Somme battlefield was frozen. Mud and water hardened into a slippery but relatively more traversable terrain. This would last until mid-February. Command, administration, and the logistics of supplying an army on the Somme required perhaps twenty men behind the lines for every front line soldier. Somewhere along the way the system appears to have failed those at the rougher ends of the trench system, for they too were set to work improving transportation infrastructure even during their rest periods out of the line.

In the main, such work centered on roads, drainage water piping, trench building and repair, and movement of munitions and provisions. In the case given here, work dealt with the extension of a narrow-gauge light railway as close to the front lines as possible. Demand was sufficient to see the addition of worn-out fighting troops to the usual pioneer and engineer battalion work forces. Edgar Rule (14th Battalion) was supposedly at rest behind the lines at Raineville:

> I was warned [ordered] to move out along with four others to go and work on the Light Railway ..... Ever since coming out of the line at Flers I'd just about dropped my bundle, and I've never been so down-hearted or weary before or since ..... Every battalion in the 4th Division were sending five men, the total amounting to sixty, and I was the only N.C.O. ..... It would be utterly impossible for me to describe the desolation of our surroundings. We were in the middle of a village called Longueval.[178]

Each member of the working party was provided with a sheet of corrugated iron perhaps four feet by six feet in size and told by the captain in charge to do two things: start work on extending the light railway and build themselves some shelter. Little of the former and more of the latter occupied the men on the first day. They were still building their shelters well into the night in the rain: four pieces of corrugated iron for four men and whatever else could be scrounged from the battlefield vicinity:

> There was just about three feet between the floor and the roof and, as the place was flat and the boys had no time to dig drains, the rain during the night just poured in and flooded everyone ..... For days this went on - short rations, disturbed rest, wet clothes and swamped dugouts. It is a mystery to me how anyone stood it.

More practical shelter was soon discovered:

> I pooled up with Sgt. Jenner, who lived in the remains of a cemetery. Someone had got down in a vault, flung out the dead, and made a home, and apart from a leak or two it was a mansion.

Such were the vagaries of being lifted from one's battalion and seconded to the broader logistical task. They completed work on the light railway through Longueval, Delville Wood, and up to Flers:

> This little line handled practically everything and it was a very great saving on horse flesh. As a man who loves our four-footed friends, the winter of 1916-1917 was a heart breaker. If they were not floundering around in the mud, they were slipping, sliding and falling down on the frosty slippery roads. Here and there one came across dead horses bogged hopelessly – their owners had blown their brains out to end their misery. To see a horse get hit and wounded is the most pitiful thing I know of.

Rule's views on mortality are morbid yet compelling. He fully realizes that he is alive and surrounded by death:

> It was a question of which was the worst – Delville Wood or High Wood. Trones Wood was a runner-up. The attitude of some of the dead was remarkable: some were sitting down, and one I saw was almost standing up leaning against the back of the trench ….. High Wood was a much smaller wood, but a far more important place than Delville Wood ….. there were three crippled tanks, and several big crosses put up by the battalions which suffered the most ….. To a civilian and a new soldier the sight of dead men is a very unpleasant thing to gaze on. To an old hand who has faced death many times it has a fascination which seems to grow. I've often wondered what it was that made a man walk out of his way to have a look at some bodies. Somehow one does it unconsciously, and often I've stood over dead men and my thoughts would run along such channels as these. I wonder who he or they were. I wonder if his mother knows. Then try and sum up all his joys and sorrows that he had on earth, what terrors he endured before he went west. These and a thousand other questions I'd find myself trying to answer. Every man who laid out [killed] was sooner or later "ratted," either by A.M.C. [Army Medical Corps] men - whose business it was to send the effects into their H.Q. – or passing soldiers who were hunting for what they could find. Almost without exception the man's haversack had been opened, anything of value taken out of it, and the rest flung all around the body.

Rule admits to being in a distinct minority who passed time in this way. He seems to be managing his own fears by engaging in such quests.

Leonard Jones held strong views on the nature of war conducted by the Germans. Cruelty was by no means the sole province of the enemy, but he was moved to record a meeting with a British soldier in December:

> I had a yarn later with a Tommy who had been in one attack, had laid out wounded and was again shot and left for dead by a German officer who had deliberately – at night – gone over the ground shooting wounded. He [the Tommy] was very bitter – it was a typical German trick. War or no war there's no milk of human kindness in this nation. Any humour they had was "heavy." Tommy sang "Good byee – Take me back to Blighty" etc. The Hun was partial to Deutschland uber Alles. Hymns of Hate. We named places "Rat Alley," "Dead Dog Farm." Fritz went in for Hindenburg Platz, Kaiser Augustus Victoria Strasse, etc.[179]

Allied soldiers, not least the Australians, could also seem cruel. In his diary, Edgar Rule (14th Battalion) has this to say of one of Australia's most decorated and heroic soldiers, Albert Jacka, V.C. The "hop-off tape" referred to has been laid well beyond the front line to reference the start point for troops who will crawl to it in darkness for an impending attack:

> Earlier in the night as Jacka and Bradley (16th [Battalion]) were out in No-Man's Land attending to their duty they were surprised to see a couple of Huns poking about eyeing up our hop-off tape. Jacka and his partner sneaked around to the rear of them and before the Huns knew what had happened Jacka was covering them with his revolver. One of the Huns started to squeal and kick up a fuss. Jacka walked up to him and, pushing the revolver into his face, pulled the trigger. Strange to say the thing never went off, and Jacka belted him across the jaw with it. After a little further attention [presumably a beating into silence] he quietened down and the pair of them were taken to our C.O. Here the Hun officer complained very bitterly of his treatment, but when our colonel told him he was a bloody lucky man to be alive he shut up.

Of course, Jacka may have been acting out of self-preservation. A squealing German in no man's land is likely to have seen the Australian pair shot at by either side. Then again, perhaps the German officer with the pistol who was shooting the injured Tommies in the previous incident was acting out of compassion. Perhaps.

Although the temperatures remained low and the snow, sleet, and rain frequent, the ground would eventually yield to a thaw, ending the short reprieve from the mud and the slime of the battlefield.

Strategic Change

During 1916, there were two commanders of the two armies on the Somme: Haig for the British and Joffre for the French. Although well to the south, the French had taken an active role in the Somme Offensive to the extent that the greatest advances were made in that southern sector. That southern sector had the Albert–Bapaume Road as an axis. North and just south of it, the British—along with the Australians, South Africans, and Canadians—had paid dearly for their advance into the German main lines. Adjoining them on their southern flank had been the French, with whom they more or less kept pace in the advance.

The cost was immense and on 27 December 1916, the French commander Joffre was promoted out of the way and his place taken by the least sullied of the remaining French commanders, Gen. Robert Nivelle.[180]

In Britain during 1916, there was a change of prime minister. Asquith was replaced by David Lloyd-George. Lloyd-George detested what he saw as the waste of humanity on the Western Front. He was and remained an "easterner," one of those who still saw merit in opening fronts further east as a means of placing pressure on the Germans. He disliked Haig and Haig clearly disliked Lloyd-George. Haig's questionable summation of his command's achievements has already been referred to. In late December 1916, Lloyd-George met Nivelle and was seemingly charmed into placing the entire British forces—including the Dominion forces—under the command of Nivelle. Haig would be subordinate to Nivelle.

Nivelle too detested the waste of life on the Western Front. He saw it as a direct result of Joffre's ineptitude and now that he had replaced him, set about convincing Haig to join in a new approach. The French would attack on the Chemin des Dames (roughly east of Paris and well south of the Somme) while Haig would extend his line further south on the Somme to supplement the French effort. Haig was also to mount an attack north of the Somme River on a line running north from Bapaume to Arras. Haig agreed, apparently eager to work with a man such as Nivelle who, like himself, harbored illusory visions of a swift and grand breakthrough. Haig agreed to these plans in a letter to Nivelle on 6 January 1917.

Haig had formed the view that Nivelle would conduct a breakthrough assault in the drier reaches of the Chemin des Dames, that Haig would draw away German reserves in an attack on the Arras sector—again a drier place than the Somme—and that Haig would then be able to concentrate on his long-held, long-forestalled breakout from the Ypres sector in the far north. What Haig and Nivelle were about to undertake was a continuation of the "short war" dream. They would fail.[181]

With or without Lloyd-George, but with a lot of support from the British royal family, Haig soon saw the command of British forces returned to him in practice, if not immediately in word. More worrying was the German announcement in February 1917 to pursue unrestricted submarine warfare against all vessels bound for or leaving British waters. Haig's interest in the Ypres sector developed into a plan for an amphibious landing on the Belgian coast to secure their ports, but nothing came of it. The Americans were now pressed to act and they declared war on Germany on 6 April 1917. Although without a standing army to send to the Western Front, this declaration of war on Germany was significant. Much of the British materiel and munitions was already being supplied by the United States. Their eventual entry to the Western Front for actions in 1918 worried the Germans. The impending arrival of the Americans would shape German military decisions for the rest of 1917.

February 1917 also saw the German high command order a straightening of their line on the Somme. This amounted to a withdrawal farther east to a new high ground of immensely strong fortifications known to the Germans as the *Siegfried Stellung*. To the Allies it was known as the Hindenburg Line.

The German withdrawal to the Hindenburg Line, coupled with the decision for unrestricted submarine warfare, can be seen as German recognition that conquering France and turning the whole area into a German economic zone was now out of the question. Rather, they chose to consolidate what they still held and would attempt to starve the British by submarine warfare as they themselves were being starved by the British naval blockade. The Germans attempted to negotiate a peace but nothing came of it.

Another distraction was the first Russian revolution in March 1917. Allied confidence in the capacity of the Russians to maintain a second front wavered. This first, relatively liberal revolution would be followed in November 1917 by a much more violent Bolshevik version that would see Russia out of the war altogether by the end of the year.

Bapaume

On 1 February 1917, the Australians advanced beyond Gueudecourt and prepared for an advance on the next main town, Bapaume. There had also been some command changes; three of their divisions now had new leaders. Maj. Gens. Smythe VC, Holmes, and Hobbs took over the 2nd, 4th, and 5th Divisions respectively from Legge, Cox, and McCay.[182]

On 24 February, the Australians finally occupied what was left of Le Barque and Ligny-Thilloy south of the Albert-Bapaume Road. It was during these advances that the Australians came to the realization that the Germans had withdrawn along the line. They left occasional reserves of strongpoints to slow the Allied advance. The retreat also evidenced an explicit example of the German military concept of total destruction. In every village and town as many buildings as possible were destroyed. Some that had not completely burned remained daubed with tar pitch. Every well was rendered unusable, every orchard tree cut down, and every animal taken or killed.

By the beginning of March 1917, the Australians had secured the areas north of the Albert-Bapaume road. Loupart Wood and Grévillers were occupied. By 17 March, they were in Bapaume. The town had been nearly destroyed by the Germans.

Chapter Eleven

Bullecourt

From Bapaume to Bullecourt

With the spring thaw, a new series of offensives was ordered by the British High Command. Arras was set as the next objective. The town lies some fourteen miles north of Bapaume, which was now occupied by the Australians.

To help secure Arras, a diversionary attack farther south was also conceived. It centered on the village of Bullecourt, which lies roughly midway between Arras and Bapaume and six miles farther east. Its purpose was to draw German forces south, thereby

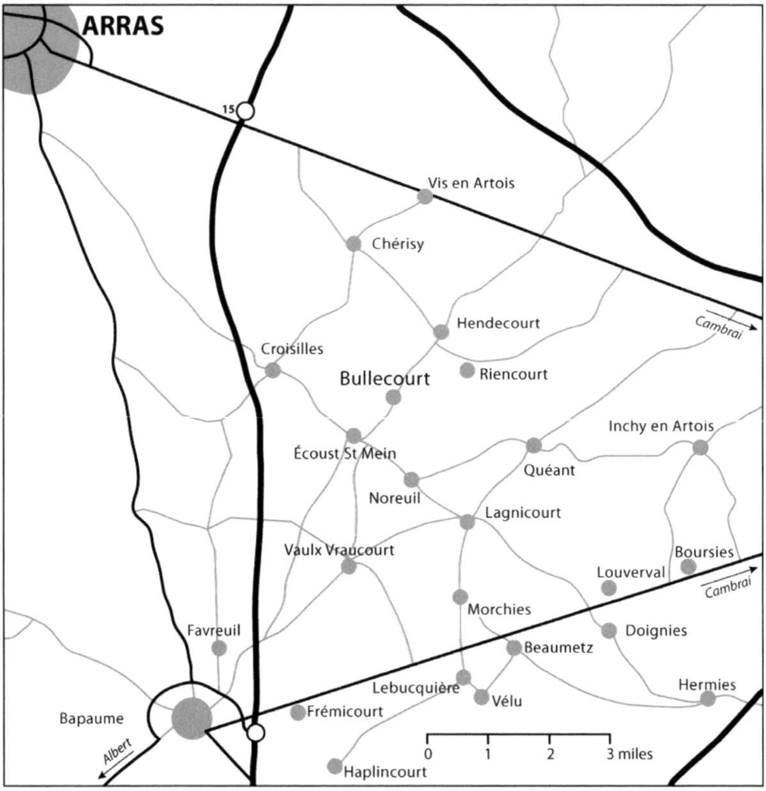

The Breakout from Bapaume to Bullecourt, March-May 1917

improving the chances for a successful assault on Arras. The attack on Bullecourt was to be undertaken by the Australians in what amounted to a breakout from the newly occupied town of Bapaume. This was higher ground. The terrain between Bapaume and Bullecourt was relatively drier and less corrupted than the Somme. The weather was improving and a more open and mobile style of warfare seemed possible. Maneuver, not mud, seemed to lie before the Australians. But the shelling from both sides, coupled with heavy snows during March-April, conspired to return the ground to a muddy state.

By 18 March 1917, the Australians had taken the village of Frémicourt, to the east of Bapaume, and Vaulx to the northeast. By the next day, Lebucquière and Vélu—even farther east—were secured. This advance was being achieved at a hitherto unprecedented pace; the Germans had, after all, retired to their Hindenburg Line, leaving only small rear guard parties to impede the advance. Between 19 and 21 March, Morchies and Beaumetz were also taken.

At this time, the deteriorating weather, extended transport lines, and stiffening German opposition was beginning to take its toll. Now somewhat compressed against their Hindenburg defenses, the concentrated German army resisted an attempt by the Australians on 19 March to take the village of Noreuil farther north. It was stopped in its tracks. On 23 March, the Australians nearly lost Beaumetz to a counterattack by the Germans. Three days later back in Bapaume, a delayed mine blew up the town hall. Charles Bean was billeted there. He wrote in his personal diary:

> March 27.Yesterday afternoon on getting back to Vaulx from the front line at Lagnicourt, someone – Wellington, I think – at Brigade H.Q. told Gilchrist and myself that the dugout in which we had been living at Bapaume had been blown up by a delayed mine ….. There were two men working there at the time, the signals sergeant and a runner - & they are still there.[183]

Harold Williams

Sgt. Harold Williams of the 56th Battalion—a survivor of the disastrous 5th Division's action at Fromelles—had just returned from a training school course for British and Colonial NCOs. His opinions of the British and Australians he met there is something of an exception to the more broadly held views and is worth noting:

> They were of great moral value in bringing together men of all countries and characters; the mixing of the English and colonial soldiers in this way broke down many prejudices. Thus we learned the traditions and the real quality of many of the British regiments – often ignorantly slandered in the AIF on the score of short-comings in some newly-raised war battalion; and on their part they learned that Australians were not all the boasters they had heard of who delighted in insulting English officers and flaunting the fact that we were the best paid troops in the field.[184]

Such observations have been overwhelmed—at the time and since—by more popular Australian sentiments about British competence. Not all British officers and men were seen by all Australians as incompetent, yet it remains a pervasive outlook.

On 3 April, Williams was near Doignies, just south of the Bapaume-Cambrai road.[185] Around here was a number of small villages: Louverval, Boursies, Haplincourt, Morchies,

An Australian 18-pound gun crew in action in the Noreuil Valley during the fight for Bullecourt, probably April 1917. Empty shell cases have been thrown in front of the gun. *AWM*

Vaulx, and Lagnicourt. All of these are east of Bapaume and represent a relatively dense set of settlements that the Australians proceeded through toward Bullecourt. He wrote:

> Presently a shell landed close to us and almost immediately one directly in front and one to the rear. One of our fellows remarked how close the three were, and I answered that the gunners had to put one right in the trench to get us. The words were scarcely out of my mouth when there came the whistle and roar of an exploding shell. I was hurled to my face in the bottom of the trench and felt as if a draft horse had kicked me in the solar plexus. My mouth was open and rigid, my hands clutched to my stomach, and my limbs felt as if they had been petrified. My face was turned to the spot where only a few minute before I had been relieved on post. Instead of a man there was a heap of tumbled earth that still smoked from the explosion of a shell, and intermingled with the smoking mass was blood, flesh and fragments of clothing. My face, arms and head were covered with the poor wretch's minced flesh and warm blood.[186]

It took Williams some time before he could stand unaided. He was in shock, concussed, and temporarily deaf. For many hours after:

> When men spoke to me their voices came from miles away, and it took me an appreciable time to realize what they were saying. Even the noise of the shells appeared not to matter. My stomach, back and ribs ached damnably.

The next night, just outside Morchies, he helped an exhausted friend. His account is counterpoise to some of the baser behaviors the battlefield could induce:

> Just as we got clear of the wood Jack Brewster collapsed in the mud ….. I was alone in the darkness with a game man whose shame at his exhaustion made me pity him. I took his rifle, and with him hanging on to my equipment we plodded up the rise down which we had advanced seemingly years ago. It was daylight when we reached the sunken road with Jack Brewster's weight hanging with both hands to the braces of my equipment.

By 6 April 1917, the Australians had consolidated their position before Bullecourt on the Hindenburg Line. They now occupied the nearest remaining villages of Doignies, Louverval, and closest of all, Noreuil, from where they had been repulsed two weeks earlier.

Prisoners' Return

On 9 April, the British Army commenced their long-planned attack on Arras. This was the signal for the Australian push on Bullecourt. Before it got fully underway, a sobering account was recorded in the 48th Infantry Battalion war diary:

> Relief of 52nd Bn completed at 2.35. Casualties 1 O.R. [other rank] killed, 3 wounded and 3 O.R. come into our lines this morning. They were members of 5th Dorsets [British] Battalion and were captured by the Boch last January and escaped from German compound last night. Enemy shelled [us] regularly through the day. Weather fine.

There is accuracy yet incongruity in this official reportage: deaths, injuries, shelling, and fine weather. The ever-present Charles Bean recorded a more sobering entry about those escaped British prisoners:

> April 9. I saw today 2 of 3 English soldiers who were brought to Corps H.Qrs. after coming into 48 Bn lines. They had been prisoners of the Germans. Butler was keen on my seeing them as they show in their bodies how the Germans treat our prisoners. I found them lying down – one man covered with boils, the other so thin and pale that he looked like dying. He seemed to have dysentery and was retching when I got to him. He (Parsey) had weighed 13 ½ stone before he was captured – he is about 10 stone now. This is due entirely to the way they were fed & worked. They were working on roads behind the line. The [captured] Germans whom we see on roads here are well fed, well clothed. These men [the British] lay on shavings; in a windy hut, had no overcoats unless they could beg them off French civilians; were given one blanket when the snow came; were butted with a rifle if they didn't get up on time or didn't work hard enough, not so much by the soldiers from the line as by the permanent base men.[187]

The Flawed Plan for Bullecourt

Although the village of Bullecourt gives its name to these battles, the plan formulated by Haig actually involved a division of British V Corps advancing west of the village and a division of I Anzac to its east. Some delay to the original timetable was incurred through the protestations of Gens. Birdwood and White. They had been clearly shown that the extensive, deep double lines of barbed wire set at angles to separate and then herd advancing troops into machine gun-swept concentrations still remained intact. The overriding desire of the British High Command to quickly follow up the British assault on Arras nevertheless brought a sense of dubious necessity to the early timing of the attack. What the Australians were about to experience was their third disaster on the Western Front. After Fromelles and Pozières-Mouquet Farm, the attack on Bullecourt would make a convincing trilogy of ill-considered use of their lives. It was still Haig's intention to deploy cavalry through the intended breaches in the Hindenburg Line, both at Arras and Bullecourt. The galloping breakthrough dream remained firm in his mind.

There was known to be a sort of second main branch to the Hindenburg Line. It commenced from the village of Quéant, behind Bullecourt, and led off behind the Hindenburg Line to the north. It was known to the British as the Drocourt-Quéant Switch. Gough was convinced that a breakthrough at or around Bullecourt and into the Drocourt-Quéant Switch would not only relieve pressure on the attack on Arras, but also neutralize this complex set of fortifications. It was to this end that he sent the British 62nd Division into the Hindenburg Line just west of Bullecourt and the 4th Australian Division to its east.

According to Gough's plan, these forces would sweep through key posts behind the line at Hendecourt and Riencourt, respectively. It then appears Gough subsequently became less concerned about the Quéant Switch being taken and more concerned about getting Riencourt first. This would require the Australians to yet again advance at least a mile on a narrow front. It was almost the same kind of advance that Gough had committed the Australians to at Mouquet Farm, except this time there was no ridge guiding the line of advance. There was, however, a positively more dangerous factor; the Australians were to attack into the middle of a reentrant, an objective on a line that is recessed behind two salients.

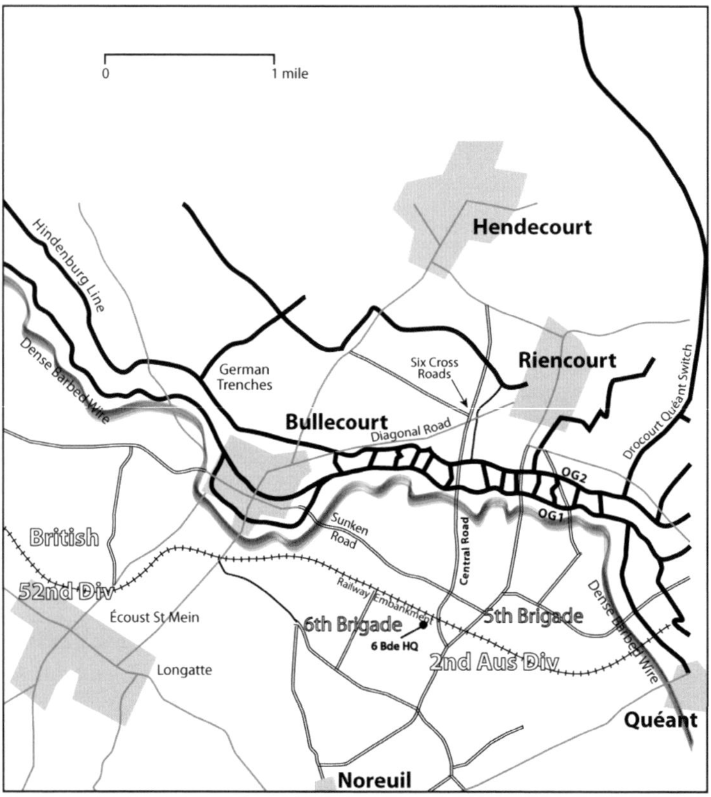

The reentrant at Bullecourt, April-May 1917

From the moment they left their trenches to assemble for the advance, the Australians would be enfiladed. How Gough imagined this would work is not clear. He too was by now well aware that the multiple belts of enemy wire remained. It would have been evident to him that murderous machine gun fire—both at the reentrant and at the wire further on—would cost the Australians dearly. He was certainly aware on the evening of 9 April that the Canadians had taken Vimy Ridge near Arras and that the British at Arras next to them had advanced some three miles. Yet here he was without even a preparatory artillery barrage effective enough to cut the wire. The fast pace of the breakout from Bapaume to the front of the Hindenburg Line had created the usual logistical problems. The full complement of supporting artillery had yet to arrive, but Gough wanted the attack to commence. The limited artillery was not given adequate time to register on the enemy line. Even when they commenced their hurriedly prepared barrage, it was weak not only in numbers but for want of adequate shells.[188]

During that evening, a British officer in charge of twelve tanks concluded with Gough that it would be feasible for the tanks to advance first, cut and crush the wire at the reentrant, allow the Australian infantry to pour through, and then provide covering fire for the advancing infantry. The tank commander was new to the field. Gough appears to have been overly impressed with the tank-led option put to him by this officer. The Australian 4th Division was unfamiliar with tank tactics. The attack commenced just before dawn the next morning, 10 April 1917.[189]

The First Attack on Bullecourt

Unseasonably heavy snows had fallen over the battlefield on 9 and 10 April. This was in sharp contrast to the relatively unscathed, green fields that the Australians entered as they moved beyond Bapaume in mid-March. Now muddy and cratered by shelling, with every village from Bapaume to the Hindenburg Line a smoking ruin, the whole place was returned to cruel winter conditions. This added to the strain of the task before the Australians. Here is Bean's personal diary entry for 10 April:

> At 2 a.m. I went up to see the attack on the Hindenburg Line with Tanks. It did not come off. About 5 a.m. Tanks could be heard puffing at Noreuil. General Gough said to Corps: if we get on in the northern part of the attack [Arras] it is up to you to do something. What are you going to do. White said: well, unless there's some worthy object to be gained we can't put a division up to face very heavy losses in front of [the] wire. But if he likes to send tanks through wire first our infantry will follow after.[190]

This is at some variance to subsequent accounts of Gough having somehow completely commandeered the Australian forces. The reason for there being a reliance on the tanks rather than a preliminary artillery barrage appears to spring from a fear that the adjoining British forces on the left might be shelled if such a barrage were put over. It seems that Birdwood and White at least acceded to Gough's proposition, but only under orders and against their better judgment. Brudenell White was very clear on how he and Birdwood had been dealt with in this matter in a meeting on 10 April 1917:

> The meeting was at General Gough's headquarters shortly after noon. We were having considerable success, I thought, in our arguments against the operation.

> When we had reached a decisive stage, i.e. when Gough was trying to make up his mind, Gough was called to the telephone and left the room. He was away for some minutes and when he returned he impressed us that he had just been in telephone conversation with the C.G.S. [chief of general staff] who had informed him that the C.in C. [Haig] had directed that the attack should be made.[191]

Birdwood and White had been trumped by a direct order from Haig himself that the tank-led attack must proceed. The first wave of Australians was already out of its trenches, assembling at the start points and under fire from the Germans. It was freezing. The men were in battle order without trench coats, lying out in the snow. Bean records the weather as so cold that he was unable to write until the next day.[192]

Those troops were now recalled with the intention of re-forming them before dawn the next day. At 3 a.m., the infantry were assembled again in front of their trenches at the start line. The first of the tanks—guided by Albert Jacka of the 14th Battalion—did not reach the start line for another half an hour. He was one of several men detailed to guide the tanks up to the start line. Seeing the obvious delay that was developing, Jacka took it upon himself to report this to the commanders of the 14th and 16th Battalions. In turn, the matter was sent to the 4th Division commander, Maj. Gen. Holmes. There had been numerous changes to successive "final" plans throughout the night of 10/11 April, including a renewed interest in taking Bullecourt village itself. There would be artillery support, but it would be limited to a time after the tanks had reached the enemy front line. Holmes—in a difficult position—decided the attack must proceed in his sector.

Around 4.30 a.m., with only three of the twelve tanks in front of the troops, the attack commenced. Some tanks were only equipped with machine guns—the so-called "female" versions of the Mark I and II. The rest were the "male" version, with two six-pounder guns. All were lightly armored, and all were now being led by one of their own crew walking ahead through the darkness and later the featureless, snow-covered terrain. Most of the other nine tanks had yet to arrive. At least three appear to have broken down before even reaching the start line. By 5 a.m., the four Australian battalions involved—the 46th and 48th (of 12 Brigade) to the left and the 14th and 16th (of 4 Brigade) to the right—were all on the move toward the Hindenburg Line objectives. Only four of the twelve tanks were in front of the infantry; the rest were behind in various states of disorder or malfunction, strung out along Central Road, which led to the enemy lines and bisected the battlefield.[193]

During this time, Pvt. William Gallwey was in a party of 47th Battalion reinforcements that had been placed at the disposal of the CO of the 46th Battalion. Gallwey was amongst reinforcements just arrived from England. This was his first action. In his account, he is not actually attacking the Hindenburg Line on 11 April. Rather, it describes his struggle to reach the British front line before Bullecourt. This party had marched from the rear of Bapaume *via* Sapignies, Vaulx, and Lagnicourt; a considerable distance in appalling weather. Just getting to the front line was exhausting. It is early morning, and they are just outside Noreuil and have crested a ridge:

> The sight that met our eyes was really wonderful. Oblivious of all risk for a few moments we stood spellbound and looked across the battlefield on the other side. It was a great open plain. In the distance about a kilometre away was the famous village of Bullecourt ..... men could be seen walking over No Man's Land. Many of these were stretcher bearers and some were walking wounded.[194]

At about 10 a.m., after hours of constant shelling and machine gun fire, the order was given to move forward—not to the Hindenburg Line, but to the support line. The "support line" was really the original front line, with the new and rapidly disintegrating front line beyond the wire and in and around the enemy trench system:

> We had about 500 yards to negotiate and had to go over open ground. Shells often fell in our midst ..... Eventually the trench was reached and we were down into it like rabbits into a hole. Water laid in the bottom and the mud was awful.

Orders were given to stand by for a bayonet charge into the Hindenburg Line when:

> We received a great shock when men of our own battalion and "A" Company began to drop in upon us from No Man's Land utterly exhausted ..... They explained they had been driven out of the front line by the enemy and had to fall back on us. Many of them had been slaughtered in the retreat and a number taken prisoner.

As the morning wore on, the Germans made a number of costly attacks on the original British font line. There comes a point where a dazed and demoralized soldier sees no more use to fighting and yet is so far advanced from his own lines that the only option seems to be to surrender. The Germans were doing this in Gallwey's sector:

> We were startled when several Germans appeared above the parapet shouting "Kamerad, Mercy Kamerad," throwing their arms away ..... [I] have never seen such dejected looking humans. They were like whining dogs. The eldest looked about eighteen. Further along the trench prisoners were coming in. In many cases they were shot dead the moment they appeared at the parapet. Some men have old scores to settle and will show them no mercy whatever.

Gallwey's party was eventually relieved after only twenty-four hours in the line by the 52nd Battalion. They returned whence they came the day before, to Lagnicourt. The place was under heavy German bombardment and was a smoking ruin. It is the evening of 12 April and darkness has fallen. The men must press on, as there is no safety here:

> The snow became heavier and it was still inches deep. Suddenly shells began to fall ..... we were all in groups at present which is not allowed. Men are always instructed to be as scattered as possible under shellfire.

One shell landed nearby:

> Just at the time the shell landed some mules were passing with a couple of limbers going for water. It fell right between the wheels of one and the driver was thrown off his mule, also another man sitting on the limber. The both limbers were broken to matchwood and round a big crater in the centre of the road was lying a terrible mess. Mules were lying dead and some of them that were only wounded were kicking. Many of our men laid there with all their equipment on. Four of them were dead. Those who had only slight wounds

> walked to the dressing station. Some of those lying there were face downwards in the mud; but we turned them over and their faces were hardly recognisable with mud and had a ghastly look. Wounded mules hopped about on two or three legs and were instantly shot.[195]

By 7 a.m. on 11 April, the 4th Division had seized its objectives on the Hindenburg Line. As for the British tanks, only four reached the wire before the enemy's front line. One had strayed well to the left of the proposed advance and halted before Bullecourt itself. Of the other three, two were stopped at the wire. Only the one remaining tank actually breached the barbed wire defenses before being stopped at the first trench. If mechanical malfunction or crew disorientation had not stopped the tanks, then the withering German artillery fire into their thin hulls had.

The German line was made up of two lines connected by a series of communication trenches. Much like the German double line at Pozières, this system stretched like a crumpled ladder across the higher contours of the battlefield. Exactly who gave the double lines at Bullecourt the names "OG1" and "OG2" is not clear, but they did resemble those at Pozières from the year before and the names have remained. It was on the OG1 line that the farthest tank got stuck.

This, along with strong German counterattacks, forced the Australians to halt and signal for a supporting artillery barrage. This barrage did not eventuate until too late; indeed, it fell on the infantry in places where they had reached the OG2 line. The Australians eventually withdrew from their newly won positions as a fall of snow commenced.

The 4th Infantry Brigade war diary records the outcome for their two battalions (the 14th and 16th) who were involved in the fighting:

> The Brigade attacked this morning at 4.45 a.m. and gained the 1st and 2nd objectives but were unable to push on to the third. After seven and a half hours fierce fighting & the supply of bombs and S.A.A. [small arms ammunition] had given out & under pressure of repeated counter attacks our men were forced to fall back. The brigade was relieved by 9 p. m. & moved back to FAVREUIL area.[196]

For 12 Brigade's two battalions (the 46th and 48th), the account is similar:

> The Brigade attacked the HINDENBURG LINE in conjunction with the 4th Aust. Infantry Brigade on our right. Tanks were to co-operate but were put out of action before the attack commenced. Both objectives were gained but owing to an overwhelming counter-attack had to be evacuated and we returned to our original front line.[197]

The appendices of both war diaries are replete with several sets of amended orders dated 10 April. In a post operational report, an officer writes this of the performance of the tanks:

> In my opinion the Tanks – probably through no fault of their officers – failed absolutely to render any assistance whatsoever ..... In fact their effect was exactly the opposite as they drew very heavy enfilade and frontal machine gun fire on the advancing troops.[198]

Lt. Col. Raymond Leane, CO of the 48th Battalion, was equally damning in a separate report. Of the performance of the tanks he wrote:

> The tanks absolutely failed to carry out their part of the attack. I consider had they shown more dash and initiative things would have been better.[199]

So much for the tanks; but what of the decision by Gough to attempt to force a breach at a reentrant? This factor, more than the performance of the tanks, led to such high Australian losses. More Australians were taken prisoner this day than any other during the war on the Western Front.

In the official history, Bean's summation is scathing:

> Gough's general conception of assisting the Third Army [at Arras] by a stroke at the enemy's exposed flank and rear was indeed sound, provided a practicable means of delivering that stroke could be discovered. But with almost boyish eagerness to deliver a death blow, the army commander broke at every stage through rules recognised even by platoon commanders. He attempted a deep penetration on a narrow front, and that at the head of a deep re-entrant.[200]

In a similar vein, British liaison officer Capt. Edward Spears concludes that Gough, in conjunction with an overly optimistic tank commander, had:

> ….. tended to give the plan the quality of a gamble, the gamble of a somewhat reckless punter plunging on the advice of an irresponsible tipster.[201]

The 4th Australian Division had broken into the Hindenburg Line without sufficient artillery support and without the tanks leading the way and then lost their gains, all in a day. The troops made their way back to the start line. In a letter to Bean in 1922, one survivor from the 48th Battalion put it this way:

> The enemy shelled lightly and kept a few machine guns going. Nobody seemed to take any notice. Men wandered back in twos and threes across the level country. The C.O. remarked, "looks like the finish of a football match."[202]

Australian casualties by 11 April were 3,191: 857 were killed, 1,059 were wounded, and a staggering 1,275 were taken as prisoners of war.[203] These casualties constitute around eighty percent of the force that attacked, and this for less than a full day's fighting. The Australians had been committed to what amounted to a repeat of the Charge of the Light Brigade at Balaclava. Like that battle, it had been "fought in a space that brought its events almost within the view of a single observer"—a most unusual occurrence on the Western Front to this time.[204] If Gough had not read his military history, he appears also not to have learned from this First Bullecourt, for in early May, he would repeat the whole thing again with more Australians.

Casualty

Between 11 April and 3 May, the Germans counterattacked the Australian positions. Some territory was lost and then regained by the Australians at great cost to both sides. We have a vivid description from Pvt. Leicester Johnson of the 20th Battalion of his experience being wounded during the ongoing battles that raged between the time of the end of First Bullecourt and the commencement of the Second Bullecourt attack. It is 7 p. m. on 14 April 1917, near Vaulx:

> The Company having been put on ammunition fatigue, I with the rest of my section, was sitting down detonating [arming] bombs, when Fritz sent over some "Whiz bangs" (i.e. 4.5s) some bursting within a few yards of us; a piece of one of them hitting me in the back of my right upper arm and cutting a deep gutter across it ..... While I was having my arm tied up in a dugout, another chap stopped a bit in the arm, right alongside me. He was lucky it did not finish him, as it blew his gas respirator to bits and shattered his pay book, merely knocking his arm about a bit.

Johnson then made his way back from the line to a dressing station, then another farther back. Still without treatment, he waited until a sufficient number of wounded were gathered to be taken by horse-drawn ambulance to a third location, the 7th Field Ambulance. Here his arm was dressed, and he was taken by motor ambulance to a fourth station (the 5th Australian Field Ambulance) a farther two or three miles behind the line:

> Where we spent the remainder of the night drinking cocoa and eating bread and butter. It was impossible to get any sleep, not being able to lie down owing to the fire being too small to allow us leaving it [it was snowing], consequently we had to sit up and nurse our respective wounds through that cold wet night, waiting for sufficient wounded to be sent in to make up a bus load for Pozières.

Here they spent another night, and at noon the next day, were put on cattle trains headed to another Casualty Clearing Station outside Albert. At Albert, their wounds were redressed:

> Owing to a shortage in ambulance trains we had to remain at this place for three days. The treatment here was none too good and the sleeping accommodation consisting merely of a bag of straw and four blankets (filthy dirty) although warm was not the best for wounded men ..... At last we received orders to move off and on walking half a mile to the railway, boarded a Red Cross train bound for Rouen.[205]

This involved an overnight trip in a train so crowded that none could lie down. Finally, at the hospital at Rouen some ten days after being wounded, Johnson received the first stitches to his wounds. He was eventually returned to England for further treatment. It would be four months before he recovered sufficiently to return to the Western Front.

There are two elements common to all the personal diaries for this period: one is the observance of the first anniversary of the Gallipoli landings on 25 April 1916, already referred to as "Anzac Day"; the second is the endemic lack of food and shelter. A hole in the side of a crater that kept you mostly dry was considered luxury. At the front a hot meal was an infrequent delicacy. Nearly all the soldiers write of constant hunger, meager and irregularly supplied rations, and exposure to the wet, mud, and the cold. Their feet are constantly wet and limbs ache from traversing broken, muddy terrain. In every area of recent fighting is the stench of the dead poorly buried or otherwise slowly decaying, exposed to the elements. These were scared, hungry men, always wet, often cold, and always surrounded by ear-splitting noise, earth shattering explosions, and the pervasive odors of death and their own fear.

Second Bullecourt

Meanwhile, farther north, the main battle at Arras continued for little gain and even greater cost. On 3 May, to reinstate the momentum lost at Arras, the British High Command launched a second offensive. This involved fourteen divisions along sixteen miles of the front line, stretching from Arras in the north to the Bullecourt sector in the south. Two Australian brigades were committed at this southern end. The entire attack commenced on 3 May, with the Australian 6 Brigade on the left and 5 Brigade on the right attacking into the same reentrant to the right of Bullecourt.

This time an extensive preliminary barrage was laid on and continued as a creeping barrage behind which the Australians commenced their advance at 3.45 a.m. This curtain of fire did not alleviate the deadly enfilade fire that the four leading battalions and then the four following battalions met as they made their way to the wire and the enemy trench system beyond, but progress was made.

The Germans were also paying a high price. Between 3 and 6 May, they launched six counterattacks on the Australian positions. A seventh was made the evening of 14/15 May. It is worth reminding the reader that the left flank of the Australian attack was not entirely in the air. The British were making similar sacrifices to breach the line at and around Bullecourt itself, and they too were paying a heavy price. It seems that German fire from the left salient of the reentrant was just as effective against the British as it was against the Australians.

It was as if Gough learned nothing from the previous disaster. After the war, both Gough and Haig came under strong criticism for the fiasco. Blame was also apportioned to the Australian commanders for failing to suppress the enfilading German machine gun fire from one side of the reentrant at Quéant.[206] This may be connected more with the timing of the attack. The Australian commanders had wanted the attack to commence at 3.30 a.m. The British farther north had wanted a start at 4.05 a.m. Haig split the difference with disastrous results by ordering the advance to commence at 3.45 a.m. At this pre-dawn time, the British—unprepared for a night advance at such short notice—proceeded chaotically. Further south, the Australians had lost a precious fifteen minutes of darkness.

Why the Australians were required to attack at all—let alone with insufficient time to advance in darkness—into the same reentrant that had cost them so dearly three weeks earlier remains unclear. The idea of such a long front for what was hoped to be a coordinated offensive over a very short time is symptomatic of Haig's incapacity to envisage the difficulties of command and control in the face of strong German defenses.[207] As Charles Bean concludes in the official history, the attack on the reentrant south of Bullecourt was, like the attack on Mouquet Farm the previous year, a subsidiary operation to a broader offensive that gained no advantage for the very offensive it was meant to assist.[208]

There is evidence that the British generals farther north were equally unimpressed. The British Third Army occupied the line from Vimy Ridge, north of Arras, all the way south to Gough's Fifth Army boundary just north of Bullecourt. The Australian I Anzac Corps was under Gough's command at the southern end of the line, in front of Bullecourt. On Sunday, 15 April, Haig called a pause in the Third Army offensive when three of its British front line major generals—each in charge of a British division—protested the orders of their commander, Lt. Gen. Edmund Allenby. They had done so by passing over Allenby's head with a direct complaint—it was coined a "resolution"—to Haig. They called for a cessation of hasty, ill-prepared, and costly attacks. Haig was the source of these directives. This "quasi-mutiny" reflected poorly on Allenby, who was promptly promoted out of the way and replaced by Julian Byng. It also reflects poorly on Haig, who maintained command and continued the offensive.[209]

John Gellibrand

Dissent was also shown in dramatic fashion by one leading Australian commander. Maj. Gen. Sir John (then temporary Brig. Gen.) Gellibrand, commanding 6 Brigade, was wholly unimpressed with the performance of some in the 2nd Division, of which his brigade was a part. He resigned and, despite attempts to retain him by Birdwood, was sent to England on staff duties. He would return to France in command of 12 Brigade in November 1917.

People like Gellibrand are overlooked in the Australian remembrance of war, be it war on the Western Front or any other front in any other war where Australians have served. Gellibrand was a brilliant, brave, and eccentric commander. Three times wounded on Gallipoli, he was wounded a fourth time on 21 May and only returned to duty at the end of June. Admired by many, he rarely wore anything other than the uniform of a private. He possessed a sense of the ironic and frequently dismayed or disenchanted his superiors, including Birdwood, with his appearance and direct attitude. Along with Cyril Brudenell White and James Gordon Legge, John Gellibrand is one of three great men we have rather forgotten. None of these men were shameless self-promoters, what Australians term a "big noter." The Australian Gen. Monash would, in confabulatory terms, describe Gellibrand as having "some tendency to uncertainty in executive action."

The Cost of First and Second Bullecourt

The Australians eventually took a substantial part of the Hindenburg Line on 17 May. That day, the British to their left finally occupied the remains of Bullecourt village and three days later secured part of the Hindenburg Line to the west of Bullecourt. Australian casualties during the Bullecourt fighting between the first attack on 11 April to its petering out on 17 May stood at 13,782: 1,746 prisoners of war, 8,338 wounded, and 3,698 dead.[210]

Chapter Twelve

Messines

After Arras: The Return to Flanders

After Arras, the British faced increased burdens. The French Army was in shambles. Poorly paid, incompetently led, and worn out, the morale of the French soldiers was very low. On 3 May—the same day the Australians commenced Second Bullecourt—sixteen separate mutinies broke out in the French Army. Nivelle's handling of the French campaigns concentrated farther south on the Aisne River had been disastrous. Even when an indiscreet Nivelle virtually publicized his plans for the French offensives of April-May and then learned the Germans were aware of them, he refused to modify them.

Between 16 April and 25 April 1917 the French took 134,000 casualties: 30,000 killed, 100,000 wounded, and 4,000 taken prisoner.[211] A terrible cost was being paid on the Western Front. To give this figure some comparative dimension, the entire Australian contingent on the Western Front at this time was little more than 100,000.

Nivelle—the one who so charmed Lloyd George—had presided over an army already broken since Verdun and led it to further disasters. With the revolution in Russia in early March 1917 and then the inconclusive, costly British Arras Offensive of April-May, this constituted bad news for the Allies. Gen. Henri-Philippe Pétain replaced Nivelle as head of the French Army.[212] Haig now stood clear of any immediate threat to his command again being subordinated to the French. For the time, the French army was in recovery.[213] In Russia, the revolution was making its continued contribution to the war effort doubtful. The Germans had yet to be dislodged in any conclusive way from French soil. It was in this setting that Haig's strategy for the second half of 1917 was developed. However, there was some continuity. How to dislodge the Germans from the high ground around the Ypres salient had been concentrating the minds of the British General Headquarters since 1916.

To Flanders

The British Commander in Chief Douglas Haig had long held designs on an advance in the north. The Germans' return to unrestricted submarine warfare was added reason to make this shift, as the initial plans envisaged a complementary seizure of the Belgian ports being used by German submarines. Between this threat and the need to take on more of the offensive burden from the rattled French command, the stalemate at Arras had been set aside for a fresh look at Flanders.

There was already a British general—the competent and capable Gen. Sir Hubert Plumer—overseeing a planned offensive in the north.[214] He had been there in charge of Second Army since early 1916 and had actively planned and prepared for a breakout from the Ypres salient.

Differing Histories, Differing Stories

Just who shaped the final plans, exactly what external influences were at play, and who succeeded in what depends on whose official history is read. The British version differs from the Australian in several respects, not least the conduct of the subsequent campaigns by Haig. It is worth noting that the British volume dealing with this period (1917, vol. 2) was initially drafted by Capt. Graeme C. Wynne. So much did its content displease the overseeing British Official Historian James Edmonds that he redrafted it on the grounds that Wynne was too critical of Haig. Wynne's response was to disassociate himself from the volume altogether; he declined even to have his name in the volume. In its final form it came out under Edmonds' name, in 1947. Bean's *Official History*, volume IV, dealing with the same events was first published fourteen years earlier in 1933.

The British official history—particularly volume two for the 1917 series and parts of the 1918 series—have subsequently been held as severely compromised. As one notable British historian has observed, "The history of the British Army on the Western Front is also the history of the writing of that story."[215] That it took so long to complete—it was not published until 1948—and that the initial author, Wynne, refused to see his name attached to it, is something of a history war in itself.

Whilst Wynne's name is absent, Charles Bean receives a strong vote of thanks from Edmonds.[216] This acknowledgment appears in Edmonds' preface at page xix. The entire preface up to that page is a remarkably strident defense of Haig's command against his British critics. Whatever may be said of Haig, it seems very evident that Arras—like the Somme the year before—was not a place of Haig's choosing. However, Flanders was.[217]

Ypres

Ypres had been a fortified city since 1385. Along with the nearby cities of Ghent and Bruges, it had been a prosperous center of trade. Such places usually owe part of their eminence to their strategic position beside rivers, astride accessible ground, and the meeting of roads with waterways. Ypres was just such a place. In result, it was also much fought over for centuries. It was a center of the cloth trade with England. From places like Ypres sprang remarkable developments in the manufacture and marketing of goods, husbanded by judicious supervision of supply and demand. It had long been a shining example of the northwest European trade center, with its elites and mercantilist guilds. This was a high status city, with much history reflected in many beautiful buildings. Prominent among these were the Cloth Hall and the cathedral.

This fine city had already been heavily damaged from the start of the war. It was the center of two battles, known as First and Second Ypres. First Ypres had seen the British hold the city but give away the higher surrounding ground in late 1914. Second Ypres—during April-May 1915—saw a desperate attempt by the Germans to take the city and an equally desperate attempt by the Allies to stop them. Here too, the Germans had used their new chlorine gas for the first time in great quantity. The remnants of the old British Army (BEF) were literally wiped out after First Ypres. Ypres had become a devastated and shell torn place. During November 1916, Haig ordered Sir Hubert Plumer to make plans for an advance from Ypres. Plumer's Second Army had been holding the sector for the past year.[218]

The rationale for an advance from Ypres was shaped in the knowledge that its position before a sort of semicircle of elevated German positions was by no means ideal. Still, Ypres constituted a salient that the British had held since the start of the war. It had taken on significance for the British much in the way Verdun had for the French. Yet it was not this allusion to sacred ground that was the sole reason for keeping Ypres. Another more geographic factor —the nature of the terrain to the north, to the coast itself—was shaping the dimension of the offensive. The canaled River Yser, next to which Ypres lay, ran north and emptied at the Belgian coast at a point almost directly north of Ypres. This was, like much of Flanders itself, low ground and had been deliberately inundated by the Belgians in October 1914.[219] The resulting morass was neither traversable nor navigable. The event had prevented the Germans from taking all the channel ports (something they did twenty-five years later). It also pushed the focus of battle south of this barrier to Ypres itself.

The Germans were well aware that any British attempt to push them off the semicircle of high ground to the east of Ypres would start from there. That semicircle of high ground has been described by Edmonds as a "crescent" and by Bean as a "sickle." Clockwise from north to south lay Westrozebeke, then Passchendaele, Broodseinde, and St. Eloi, with Wytschaete and Messines at the southern end. All these places were in Belgium and all were proximate to the Franco-Belgian border. To take Bean's description further, he usefully described the handle of the metaphorical sickle as being the Messines-Wytschaete ridge. As Bean puts it and Edmonds largely concurs: "No British commander could attempt to capture the blade of the sickle leaving the Germans in possession of the handle (Messines-Wytschaete) behind his southern flank."[220]

Bean's "sickle" and Edmonds' "crescent" descriptions are reflections of the plans Plumer now finalized. The southern area centered on Messines Ridge would be taken first. The second attack would commence to the north and directly east of Ypres.

Messines

Messines was itself a German salient positioned perilously close to Ypres, some seven miles to the south. This most threatening part was the object of the first British attack. Although constituting the first stage in the breakout from the Ypres salient, it was to be conducted by a smaller force than the subsequent, main thrust out of the Ypres area (discussed in chapter 13). The command of the larger, northern force was given to Gough. Command of the southern force to attack Messines went to Plumer.

Since September 1915, serious preparations to assist a future British offensive had commenced in the form of mining. Shafts were constructed as deep as ninety feet through the unstable soil. These shafts had been driven down some 400 yards to the rear of the British lines before being horizontally extended to points under the German lines at depths varying from eighty to 120 feet. Amongst many others, the Australian 1st Tunnelling Company was active in this endeavor and the 2nd in support work. This was a dark, dirty, and terrifying business involving its own forms of subterfuge. Defensive explosions known as *camouflets* were used to wreck the enemy's simultaneous mining activities, and at times an eerie, subterranean shooting war would take place when the miners broke into each other's galleries.[221] Much of the inspiration for and subsequent project management of this mining program can be attributed to British officer Maj. John Norton Griffiths. Seemingly by initiative more than directive, he commenced the extensive tunnelling well before official orders were given. There is something providential in this, for his work was completed by the time of the 7 June attack on Messines. Twenty-four mines were laid. They held a total of nearly

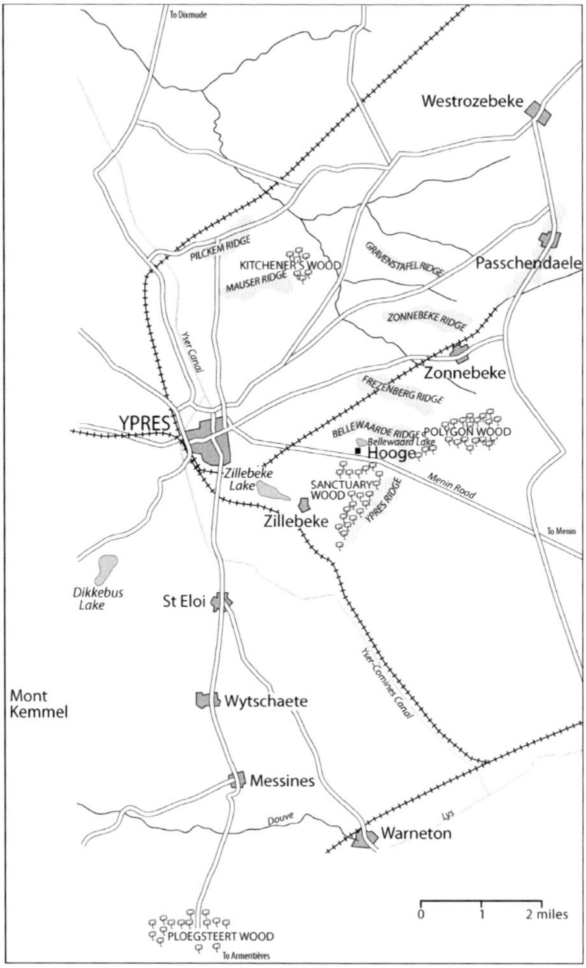

Flanders: Messines, Ypres, Passchendaele

a million pounds of explosives: ammonal, blastine, and guncotton. So extensive was the preparatory work that in most cases the charges had been laid for nearly a year, their access and electrical detonation devices being constantly checked and maintained.[222]

Without doubt, Plumer was the chief architect of both stages of the Ypres offensive. It was he who had quickly grasped and then adopted the "bite and hold" approaches used by Rawlinson on the Somme a year before. Indeed, Rawlinson had some part in the initial plans for this third Ypres, although he was set aside by Haig in favor of Gough to command the second, northern stage. Plumer also saw to the useful inclusion of over seventy of the new British Mark IV tanks—a vast improvement in speed and reliability over the earlier models. He even instigated overflying the German lines by the Royal Flying Corps the night before to drown out the sound of the tanks moving up to the start line.

In addition to the mines, Plumer also laid an effective artillery barrage. Between 26 May and 6 June, from stores holding over 144,000 tons of ammunition, over 2,200 pieces of artillery fired around 3,250,000 shells into the German lines.[223] Plumer had also ensured that giant tennis court-sized models of the terrain and smaller versions were made available for all officers to view as they finalized their plans. It is believed that nearly every available soldier—including those from the ranks—viewed one or other of these models.

Three corps were to make the Messines attack. From north to south these were the British X and IX, and the II Anzac. II Anzac was a cosmopolitan corps. It comprised four divisions: the British 25th (North Western) Division, the New Zealand Division, the 3rd Australian Division under Maj. Gen. John Monash, and the 4th Australian Division under Maj. Gen. William Holmes. This was the first test of battle for the 3rd Division, which was newly arrived from England. The Australians were at the southern end of the front in the vicinity of Ploegsteert Wood. To their left and north of them were the New Zealanders.[224]

At 3:10 a.m. on 7 June, the mines were blown. The sound was heard in London. Some thirteen miles away in the German-occupied city of Lille, German soldiers and civilians fled into the streets, believing an earthquake had occurred.[225] Nineteen mines had been detonated; three of the five remaining mines were subsequently salvaged after the war. Of the remaining two, one detonated during a thunderstorm on 17 June 1955. The location of the last mine remains unknown or unrecorded. It was Norton Griffiths' intention to create an earthquake under the Germans on 7 June 1917, and he did.[226] German soldiers above and near the mines were atomized. At the farther edges, the injured, concussed, paralyzed, and shocked were mingled with the dead.

We have an excellent eyewitness account of the attack on Messines from Capt. Robert Grieve of the 37th Battalion. He was leading a part of the advance of the second wave on Messines Ridge the evening of 6/7 June 1917. Ahead of them and first in the line of attack was the 38th Battalion. We can chart Grieve's progress.[227] They are heading in a roughly east-northeasterly direction toward the western edge of Ploegsteert Wood. They are being heavily bombarded with gas shells:

> All gas masks were to be worn. This was a tremendous hardship because it nearly reaches a point of suffocation to be subject to continual exertion with a mask on ..... it was pitiful to see the horses and mules affected by it – gasping for breath as we passed them.[228]

The gas shelling increases:

> It was most trying to the strongest nerves to sit tight in this open field while it actually rained gas shells. They were falling all round and you could plainly hear the snap of the detonator that burst the shell sufficient enough to liberate the liquid that formed the gas.

They then enter the remnants of Ploegsteert Wood, where the incessant shelling becomes a combination of gas and high explosives:

> Words fail to describe the conditions in the wood. Shells rained into it without ceasing – trees were falling in all directions and the whole place was full of gas. The duck boards in many places were smashed to atoms by direct hits and yet through all this we came safe and sound.

They traversed the remnants of Ploegsteert Wood, emerging from its northern edge somewhere to the right of the crest of Hill 63, about one and a half miles southwest of the remains of Messines village, which sits on the crest of Messines Ridge:

> Our first formations were due to attack at 3.10 a.m. and at that hour the barrage was to open and the mines sprung. Suddenly Bedlam was let loose. It would be impossible in words to describe the inferno. The earth seemed to vomit fire and was shaken as though by an earthquake.

This was not the detonation of the mines; rather, it was the effects of the Allied artillery barrage on the Messines Ridge. The mines blew shortly after:

> Then the whole earth was shaken by the effect of the mines. The trenches rocked and trembled and I fully expected that they would cave in – the whole surroundings right along the battle front were weirdly lit up by the flash from them. The largest mine on the front was close to us ….. Our first warning that she was fired was by sounds like distant rumblings of thunder – then gradually getting closer – then directly to our front the earth was seen to be rising like a huge mushroom – suddenly to be flung into space with an awe-inspiring roar.

Grieve estimated the crater was at least 300 hundred feet wide and ninety feet deep. This started as a most coordinated attack. The barrage had been heavy, accurate, and effective. A year and a half of tunnelling had permitted the detonation of nineteen underground mines almost simultaneously at strategic strongpoints in the German defenses. In many places, tanks advanced behind the barrage and preceded the infantry:

> Just ahead of the infantry nosed twelve tanks squirting [gun] fire along the enemy trenches and butting into any concrete emplacements that held a machine gun.

The section of front along which the Australian 3rd Division attack proceeded traversed the ground to the south of Messines. Messines village itself was taken by the New Zealanders. Grieve watched them advance:

> The New Zealanders attacked the Messines Ridge and they looked like ants as they swarmed up the face of the hill – through and round the ruined houses that every now and then seemed to vanish into clouds of black-red dust as an enemy shell landed with a crump into them.

Above them, British aircraft observed and strafed the enemy lines. Behind, observers aloft in sausage-shaped balloons sought out enemy strongpoints for the artillery. Here was the best of planning and the most advanced, coordinated use of infantry, artillery, tank, and airpower yet seen in this war.

Someone had given consideration to the limitations of troops normally employed without adequate support. Haig oversaw the battle. Plumer, in charge of this southern aspect of the advances, was responsible for its meticulous planning. The Australian Gen. John Monash, in charge of the Australian 3rd Division, had taken some part in the planning, as had the leaders of the other three divisions making up this attack, but it was the British Gen. Herbert Plumer who found a way to undertake an advance ordered by Haig and turn it into something far more successful than a 1 July 1916, a Pozières, a Mouquet Farm, a Flers, or a Bullecourt. We return to Capt. Grieves' account. At this point, the second wave has yet to attack:

> At last our time came to move and all our energies had to be concentrated on our own particular part. Moving by platoons in file from our trenches we went through gaps in our own wire and advanced towards our own front line.

They were now south of Messines village and about to turn left toward the eastern side of Messines. They needed to negotiate a stream (the River Douve), for which a number of parties from the preceding wave of sappers had carried portable wooden bridging structures:

> When our first attack was made parties were to carry out bridges for the attacking troops to cross by and it was here that the first bridging party had fallen at their posts. Evidently a shell had burst just as they had their bridge in position because they all lay there dead – two or three of them in their death struggles still retained hold of the rope carrying handles. There was no time to mourn the loss of brave comrades, so we pushed on to our first objective ….. We at last reached Schnitzel Farm ….. The old farm which was to have been our main objective in the first plans of attack was now nothing but a mass of torn and crumbled bricks. Behind this again was Bethlehem Farm ….. blown to pieces, but round in the hedges were numerous concrete dugouts in the largest of which we captured a battalion commander and the whole of his staff.

By then, they had advanced some three miles and found themselves in front of a series of German fortifications and trenches known as Hun's Walk. This was actually a road that ran east from the northern end of Messines village to Warneton. They paused:

> While waiting here we had several casualties – one man killed by a direct hit from a shell which failed to explode. Another man was hit on the arm by a big fragment that came humming through the air like a big top ….. It was about this time that the enemy commenced to mass for counter attack.

The counterattack was broken up and the advance to the final objective—a trench system north of Hun's Walk—was finally made. It is now 3:30 p.m.:

> Here we suffered many casualties – the whole of our Stokes [mortar] and Vickers [machine] gun crews were knocked out ….. the company was held up by the fire from machine guns in a concrete building. These were put out of action by the aid of Mills Grenades and the company were able to get forward onto the objectives allotted to us ….. At this stage I was struck through the right shoulder by a sniper's bullet but managed to keep going for a few hours after this. We got the sniper who was up a tree about 75 yards away. One of Our Lewis gunners put a magazine through the tree and he dropped like a stone ….. I was personally forced to retire after losing a lot of blood ….. I slowly made my way back towards our rear lines.

Grieve appears to have walked unaided back through the lines for about three miles, stopping briefly at battalion headquarters to report the advance and provide what he describes as "suggestions for further actions." He reached a dressing station. Finding it too crowded, he walked farther back to the next. Receiving no treatment there, he walked farther on and after a wait of several hours, finally received an anti-tetanus injection. From there, he was taken by lorry to a hospital at Steenwerck.

Grieve provided perhaps the clearest first person account of this battle from an Australian's perspective. His account is an unassuming one, much of it taken up with praise for the other officers, troops, and stretcher bearers. He tends to the unremarkable in recording his own effort. It was Grieve who had advanced on the German pillbox and "by the aid of Mills Grenades" that he threw into the machine gun aperture, neutralized it. For his actions that day Grieve was awarded the Victoria Cross.

At about the same time, Lt. Walde Fisher of the 42nd Battalion was moving up in support of the attack. Fisher in the 42nd and Grieve in the 37th were somewhere alongside each other in this second wave. Their task was to advance from a line taken by the first wave and continue the assault. However, both battalions were not moving through some recently pacified area; occasional surviving enemy strongpoints had to be dealt with and the entire area was under intense shellfire from the Germans. Fisher's account illustrates the vagueness of a front line in such a battle:

> Thursday 7th June 1917. At a certain hour the guns roared out in a tumult of sound, the starting time of which was given by explosions of two mines. Their concussion shook the earth for miles around. Certain of our troops then went over to take with very little effort the [Black] line set as a task for them. The foe's lines did not exist – there was nothing but a tumbled jumble of heaved-up brown earth for hundreds and hundreds of yards. Nothing could have existed in that hell. No wire was left ….. There we are yet and carrying to the troops in the front line ….. all was shell hole – lip on lip – up and down, up and down, all the time ….. At the moment of writing, our guns are pouring in a hurricane of drum-fire, so that one cannot hear one's neighbour even at a distance of a few feet.[229]

Fisher's next entry in his diary is 12 June. It covers the period from 7 to 10 June 1917:

> Since last writing I have had a terrible time. At 1 p. m. we moved up to our position whence the foe had been expelled some few hours previously. There was no line, just the position given on the map, and there we set to and dug in for our lives.

Fisher's company endured intense German artillery barrages in the afternoon. From their half-dug pits and shell holes they repelled several German counterattacks. The artillery barrage returned in greater intensity during the evening. After this twenty-four hour bombardment, the reduced ranks advanced on the German positions:

> One platoon was wiped out – men blown to pieces, terrible to view, others buried and shell-shocked. To right and left shell after shell, coming over incessantly in streams, poured upon our fragile lines, bringing death and wounds to great numbers. Men were blown up and killed all along – it is impossible to describe the scene ….. The stretcher bearers were magnificent, doing great work all the while. The company was reduced to 58 men! Next day, we, the remainder, sat in our positions while the guns went all day long. The stench from the dead was dreadful – many were in pieces and could not be identified – while the dead and unburied enemy in front of us added to the nauseous horror. We were all much shaken and gladly, very gladly, were relieved after 72 hours of hell.[230]

At least one Australian was serving in the British corps to the north. Lt. Eric Dark qualified as a medical practitioner from Sydney University in 1914 and had volunteered at the outbreak of war. He was one of around a hundred doctors sent immediately to the British Army, in which he served throughout the war. Dark was attached to the 9th Field Ambulance, Royal Army Medical Corps, and was present at the Messines Ridge attack, but well to the north of II Anzac. By now, both sides were making full use of airpower. The Germans were regularly bombing the Allied lines and rear positions. Here is Dark's account of the damage and destruction:

> In the early summer of 1917 the division moved back into the Ypres sector, having a good rest in pleasant country. It was here that I had my first experience of aerial bombing, and found it much more frightening than shelling. During dinner in the mess tent one evening we heard the sound of a plane overhead, and then the whine of descending bombs; we ran out of the tent and threw ourselves flat on the ground just as the bombs began to explode; eight fell in quick succession just a few yards from us. They fell in a straight line, making quite small craters about 5 yards apart. Most of the damage was done in the horse lines where several of the transport men were killed or wounded and 70 horses and mules were killed or so badly wounded that they had to be shot at once. Going along the lines I found the transport sergeant lying on his back, most horribly mutilated; his left leg was curved in a rough semicircle, with his boot against his ear; his belly was torn open, but he was quite conscious, and begged "Please Sir, put me to Sleep". I had morphia with me, so gave him a whacking big dose, assuring him "Alright sergeant, you'll be asleep in a couple of minutes." He went off very quickly, and, of course, never woke up. [231]

Fisher came through this battle unscathed, only to die in action at Dernancourt in April 1918. Grieve never fully recovered from his shoulder wound and was unfit to serve out the war. He was repatriated to Australia and was discharged in May 1918, a few weeks after Fisher was killed on the Western Front. He would reenlist for the Second World War. He died in Melbourne in 1957. Dark survived into his eighties and died in 1987.

One Australian did not hear the mines explode. Lt. Henry Neaves of the 45th Battalion was now part of the 4th Division reinforcements before Messines:

> The night of the 6th was spent discussing the operations and everyone was confident of success. Early on the 7th the offensive opened with the explosion of a tremendous mine at Messines, and then the artillery barrage opened. I was sleeping in a tent some two miles from where this mine exploded but it didn't waken me although a few days later I read in the papers that Mr. Lloyd George had heard the explosion in England. I did not even hear the barrage that was laid down ….. At 6.30 a.m. the weather was beautiful, clear and warm. Not a gun was firing and it was very silent. I thought at first the attack could not have taken place.[232]

Neaves must have been sleeping very heavily; the area where he was included a substantial part of the artillery used for the opening barrage. Neave's battalion was part of the 4th Division reinforcements that would encounter very stiff resistance in the second advance on the Oosttaverne Line later that afternoon—a system of trenches that run roughly north-south to the east of the Messines high ground. This account of the situation is for 8-10 June:

> As I went up through Messines Fritz was pounding it with 5.9s and shrapnel and I was forced to duck into trenches a few times ….. In an advance it is largely luck whether you find your unit at once or search for them for a couple of hours. This morning I had luck with me and found Battalion headquarters in a shell hole just behind the line ….. The C.O. was sitting in a shell hole writing a report when I arrived. The shell hole was full of wounded men that had been brought in. The adjoining shell hole was also full of wounded and the M.O. [medical officer] was busily engaged attending to them.

Neaves describes the case of a shell-shocked fellow officer. He would have been but one of hundreds of such cases on any day on any Western Front battlefield during an attack:

> During the afternoon of the 9th a party of our men were blown up with a shell and one of the officers had shell shock rather badly. As he was then no use for the line the C.O. sent him back to have a rest for a few days. He got back as far as the Cooks' possie [field kitchen] and remained there until night and when I arrived I gave him directions how to get back to the Transport lines. He set off on this journey but didn't get there and next day I found him back again at the Cook house and I was told by the men that during the night he had gone about with a revolver, threatening to shoot chaps and that finally the revolver had to be taken from him. He remained in the unit for several days but eventually had to be evacuated, as his condition got worse.

Bean's Diary Entries For Messines

Charles Bean was at the opening of the Messines Battle. Aside from his close narrative account of the battle, his personal diaries, as opposed to his official history, make two additional observations: about the use of cavalry and command.

There were vestiges of the old cavalry attached to the Australian forces in the form of mounted reconnaissance squadrons. As commander of II Anzac at Messines, British-born Gen. Alexander Godley appears to have put them to what Bean saw as a very dubious use. Here he refers to them as cavalry and as "L.H." (Light Horse):

> June 11. At about 12 p. m. much firing – possibly Cavalry putting out [forward observation] posts. Fancy Cavalry! They led their horses along Hun's Walk [a recently occupied German line] today and were heavily fired at. They are to put these posts beyond 9 Brigade today – pure eyewash.
>
> June 12. The "Cavalry Patrols" sent out last night established one post that we know of ….. Godley [in command of II Anzac Corps] altered the orders for the L.H. about 4 times yesterday – giving them an entirely new objective the last time, after they had actually started out. This was sent through Monash [commanding 3rd Division] by car to the C.O. who was found en route – but whether it ever reached the patrols is uncertain.[233]

The use of cavalry for scouting appears to be redundant by this stage of the fighting on the Western Front. But Godley was in command of an attack that whilst not entirely one of maneuver, was relatively open: Messines was a battle conducted over dry ground. There were trench systems on both sides, but the defense-in-depth approach of the Germans was marked more by the presence of pillboxes and strongpoints. It is ironic that Godley changed the orders for the patrols four times and that the final, amended orders to a horse-mounted patrol already in the field were sent by motor car.

Bean then turns his attention to the command and control situation as he sees it. He was in regular contact with all levels of command up to corps level and often conferred with them. He frequently dined with them. He continues his 12 June diary entry:

> All these [Australian] divisions are longing to get back under Birdwood and his staff. Salier of 12 Brigade told me so – Holmes of 4th Division [commanding] – Leane of 48 Battalion [commanding] – even Blanchard, Field Cashier of 3rd Division.

And on 15 June:

> Got a message from Godley that he was going to review the third Division – meeting General Monash at Doulieu – which meant: "come and report my speech." This was a nuisance.

Doulieu is at least thirteen miles southwest of Messines. The review would have involved only a token number of troops from the battalions. Bean attended the review on the fifteenth and made some strident observations about the battalions represented and the commanders at various levels. He continues his entry for the fifteenth:

> The 3rd Division units were in splendid condition – the men stepped out well. The 33rd and 34th looked splendid, but the 35th looks like what I believe it is – the weakest of the lot. It has a miserable poor old moaning weed of a colonel in Goddard.

Nor was Bean impressed with Godley's speech. He was someone "who never strikes me as being in the least sincere." Bean concludes his diary entry for the fifteenth with this summary of matters as he sees them:

> Had dinner at Steenwerk Café with some 3rd Division and some 4th Division officers. The 3rd Division men were a little shy of 4th Division to start with though they were from the same states – South Australia and Western Australia. But 3rd Division is finding its feet. Only the C.O.s are a bit shy of fire in some cases and Monash is not the man to keep them up to it. In 9 Brigade that General Jobson, though a clever man, does not visit his front line at all – and does not make his staff do so; and only one colonel – Morshead – who has the old 1st Division tradition – does so sufficiently. The 33rd Battalion with Morshead [commanding 33rd Battalion] and Massey is splendid – 34th good – 35th, they say, rotten –McNicoll [Brigadier General commanding 10 Brigade] visits his front line as much as he can and Cannon [commanding 11 Brigade] of course, is splendid.

> Jackson, GSO1 [General Service Officer] and Peck, GSO 2 go round their front in battle; and Pain, though much shocked, does so also, but Monash doesn't and that makes a great difference. The staff captain of 9 Brigade doesn't – only Borwick, the old 2 Bde major. It is a great drawback and I have not the least doubt that Jobson ought to go.

Bean notes a further grievance in his diary on 17 June:

> Second Anzac [Corps] is rather a wretched staff and I cannot get over Godley having no Australians on it in a responsible position. When I asked for a photo of it they said: "Oh I suppose it's the clerks and warrant officers you want" because they and the other subordinates were the only Australians.

Laid bare is the profound difference between personal view and public, official history. Such observations do not appear in official histories.

The Results and the Cost

The almost simultaneous detonation of nineteen mines under Messines Ridge has been described as the largest man-made, pre-nuclear explosion.[234] Under Plumer's command, the ridge from Messines northwards to the southern edge of Sanctuary Wood had been taken after two days of fighting. The Australian contribution in the far south of the advance was part of this largely British attack. The Germans were pushed off the high ground. In the north, they had fallen back to a point east of Hill 60. It now remained to clear them from points even farther north. Some three miles east of Ypres on the Menin Road, the Germans still held Sanctuary Wood and the fortified village of Hooge.

The battle for Messines Ridge cost the Allies dearly. For the three corps involved, total casualties stood at 27,303. The British IX Corps and X Corps lost around 4,000 and 8,000, respectively. It was II Anzac that made up the balance: 15,303. Total Australian casualties for the 3rd and 4th Divisions at Messines was 6,964, of whom 1,513 were killed or died of wounds from 6-15 June. Wounded totaled 4,928. The rest were taken prisoner, gassed, or were shell-shocked.[235]

About Gas

The use of nonlethal and lethal gasses arose from the obvious limitations of traditional means of breaking through an opponent's lines. Artillery shells and gunfire could kill but in insufficient quantities to always guarantee a breakthrough. There existed a general knowledge of the lethality of certain gases and this was harnessed to give one side an edge over the other by more efficiently incapacitating the enemy than with explosives and bullets alone.

The first use of gas was by the French in 1914. The effects of these rifle-fired projectiles and hand-thrown grenades were minimal on the Germans. The French developments appear to have sprung from prewar development of tear gas for riot control.[236]

It was the German High Command that took the use of gas to new levels of lethality and industrial production quantities. They first used lethal gas in battlefield quantities near Ypres in April 1915.[237] The gas was chlorine, released from cylinders and allowed to drift with a favorably prevailing wind onto the British. By early 1916, the Germans had improved on this haphazard delivery system by putting gas in artillery shells. At Verdun, they introduced phosgene. At Messines, the Germans used both gases and shells that contained a mix of the two. By this time, the French and British were also employing similar technologies to deliver similar lethal formulations.

All of these gases injured soldiers exposed to them. All gases induced fear and panic, often heightened by the requisite donning of claustrophobic and often inefficient gas helmets, masks, and respirators. Chlorine and particularly phosgene were lethal. The classification of gases used is complex and lengthy: acute lung irritants, lachrymators, paralysants, sternutators, and vesicants.[238] All had the potential to cause lifelong, debilitating health problems. Most, in sufficient quantity, could kill. The lives of many returned Great War servicemen were miserably shortened by their exposure to gas. The worst and most commonly used by both sides appears to have been chlorine and phosgene—both acute lung irritants—and mustard gas, a vesicant (introduced by the Germans at Ypres in July 1917). Eyes would run, and breathing would become labored and increasingly difficult. The walls of the mouth, throat, and lungs would progressively and irrevocably deteriorate and victims of serious doses were only able to be comforted until their blue-lipped, agonized shallow breathing gave way to suffocation as mucous fluids filled their lungs. For those who came home, the effects of gas would linger: chronic ear, nose, and throat, bronchial, and skin complaints; hacking coughs; a slow, debilitating drowning from ever present fluid in the lungs; boils and blisters; dizzy spells; and recurring eye problems.

The Next Step

The Allies had performed remarkably well at Messines. This was done without the French Army; Pétain had revoked the order to support the attacks at Messines on 4 June, three days before it commenced.

In Flanders, Haig was now commanding at a place of his choosing. He had done so with the knowledge that the British and Commonwealth forces would have to bear the burden. The French were recovering from mutinies and had played no significant part. On the Eastern Front, the Russians were effectively out of the war. It was now obvious that the Germans in the east would soon reinforce those holding the Western Front. It was tactically imperative that the British retake the ridges to the east of Ypres. It was the same high ground they had lost at Second Ypres in 1915. So far, this had been undertaken successfully with the capture of the Messines-Wytschaete section. This was in large part due to Plumer's effective planning and command.

Messines was essentially an opening, subsidiary operation. Haig now needed to oversee the retaking of the rest of the ridge line from Sanctuary Wood to Passchendaele. Only then would he realize the strategic goal of dislodging the German armies from the northern end of the Western Front by taking Roulers and Bruges. Could he do this without giving in to his tendency to overlook the "bite and hold," step-by-step method? Could he conduct the next stage without giving in to the temptation of one of his recurring grand breakthrough ambitions?

Chapter Thirteen

THIRD YPRES

Background

"Third Ypres" covers several phases of fighting between 31 July and 10 November 1917, in which most of the ridge system around Ypres would be retaken at appalling human cost. This Third Ypres would also be known by the name of the ultimate objective, the village of Passchendaele. Today, the terms "Third Ypres" and "Passchendaele" are used interchangeably. The tendency to periodize battles and draw some sense of cause and effect has already been discussed, and Third Ypres is yet another example. It is useful to remember that perceptions still differ. These battle titles were conferred after the war by the British who, for the purpose of giving sequence and continuity, had established a "Battle Nomenclatures Committee." At the time these actions took place, the "sequence and continuity" would have been less obvious to the participants. Some significant actions did not necessarily pass the Battle Nomenclatures Committee's test to qualify as a battle. Take the disaster at Fromelles of 19-20 July 1916 that saw the 5th Australian Division cease to be an effective fighting force in twelve hours. This does not rate as a battle under the British nomenclature system. Australians understandably see it as a battle.[239]

The strategic intent for this Third Ypres was to move toward the Belgian city of Bruges and continue to the Channel coast, thereby cutting German access to their submarine bases and at the same time gaining considerable Belgian territory. The first step had been to take control of the southern flank, the Messines Ridge. This was now followed up with the taking of the rest of the heights to Passchendaele. Different sequences can be applied to what happened next.

Matters of Periodization for Third Ypres

One is the eight battles sequence. This breaks Third Ypres into the Battles of Pilkhem, Langemarck, Menin Road, Polygon Wood, Broodseinde, Poelcappelle, First Passchendaele and, finally, Second Passchendaele. The first two did not involve the Australians, except in an artillery support role. The Australian infantry was involved in the six subsequent battles. Another method is to include Messines as part of Third Ypres. These battles are dealt with in immense detail in several works, not least among them being the British and Australian official histories.[240]

Given that this is primarily an account of Australians on the Western Front, phases suitable to their involvement are employed.[241] In his official history, Bean employs three phases to cover the battles that followed Messines.[242] The separate *Official Australian Army Medical Services History* also uses three phases, but they do not synchronize with Bean's. However, the medical history version is a clearer periodization and is used here.[243]

The first covers the opening battles of 31 July to the end of August. Only Australian artillery took part in this phase, albeit at considerable cost. The second phase is covered in chapter 14. It covers the Battle of Menin Road, then Polygon Wood, Broodseinde, Poelcappelle, and First Passchendaele. This covers the period 20 September to 12 October, which saw the greatest participation by the Australians. The third phase—from 14 October to 10 November—is covered in chapter 15 and includes Second Passchendaele, which saw less action on the part of the Australians.

The First Phase: 31 July to the End of August 1917

The success at Messines in early June saw an elated Haig revert to type. Convinced the Germans both on the front and in Germany itself were close to collapse, he saw a breakthrough looming. Haig couched his plans to the War Cabinet in step-by-step "bite and hold" terms, but took remarkable liberties in estimating just how long a step should be. In his diary, Haig recorded on 7 June that Plumer's careful approach to taking Messines met with his approval. He then recorded his personal view on where lay the real credit:

> The operations today are probably the most successful I have undertaken.[244]

What to do next? Haig was under much pressure from the War Office and War Cabinet to continue the offensive, but without unbearably heavy losses. Lloyd George, who by this time appears to have lost confidence in Haig, again mooted the idea of opening another major offensive—perhaps on the Italian-Austrian border—rather than see the endless waste continue on the Western Front. The idea failed to convince anyone. Meantime, the French could not yet be counted on in any great strength. Attention returned to the execution of Third Ypres with the knowledge that it would be British and Commonwealth troops bearing the burden. Haig remained in charge.

A further complication arose, and it brought Haig's competence into question yet again. The Chief of Imperial General Staff Sir William Robertson was Haig's main liaison with London. Robertson had supported the offensive moving to Flanders, but now appeared to waver over Haig's suddenly renewed flush of optimism in a grand breakthrough and advance to victory. Haig, aware of what he saw as Robertson's at best conditional support, tried to have him removed, but he did not succeed.

Other intrigues abounded. Plumer, the careful architect of Messines, was already aware he had been overlooked for the main thrust toward Passchendaele. Rawlinson, the man who personified the step-by-step methods on the Somme in 1916, was sent out of the way, north to the Channel area. Haig maneuvered the aggressive and thoroughly loyal Gough into the command of Third Ypres.[245]

Gough too talked "bite and hold," but like Haig, now proceeded to dramatically reinterpret the concept with a planned initial giant leap forward of between some 1,500 and 3,000 yards for the opening day, 31 July. Under pressure from others at GHQ, Gough reworked the planned advances to coincide with the three German defense lines. Their approximate distances from the British front line were nevertheless overly ambitious: 1,000, 2,000, and 3,500 yards, respectively. Gough believed the 2,000-yard second line should be the objective for the first day. This was by no means a restrained, step-by step approach. He also believed that any part of the attacking force successful enough to go beyond that 2,000 yard limit should do so.[246] Haig approved the plans. It is not clear whether he actually examined them.[247]

In preparing for the main attack from Ypres toward Passchendaele, the British and Commonwealth forces were again acting almost alone. Of forty divisions to be used in the offensive, only six in the north were from the broken and demoralized French Army.[248] The attack commenced at 3:50 a.m. on 31 July. Three armies advanced from the front lines: the few French divisions well to the north, British V Army in the center (to the east of Ypres), and the British II Army from the Messines area in the south. The Australians—represented by the 3rd Division—were well to the south of British II Army's sector and took no significant part.

A considerable but uneven advance was made. In the center, initial gains were made and then partially lost to a German counterattack. Farther south, the British were unable to occupy their main objective; a plateau that gave on to the village of Gheluvelt. Haig was nevertheless satisfied:

> This was a fine day's work ….. Wounded very cheery indeed.[249]

The Menin Road, east of Ypres—almost certainly July 1917, given the relatively dry and warm conditions. Soldiers in short trousers walk through the detritus of war. Two dead horses straddle the road. A disused or damaged light railway can be seen to the left. Debris has been pushed aside to clear a path for traffic. Constant shelling has stripped the trees bare of all vegetation and most of the branches. *AWM*

Yet it was not really the sort of advance consistent with Haig's or Gough's now overly optimistic interpretation of the step-by-step method. Then, at 4:00 p.m., it started to rain and did so, on and off, until the end of August. The impact of such unseasonably heavy rain turned the shell-pocked ground into mud. Movement of men, artillery, ammunition, and food became almost impossible. By late August, Gough advised Haig that unless he received support from Plumer's army, there seemed no apparent means to advance the line or continue the offensive. Gough had already mentioned this to Plumer. By now, Rawlinson had prepared a paper that essentially stated the obvious: that the step-by-step method was, despite claims to the contrary, yet to be put into practice. He summed up:

> We have never yet set ourselves deliberately to carry out a battle of attrition on absolutely definite lines, with successive objectives well within covering range of the artillery and well within the physical capacity of the infantry. We have never issued hard and fast orders that these objectives are not to be exceeded however easily they may have been gained.[250]

This was the clearest, unambiguous appreciation of the folly of setting aside the step-by-step method for the rapid advance to some dreamed-up breakthrough. It was Rawlinson who attempted to apply the method back on the Somme in 1916. It was Haig who bent Rawlinson's careful plans to his own willful breakthrough fantasies on the Somme, not least with the Australians at Pozières and then at that ridiculous, almost in-grown salient at Mouquet Farm. A more compliant Gough had raced—again with Australian troops—into the absurdly conceived attacks in March and May 1917 at the reentrant at Bullecourt. Now Gough himself could see no end to the slaughter outside Ypres; the August rains had seen to that.

Amongst the Australians, Gough was generally considered an incompetent and insensitive waster of lives. Four men—Charles Bean, Brudenell White, Keith Murdoch, and the English journalist Philip Gibbs—had discussed the problematic situation and set about having Gough removed.[251] This did not eventuate, but Bean did write a letter to Lloyd George. It was a much diluted communication. Gough did not get mentioned, but Bean's letter to Lloyd George was blunt. It called for the Australian divisions to be gathered under one command, preferably an Australian. In that letter Bean came to the point:

> You in England have an understanding of the strength of Australian nationalism as the one great motive working in our people but I do not think that [British] G.H.Q. has the slightest comprehension of it ….. I think G.H.Q. is actually hostile to it, and regards it if anything as a drawback and a nuisance that any such motive should exist; a sort of treachery to the old idea of Empire which I suppose naturally lingers amongst regular [British] soldiers.[252]

Bean proceeds to strongly criticize the quality of sections of the British infantry, citing their poor performance alongside the Australians at Fromelles and First and Second Bullecourt in particular—a thinly veiled reference to Gough's command. The letter is scathing of British censorship of reports and photographic activities in the field and directly challenges the British to give the Australians more freedom of maneuver in the collection of records, including battle reports that the British High Command withheld from the Australians. They always seem to find a rule the Australians are breaking:

> Some rule which the British authorities are welcome to apply to the British, but which surely ought not to block us from building up our records.

Even the collection of relics for a future Australian war memorial was the subject of confiscation by the British. In his diary, Bean records that a sign marking Centre Way Trench (and now on display in the Australian War Memorial) was only collected from the old Pozières battlefield by a British writer and poet who gave it to Bean in England. That person was John Masefield, who in 1930 would become Poet Laureate of the United Kingdom until his death in 1967. Should Bean ever be considered excessively Anglophile or somehow permanently immersed in British classical scholarship, his letter to Lloyd George and his personal diary entries indicate otherwise.

Meanwhile, Haig seems to have remained oblivious to the problem of Gough's command. Even the troops on both sides could see that advance and counterattack in these conditions was futile. Gough himself appears to have come to realize this futility not only from his own staff, but from captured German troops as well. During that rainy, muddy month of August, it was British, not German morale that was being worn down. Still, Haig could inform a meeting of senior staff officers as late as 19 August that:

> Our Army's efforts this year have brought final victory near. Indeed I think that, if we can keep up our effort, final victory may be won by December.[253]

But by 26 August, Haig was sufficiently aware of the problem to bring Plumer's Second Army in to replace Gough's II Corps at the southern reaches of the ridge. How Gough ever got the job over Plumer in the first place appears to lie with Haig's favoritism for Gough. By now confidence in Haig had dipped further. On 23 August, Lloyd George again raised the matter of halting the Ypres offensive and diverting resources to the Austro-Italian front. This did not occur, but the sentiment in London was understandable.

Except for the important and costly work of sections of the Australian artillery batteries outside Ypres, there were no significant actions by the Australians during August. By the end of August 1917, it was clear to Plumer that the British II Corps (part of V Army) would have to be replaced by I Anzac Corps, with II Anzac to its left. This was where the fighting had stalled, where overreaching advance and subsequent German counterattacks had seen ground just as quickly lost as it was gained. For the time being, and until the weather improved, the advance would be halted. By September the rain had eased, though the mud remained.It was into this morass that the Australians would be drawn. Of the more than one million British and Empire troops who died during the Great War, the Ypres sector would claim one in four of them.

It was around this time that the Australian infantry took up the description "Diggers"; it was rapidly adopted by the Australian infantry. Bean assures us that its provenance lay with the New Zealanders and that the term would be used by both for some time to come. Only later, perhaps after the war, did the term transform into a very Australian possession.[254]

The intrigues and maneuvering of British GHQ have taken considerable space here. They illustrate the extent to which dissatisfaction with and resentment against Haig as commander had developed. British commanders and politicians were at the heart of this. Australian criticism of British command in general and of Haig in particular existed then. Criticism of Haig's performance is definitely not the product of the postwar blame game his defenders claim it to be, as it was evident since mid-1916.

Chapter Fourteen

Menin Road, Polygon Wood, and Broodseinde:

20 September to 12 October 1917

The opening phase of Third Ypres bogged down in the August rain and mud. British losses between 5 August and 9 September amounted to 109,000.[255] The misfortunes of weather alone had not led to such loss; the commanders, Gough in particular, had squandered men and morale in a number of subsidiary, narrow-front, minor offensives. These were much in the style of his adventurism with the Australians at Mouquet Farm the year before. In result, Gough and his Fifth Army were now relegated a secondary role to Plumer's Second Army.

It would fall to Plumer to get the campaign reorganized and restarted. He brought with him the principles he used successfully at Messines: set-piece battles with limited but attainable objectives. The offensive reopened on 20 September, and the Australian 1st and 2nd Divisions took part.

The Battle of Menin Road, 20 to 25 September 1917

It was a well-rested I Anzac that went into Third Ypres. They had fought continuously since July 1916: at Pozières, Mouquet Farm, and Flers-Gueudecourt, then into 1917 at the German withdrawal, Lagnicourt, and First and Second Bullecourt. In that time, the only rest they received was an abbreviated break in the Ypres sector before a premature return to Flers in late 1916. Yet for the last two months they had been rested, refitted, and replacements were brought in and trained. On 20 September, I Anzac (now 1st, 2nd, 4th, and 5th Divisions under Birdwood) was committed to Menin Road. II Anzac (now 3rd Australian, 59th British, and the New Zealand Division under Godley) would enter the battle at Polygon Wood on 26 September.

On 15/16 September, the 1st and 2nd Australian Divisions marched out of Ypres along the Menin Road to the western edge of Glencorse Wood. For the first time on the Western Front, two Australian divisions would fight side by side. Also for the first time, they would be facing a most complex German defensive system. This was a blasted place. Leonard Jones of the 3rd Battalion was carrying equipment from Ypres:

> Off we went, quite a mob, for [1st] Division was sending up a wireless set. We were loaded with scopes and lamps. And we were shelled all the way. Heavy stuff. We missed a lot of congestion going across country, but the ground – it

The Menin Road, 20 September 1917. These Australian wounded are well back from Edward's Aid Post. They are somewhere on the remains of the Menin Road near Hooge. The walking wounded and shell shocked make their own way or are assisted by fellow soldiers. Those unable to walk lie on stretchers, waiting for bearers. Beside the road lies a wrecked vehicle, quite possibly an ambulance. This photo is a particularly candid example of the muddy conditions and was taken just before a German shell landed amidst those on the stretchers, killing them all. *RAAF Archives, Point Cook*

> was quite spongy, for underneath were mules, horses, Fritzes and Tommies of 1914 vintage on, and the stench rising from cracked drying ground was pretty awful ..... Looking across to that dreadful Menin Road, I saw mules, men and ammunition go up with a roar. Noise everywhere and up aloft scores of planes.[256]

On the same day, another Australian soldier used the very same diversionary route as Jones. Avoiding the heavy traffic and intense shelling of the Menin Road itself was English-born accountant Lt. Leslie Newton of the 12th Battalion. Like Jones, he was part of the 1st Division. Unlike Jones, he moved much farther into the front line area, for his purpose was reconnaissance prior to the 12th entering the line:

> Ypres is in a terrible state – hardly a wall stands – the Cloth Hall is a pitiful shame. We debussed at the Lille Gate and proceeded via Warrington Road, Halfway House, Hooge, and Chateau Wood. We then ducked overland to the Menin Road and up to Clapham Junction, where the 7th London H.Q. were. They provided us with a guide and we proceeded up the line and made a good reconnaissance.

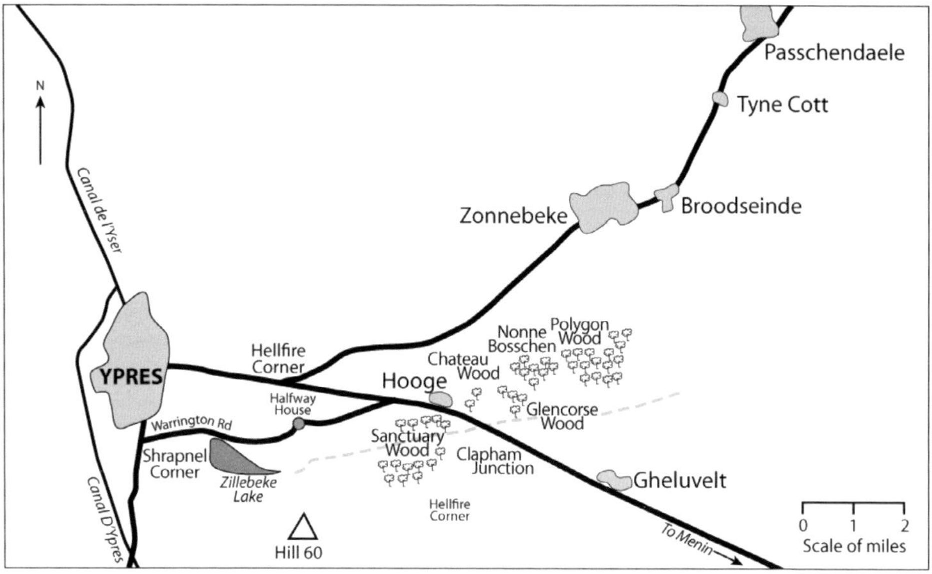

The Ypres Sector,. 1917

The group had just got back to Clapham Junction when artillery fire fell on them:

> I turned round to tell them to scatter but found that only Bovell was following me as Holyman and Keen had turned back. The shelling was most intense and [German] 5.9s were falling all round us, it is a marvel we were not hit. We ran for all we were worth. At one time it got so bad we stopped in a very shallow trench but this was worse than useless so we still ran on. At last we seemed to get out of his barrage and had a spell in a trench. Bovell suggested going on which we did along the Menin Road, side by side, when he [the German guns] started again – we commenced to run when a shell came and exploded right against us – I felt the heat of the flash and it knocked me over. When I got up I saw Bovell wounded on the ground. I spoke to him but he did not answer but moved slightly. I remembered seeing some Tommies in a possie[position] about 50 yards back, so ran back to them for a stretcher, and when we arrived, he was dead.

Newton would return with the battalion to the front line the evening of 19 September. By 2:00 a.m. the next morning, they were back in Chateau Wood and, by 4:30 a.m., crossing the marshes north of Glencorse Wood:

> It was a terrible place. You sank to your knees everywhere you walked. I got out of it alright and went through Nonnen Boschen. The barrage kicked up such a dense smoke that you could not see 50 yards in front of you and a compass was essential to maintain your direction.

This was indeed a horrible, corrupted place. The entire struggle to obtain the heights would subsequently segment into neat, official battles, but these were not necessarily apparent to the troops. What was obvious was the slaughter of men and animals on both sides.

Cpl. William Ryder

Cpl. William Ryder was with the 25th Battery, 7th Australian Field Artillery Brigade. He participated in the artillery barrage that was part of the advance of 31 July. On 23 July, during the preliminary stages of that bombardment, he noted in his diary:

> In one spot there must have been a particularly heavy fight as for some distance around can be seen the remains of dead Germans, while the ground is torn to ribbons from the shell fire. No doubt hundreds have been buried about here as the stench is awful.[257]

Ryder was subsequently involved in the preliminary artillery bombardment for the Battle of Menin Road. On 16 September, he recorded in his diary:

> It has been a black day for us, and all the boys are feeling depressed. We fired one more of our usual stunts at 10 o'clock this morning. As usual Fritz retaliated with his heavies, but for a time no shells came too near us. However just after we had ceased firing a shell landed direct on number 4 pit and three of our boys were killed and one wounded. The two killed (Cliff Richards and Roy Willis) were absolutely blown to atoms. The third (Arthur Redman) died in our arms a few minutes after. They are all from the same pit as those three who were wounded yesterday, and this practically wipes out the whole gun detachment.

Ryder was 21 when he enlisted in February 1916. Like so many others, at 5 feet 8 inches tall he was relatively well below the popularly imagined height. He was wounded in action during May 1917, but stayed on duty with the battery. During August—that very wet month in Flanders—he was admitted to hospital with pleurisy. The deaths of several members of his field battery during mid-September was taking its emotional toll. On 19 September, he was taking part in the final preparatory artillery bombardment for the next morning's advance on Menin Road when he received word that a close friend had been badly wounded. This from his diary:

> Wednesday, September 19th. I received today the worst news since we have been in the line and that was that my old chum Frank was seriously wounded and was not expected to live. It is a terrible blow and for the rest of the day I have felt like going mad. It appears that a shell landed right in the pit whilst Frank's gun was firing and the four men on the gun were all wounded, Frank being the worst of all as a piece of shell went clean through his steel hat and into the head.
>
> Thursday, September 20th. I obtained leave and with a horse started off for Poperinge, a distance of some five miles from here ….. I found my old pal and my God it

> was good to see him still alive although he was unconscious at the time. However, he was breathing well and that put new hope into my heart. I stayed with him until the train was about to start and then fearing that perhaps the worst would happen I played the woman's part and kissed him.

Ryder got back to the lines that afternoon and made two wagon load trips, carrying supplies and ammunition to the battery. It was the second trip along the Menin Road that unnerved him again. A shell had exploded farther down the road and the wrecked wagons and teams were blocking it:

> Whilst waiting near the wrecked road we heard a moaning sound coming from a big shell hole some yards from the scene of the disaster. On investigation we found a poor brute of a horse buried up to its neck in the mud. It had been blown in by the shell burst, and when we saw it, was struggling about and moaning piteously. We decided to shoot the poor brute but as luck had it no rifle was available, so we did our best to put an end to its misery with a nearby beam of wood. However this failed, so we left and on the way down the wooden road told a party of infantrymen who promised to shoot the poor brute for us.

On 25 September, whilst preparing the guns for the Polygon Wood battle, Ryder himself was injured by a blast from a German shell that shattered his left arm. By 5:00 p.m. his wounds had been dressed, and the next day he was on a train to the rear for further treatment. Like other walking wounded, he slept on the floor of the overcrowded carriage. He was hospitalized until 9 October, when he sought and gained permission to return to his unit. As he put it:

> I think I would have gone mad if I had stayed any longer as there was nothing to do but think of the boys and wonder how Frank was.

He was back in the line with the 25th Battery the next day. On 25 October, he learned of Frank's death:

> Goodness knows it struck me hard enough when I realised that I had lost the best pal in the world.

On 6 January the following year, they were in the back lines, and Ryder got permission to locate Frank's grave on the Channel coast:

> Sure enough I found the cemetery – a little well-kept place in a slight hollow in the sand hills. It was almost dark by this time so I did not stay long but started out for Etaples.

Ryder would be wounded in action again in April 1918, this time by shrapnel in the thigh.

Breaking through the German Defense In Depth

The Germans had first developed defense in depth systems during the second half of 1916. By the end of July 1917, their defenses outside Ypres were the purest expression of these principles. It was not a strictly trench warfare scenario. The front defense line did include trenches, but relied much more on newly constructed and very strong reinforced concrete pillboxes systematically built to hold strategic high points and positioned to provide mutual cover for other pillboxes in a defensive net. Interspersed with these pillboxes were further machine gun strongpoints. What the 1st and 2nd Divisions were about to encounter was the same defensive system the 3rd Division confronted at Messines over two months earlier. The farther back the defenses went, the more concentrated they became. At the rear of these were the bulk of the infantry, ready to eliminate what was presumably left of the advancing troops that had survived the crossfire of the forward systems.

The British had to establish some sort of objectives amidst this complex defensive network. These took the form of "lines." Each line represented attainable objectives. They were based as much on areas of high ground as they were on particular enemy trench systems, strongpoints, and concrete pillboxes. The Australian I Anzac Corps commanders (Birdwood and White) paid particular attention to setting realistic objectives. There were three: the red, then the blue, and then the green line. These receive mention in the accounts below. That final green line was perhaps 1,200 yards from the Australians' jumping off point.

Both divisions had two brigades each at the front for the attack. Each of these four brigades then had two to four of their battalions acting as first and subsequent waves. We have an after action report prepared by Lt. George Vaughan, commanding just one company ("A" Company) of the 12th Battalion. All four battalions of 5 Brigade (the 9th, 10th, 11th, and 12th) took part. The 12th was part of the second wave. His report shows how the best plans could go astray. He describes the final part of the march to the start line—which for the 12th Battalion was at the northwestern edge of Glencorse Wood—the evening of 19 September:

> The Company moved into position without incident and the guiding tape was of greatest assistance but had it been necessary to wear gas helmets it would have been extremely difficult to move from Chateau Wood forward, owing to the absence of tracks.[258]

In front of them as the first wave was their sister battalion, the 11th.

There was a lot of low whistling—evidently for communication—as the 11th Battalion moved into position. It would have been audible to enemy scouts. Men did not take cover, even when on a skyline when flares went up and they were evidently seen by the enemy.

Vaughan's "A" Company then advanced for the red line:

> On the right of the Brigade sector all units were mixed up and there was little control, consequent on the enemy's shelling and the rough nature of the ground. A strong concrete post [pillbox] which resisted in Nonnen Bosschen [Nun's Wood, adjacent to and north east of Glencorse Wood] was quickly surrounded

> and rushed, but the three waves of the attack [the third wave being the 9th and 10th Battalions] were so close to one another – really in one mass, that the post inflicted undue casualties on us with machine gun fire.

They continued, meeting less resistance than expected. All the time they moved behind the artillery barrage as it gradually crept forward:

> The Blue objective was reached as soon as the barrage passed it and the only strong post there either did not have sufficient time, or the men were too much demoralized by our shellfire, to resist. They surrendered with two machine guns complete.

The 9th and 10th then passed on to the green line and held it. Vaughan concludes:

> The enemy's morale was undoubtedly bad. He was evidently demoralised by the weight of our artillery fire and our infantry were upon him before he could recover.

And in his report under the heading, "Lessons Learnt":

> Our heavy barrage starting at the same time as the infantry is an affective counter to the enemy's principle of defence in depth. The necessity for keeping close to the barrage, each man knowing as much as possible about his objective, line of advance and method of advance were both emphasised. The value of a rapid converging attack on strong points was obvious.

Well trained, well rested, battle-experienced infantry, with clear goals and advancing behind a creeping barrage of sufficient weight could indeed be successful against the most advanced German defense in depth systems. And all this was conducted over ground that for the last ten days had been soaked by persistent rain. The key to success was the preparation and the choice of attainable objectives.

There are several written operational reports like Vaughan's from companies of various battalions for 19-21 September.[259] All account for a successful action under the *pro forma* headings: "First Phase," "Second Phase," and so on, then "Consolidation," "Counter Attacks," "Relief," "Lessons Learnt," and "Enemy Morale." Matters of mud, misery, and disorientation are barely dealt with; such information is more readily found in the personal accounts. John Edwards provides just such a personal description of conditions in the Battle of Menin Road.

The Personal Account of John Edwards

John Edwards was nearly thirty-six years old when he enlisted in March 1915. At five and a half feet tall, like so many other Australian soldiers, he was not representative of the nationally imagined, strapping six foot tall bronzed Anzac. He was a professional accountant and, like many professionals, served as a private. He served with the 27th Battalion and was hospitalized for shell shock on the Somme on 4 August 1916. He was back with his battalion only eight days later. His military records show he transferred to the 7th Field Ambulance in early October 1916. This unit was attached to the 27th Battalion.

On 19 September, at about the same time Vaughan was leading his company, Edwards was leading a party of stretcher bearers and orderlies through the Menin Gate at Ypres and out onto the Menin Road, headed for the start line at the northern end of Chateau Wood:

> We went into the line on the night of the 19th September and were in a mess from the jump ['from the outset'] ..... We stood for an hour in the blackness, with the rain quietly falling and making everybody pretty dismal.[260]

The party traversed the northern end of Chateau Wood by way of slippery duckboards near Bellewaarde Lake. Continuing about 400 yards farther east, they came to the start line on Westhoek Ridge. This "ridge" runs through the forty and forty-five meter (131 to 148 ft) contour lines. The difference—about five meters, or twenty feet at most — typifies the undulating but essentially low lying, low relief character of the terrain. At this point, the confusion rarely mentioned in the officers' official company and battalion reports manifests:

> Just as I was hoping we could get away from this spot, one of the Intelligence Section – Andrews – came along, and when I spoke to him he whispered: "Why Jack, they've been sending back messages, Sergeant Edwards wanted at the head of the column, ever since we left Ypres." I murmured "Where is H.Q.?" he said, "The R.S.M. [Regimental Sergeant Major] is in that trench." I'm damned if I could see the trench. He got hold of my arm, saying, "Look out, or you'll bloody well fall into it," and there I was within a few feet of the parados.[261]
> I scrambled into the trench, which was a yawning, broken down cutting but gave pretty decent cover. It was absolutely choked with men and equipment. I stumbled over them and found Dick Pearce, the R.S.M. We exchanged curses and I said, "Where is the Doctor and where is the Aid Post?" Dick only knew that the Doctor was at the 25th Battalion Aid Post, and said he would try and get me a guide, a 25th stretcher bearer, however, gave me the direction of the Aid Post and said it was only about 100 yards away "over there," pointing to some spot in the inky darkness ..... It was rather a nightmare of a journey.

Edwards records the attack as a success. Objectives were taken and consolidated, counterattacks were repelled, and German counterbattery fire was completely overwhelmed by the much greater weight of shell coming from the British lines. Their Aid Post was a sunken, sandbagged affair surmounted by a corrugated iron roof with earth heaped over it. A stretcher served as an operating table for stabilizing the more serious cases. Those less wounded and already treated and awaiting stretcher bearers were laid outside. There were many wounded. Their treatment was the best that could be offered. The condition of many who were required to make their own way back through the lines is recorded, the first being one of their own stretcher bearers:

> I thought a bit of shell had hit the earth by the door, but, hearing a groan, dashed out, and found old Bill Haggerty ..... We brought the poor old boy inside. Standing in the little trench he had cover to his waist, but this splinter

> hit him below the shoulder and went through the lungs. The ambulance bearers had not arrived to carry from our post, so we gave Bill the option of waiting for the bearers or trying to walk down. Bill, as game as they make them, decided to walk and off he slowly went.

This took place around dawn of 20 September. Later in the day, the casualties mounted:

> At one time we had 53 men lying on stretchers, waiting to go away and we of course were making everybody walk who could possibly do so ….. Soon after we had a lot of wounded to attend to, and some very bad cases came in. George Bulley was terribly knocked about – both feet smashed and one arm in a bad state ….. One chap, Iredale, was brought in with his right arm shorn off at the shoulder. The upper arm had been blown clear away, and his shoulder was exposed like red beef clean cut with a cleaver. The forearm, including the elbow, was attached by a few threads of tissue. Dr. Ross said: "Cut it off Sergeant," and with the scissors I snipped off the forearm. The hand, forearm and elbow were completely intact, the piece of shell having simply blown away the humerus, biceps and surrounding flesh. Iredale was a fine stamp of a man and though conscious, never batted an eyelash. The doctor pinched up artery and vein with a couple of nickelled forceps. I then bound up the lot with shell dressings and wool, and sent the poor chap on.

Iredale walked back to a medical station in the rear of the lines. Edwards served out the rest of the war, surviving without a scratch.

By late morning, the green line had been reached, consolidated, and held against scattered counterattacks. Menin Road was really more about pushing for the next high ground toward the Passchendaele Ridge than just the road. The southwestern part of Polygon Wood had been secured. To the south, the Australians and British on their right had also secured the western sections of the Gheluvelt Plateau. Control over this particular area had remained problematic during the Battle of Messines in early June. The eventual capture of its eastern section would form a main part of the events of 26 September, the Battle of Polygon Wood.

The Battle of Menin Road officially ended on 25 September and the next battle—the Battle of Polygon Wood—officially commenced the next day, running from 26 September to 3 October. It needs be stressed that these are postwar committee allocations. Just how arbitrary these time frames can be is evident in the British official history. Edmonds adheres rigidly to the official dates to the extent that some events in the Polygon Wood battle are held over for the subsequent chapter on the subsequent Battle of Broodseinde.[262] There is little evidence the troops could tell much difference. Their temporal reality was going in to battle, hopefully surviving the mental and physical onslaught, then being relieved by fresh troops. By 25 September, the 1st and 2nd Divisions had been replaced by the 4th and 5th.

The Battle of Polygon Wood: 26 September to 3 October

There is no clear, discernible gap between the Battle of Menin Road and the Battle of Polygon Wood. Both constituted a continued easterly push into the ridges that reached up to Passchendaele. The purpose of taking the rest of Polygon Wood was the same as that for the Menin Road; to push the Germans back off the high ground.[263] The battle maps use lines to show where each battalion was meant to be and meant to advance. In reality, the troops were not always so neatly positioned. One Australian stretcher bearer named David Whinfield (60th Battalion) was in the relieving 5th Division. Here is his diary entry for 25 September:

> We came up with only a waterproof sheet for bedding. Our Corporals, Milne and Hay get on Harry's, Jim's and my nerves. We have some machonochies. About 11.00 a.m. a real bright day, we all moved through the Middlesex Regiment being forced back. The enemy had a terrible and thick barrage which we had to pass through. We passed many killed Tommies and Scotties in useless shelters – were devilish-scared. Passed Glencorse Wood [south of it]. We dug in the shelter of a pill box where we were subjected to the shelling of the heaviest guns fired at an average of four a second. It was more than a man could stand.[264]

It is evident that Whinfield's party had veered south and off track of the Australian sector. The presence of dead English and Scottish soldiers indicates their position in the British X Corps area. They were aware they were in the wrong place but carried on. This entry is for the next day:

> We didn't re-join our unit but slept where we were the previous night. We found some bread, meat and butter at 10.00a.m. It was our first since 7.00p. m. [the night before].

And for the third day (the 27th):

> We went past Glencorse Wood, Inverness Wood [also known as Inverness Copse, located even further south than Glencorse Wood] ..... we carried [wounded on stretchers] back to the post one and a half miles back. The snipers didn't fire at us. We kept carrying till about 11.00p. m. and should have been killed a hundred times. We surprised the Tommy stretcher bearers.

These Australians were in the wrong place and had continued stretcher bearing duties, living off scrounged food. It is another good example of the innate initiative that characterized most (but not all) of the AIF.[265] Those three days (25 – 27) encompassed the official end of the Battle of Menin Road and the official commencement of the Battle of Polygon Wood. Whinfield and his party saw nothing but continual death and shellfire. They were oblivious to any end of one battle or commencement of another.

There are several reports from officers in various battalions about Polygon Wood. Amongst them is a report titled an "Unofficial Narrative Summary" that provides excellent insight into the attack on Polygon Wood by the 29th Battalion. This report was prepared for Brig. Gen. Edwin Tivey (commanding 8 Brigade) by Lt. Sidney Gullet (29th Battalion). Gullet wrote the report during a stay at the 3rd London General Hospital in Wandsworth. It is dated 2 November 1917, and its unofficial nature makes for more insight than the official reports. Along with contributions from other eyewitnesses, we can create a vivid picture of events at Polygon Wood.

Gullet was a twenty-five-year-old engineer when he enlisted in July 1916. In March 1917, he was severely wounded in his jaw, the rear of his throat and palate, and his right thigh. It took several operations and bouts with septic wounds before he returned to the lines. Now he was back in the line for the Polygon Wood battle as intelligence officer for the 29th Battalion. During the night of 25/26 September, the battalion moved out of Ypres using the Menin Road and formed up opposite the so-called race course in the center of the wood (this was in fact a horse-drawn artillery training circuit formerly used by the Belgian Army).

As was often the case, the best of plans then went awry. Although meant to be following the 59th Battalion, the initial stages of the advance saw most of the 29th somehow end up in front of the 59th. Disorientation quickly developed as Gullett:

> ….. with a prismatic compass to direct the line of advance and with two intelligence men carrying tape, which we were going to lay as we advanced. Owing to one of these men being killed and the other wounded, and so losing the tape practically at the start, and owing to the inevitable tendency to get drawn into the fight, this scheme was abandoned.[266]

The heavy barrage did not completely suppress the enemy machine gun posts and many casualties were taken:

> But most of the success was due to good bayonet and rifle work; here and there, where garrisons stood their ground, resulting in some fierce hand to hand fighting, but the enemy was outmatched by our men ….. in one case the German machine gunner with his dead comrades round him was finally bayoneted when still gamely firing his gun.

Proceeding through the lines, the attack became less one of integrated units and more of a mixture of small groups of 29th and 59th Battalion troops advancing from shell hole to shell hole until the final blue line was reached. By the afternoon of the 27th, the troops were still encountering resistance from the isolated remnants of the German defense in depth system:

> Soon after reaching the Blue Line our troops on the left noticed an occupied dugout ….. Evidently the garrison was afraid to come out, so a Lewis Gun team covered the opening with their gun, and had a thoroughly happy afternoon shooting the enemy whenever he attempted to emerge, accounting for a large number in this way. Next day the remaining garrison surrendered to us, and came into our line under a white flag. Owing to the non-arrival of any rations or water, Colonel Purser ordered us to eat our emergency ration, which we did, and drank shell hole water.

A few days later on 1 October, Gullet was gassed. He carried on his duties until the fifteenth. The continual exertion only pronounced his shallow breathing. He was vomiting and experiencing difficulty swallowing. A subsequent medical report stated:

> His voice is still hoarse, only slight cough, can walk all day at his own pace but cannot run or climb stairs without distress. Still very thin.[267]

By 1920 he had lapsed somewhat, especially with the onset of each winter season. A subsequent medical report cited disturbed sleep, wheezing, and the symptoms of effort syndrome, a condition likened to the symptoms associated with angina. Gullett's gas poisoning entitled him to a pension based on "Disability, 30%."[268] Presumably, he was still seventy percent well.

The kind of bunching up and even passing through battalions Gullett describes appears to have been a common occurrence. Often, when a particular objective was reached by the first wave, it was indeed their role to establish themselves and let the following battalion through to the next objective. This is not what is being described above. This was traffic congestion and disorientation across hostile and often featureless landscapes, with parts of various waves arriving at the same place together or in the wrong order.

While the advances were proving successful in terms of ground gained, they were also costly in terms of soldiers killed. Still wrestling with his gambling problem, Pvt. Arthur Kilgour (1st Field Ambulance, attached to the 2nd Battalion) had survived the slaughter at Pozières, then Mouquet Farm, and then the horrible winter at Flers the year before. There, he was briefly hospitalized for two weeks with a lung infection and trench foot. Now, a year later at Polygon Wood, he was suffering in the cold and mud again. He was serving as a stretcher bearer whilst plagued with sore ears and throat and shell shock. He had already lost three friends and by 5 October, in the Battle of Broodseinde, would lose another two. By 13 October, he records the deaths of the seventh, then the eighth:

> My dear friend and chum Private William Metcalfe of this battalion has been killed in action. The news has fairly stunned me. I have never missed a mate as much as I miss dear Will. Such a fine Christian man.[269]

Kilgour's gambling lapses continued:

> For the last few months I have been gambling heavily. From now on I must rid myself of this vice. I do not forget the promise I made my fiancée a few years back but there are so many temptations out here.

It got worse:

> For the last three days I have lost £5 playing cards. It is indeed marvellous how the game grips one. Oh how I wish I could shake the grip off me ….. For the sake of my wife-to-be I am going to exercise my will power and give up gambling. I have lost heavily this week. From now on I have finished with cards.

Others saw no attraction in it. Pvt. Leicester Johnson of the 20th Battalion:

> Plenty of gambling going on after pay this afternoon. Can't understand why some chaps can be such goats as to waste their hard earned wages in this manner. I can generally manage to spend my little on stores, as our rations are none too plentiful these days.[270]

And always there were the dead: the mutilated and the intact. Different insights into injury and death were being experienced all around. Lt. Henry Neaves of the 45th Battalion was in charge of a party bringing supplies by mule up to the line held by the 48th Battalion in Polygon Wood on 27-28 September:

> The first night after much difficulty in ploughing through the round shell holes and wires the 48th Battalion was reached. Fritz was shelling round about heavily at the time so I gave orders for the loads to be taken off and for the mules to return. I then went to find 48th Battalion Headquarters. I looked in the door of the first pillbox and saw a sergeant and a number of men sitting up, it was moonlight and I could just see inside. I said "Sergeant, can you tell me where your headquarters are?" I waited but no answer. I asked again still no answer. I then looked in more closely and found that they were all dead, 15 of them having been killed by concussion earlier in the evening through a German shell landing on their pill box.[271]

There could also be disorder behind the lines. The Australians were generally unimpressed with the Portuguese soldiers. They were held to be less than committed and less than likely to fight. Heckling them with cries of "pork and cheese!" added to the mutual rancor. Nor did the Chinese labor parties and Australian soldiers always mix. Pvt. Thomas Cleary (an electrician) had twice failed in his endeavors to enlist; the third time he was successful. He was with the 2nd Pioneers Battalion. Somewhere behind Polygon Wood on 31 September he recorded in his diary:

> Maffesini punched one or two of the Chows recently, so a deputation waited for him the other day to show him the error of his ways, he knocked a couple of them but eventually had to run for his life.[272]

Cleary apparently had no personal grievance with the Chinese laborers, but he did with the army's approach to replacement clothing. This entry from his diary dated 2 October 1917:

> I got a pair of underpants and a shirt from the Quartermaster after a row [argument] with Lieutenant Smith. The Quartermaster refused to give me a shirt because I didn't have one to hand in, having only received an undershirt at the Baths. I had already been carrying on well into winter with this undershirt only. I complained to Smith and the dopey coot agreed with the Quartermaster. I asked him did he think I was going to finish the War without a shirt just because the Baths had none to give me to hand in. After a brisk argument he had to give in. Raining and bitterly cold today. I get awfully wild when I think of that well clothed Smith half stupid with whiskey grudging me a shirt.

Only in the AIF could a private argue, let alone answer back and make his point to an officer and a quartermaster and get his way.

The Battle of Broodseinde: 4 October 1917

The Battle of Broodseinde was essentially an attack on the next part of the ridge that swung north from the now-occupied Gheluvelt plateau. It involved twelve British and Commonwealth divisions attacking along an eight-mile-long front. Those Anzac divisions involved started on a front of nearly four miles that ran diagonally from the northwest of Zonnebeke to the southeast of that village. The New Zealanders took the northern third of the front and the Australians the larger southern two-thirds. Within that Australian sector, II Anzac Corps' 3rd Division was in the middle. To their right and farther south were I Anzac's 2nd and 1st Divisions, in that order.

Despite some rain during the evening of 3 October, the attack began on 4 October. By coincidence, at 5:30 a.m., the Germans shelled the Australian positions. At 6:00 a.m., the Australian barrage commenced and the troops went forward, only to find a line of German troops attacking them some thirty yards distant. Immediately, the Australian machine guns responded, and their firepower was sufficient to break up the German troops. The Australians advanced and by successive waves reduced the usual system of pillboxes and fortified posts.

Leicester Johnson

Private Leicester Johnson of the 20th Battalion was in the second wave that moved up after the initial barrage at dawn. By 10 a.m., they had advanced well over a mile onto the ridge line, where they took up positions in shell holes. From here they advanced another half mile. That evening, the platoon was put on ration duty. This required them to retrace their steps back down the line, collect the rations, and return to their original forward position. The food did not arrive. They remained behind the line. Later that evening, they were transferred to ammunition carrying and sent back up the line. It had been raining steadily since that afternoon:

> Each of us was given a box of trench mortar bombs to carry up to the front line. Oh, that awful walk, struggling along through mud and slush with that heavy box on our shoulders ….. On the way back I stumbled across poor old Maclean being helped along by a mate of ours (Sid Hills) having received a nasty crack

Broodseinde Ridge, Ypres sector, October 12, 1917. In the foreground lie the remains of a dead German soldier. Alongside the huddled Australians lies one of their number. Three Australians have dug a semblance of shelter in the bank of this railway cutting. *AWM*

> in the leg. Well this was just about the limit, there were three of us fagged out [exhausted] and not being able to keep up with the crowd, lost our way and were wandering about trying to find a way out. Both Hills and I being just about knocked up [Australian for, amongst other things, being something worse than exhausted] had all we could do to support Mac. We would take turns, one leading the way and trying to find some sort of track, while the other helped Mac along. After wandering about an hour or so, Hills came across a dead Australian officer and being badly in need of water, quenched one third [each] from his water bottle and helped ourselves to any eatables he had in his haversack, also some cigarettes.[273]

They eventually found an aid post where Maclean received rudimentary attention. In the absence of any spare stretcher bearers, they decided to help Maclean back to the next Regimental Aid Post. Johnson and Hills left their friend there and returned to find their battalion:

> Poor old Mac, I wonder where we will meet again. This is the second time we two have been parted.

There is no intimation in Leicester Johnson's detailed diary account of Broodseinde that the battle was somehow done with and completed by the end of 4 October. It just simply drags on: injury, death, disorientation, rain, mud, and always the cold and the tiredness, until the place "Poelcappelle" appears in his diary. On 8 October, Johnson wrote:

> No rations coming up last night and no water, "D" Company had to share their rations with us, which, by the way proved quite sufficient, both companies having been cut up so badly. We had no water at all, so had to go thirsty all day. In the afternoon during some rain we managed to catch a little on a water sheet ….. As soon as it was dark another chap and myself went out and got a water bottle from a dead chap.

On 9 October, in the advance on Poelcappelle, Johnson was hit:

> I received a slight crack in the hand, a shell bursting on the parapet right alongside me, a lot of little splinters going into my right hand sending it stiff.

The same spot at the cutting today. *Photo courtesy of Mark Banning*

He made his own way back to a field ambulance and was evacuated. There followed a succession of evacuations farther back through the medical chain; draughty tents with no flooring, trains so full that even the floor was crowded with wounded, and always being hungry. This was the second time Johnson was wounded. The previous April saw him evacuated for treatment for a shell wound to his right arm. He was back in the line within ten days. He would be gassed in July the following year and that saw an end to his military service.

Donald Gibson

That same day, 2nd Lt. Donald Gibson of the 19th Battalion was also advancing on Poelcappelle. His older brother Samuel was in the same area. This from Donald Gibson's diary for 9 October:

> So far I have not met Sam, however on leaving our position I salvaged a waterproof sheet and today I found it marked 7201 S.J.G. I hope he is safe.[274]

The remains of Chateau Wood, near the Menin Road, 29 October 1917. This image bears the creative hallmark of the Australian official photographer Frank Hurley. A party of unusually well-groomed artillery men pause on the duckboards for this evocative, almost tranquil scene. Hurley was also the official photographer on Ernest Shackleton's Antarctic Expedition in 1914 and was marooned until August 1916, at which time he first learned of the war. Behind the romanticized imagery is the stench of tepid water, corrupted earth, and the dead. The image nevertheless provides an accurate depiction of what a "wood" usually looked like during and after a battle. *AWM*

It was not to be. Over a month later on 24 October, he wrote:

> Heard the sad news yesterday that Sam was killed. Found the 34th Battalion today and got what particulars I wanted. He was killed instantly by a piece of shell at the spot where I found his waterproof. I know the spot and will make every effort to have a cross erected. His watch and disk were left on him and all other personal property was handed in to be sent home. It is indeed sad news but war is war. My commission came through 22/10/17.

Six months later and now on the Somme, Donald Gibson made his last diary entry on 3 April 1918. Less than two weeks later on 15 April 1918, he was wounded. His records show wounds to the face, eye, and hand. He was still in hospital in England in August 1919. On 8 August 1919, a note was entered on his "Service and Casualty Form Part II":

> Officer is making excellent progress with studies as blind man. He will be with us for 3 or 4 months more.

Gibson was still in a London hospital in February 1920. He eventually returned to Australia. On 17 August 1967, his widow wrote to the authorities, requesting that his

Ypres, 25 October 1917. Australian soldiers pass the ruined Cloth Hall (left) and the remains of the cathedral (right). They are moving directly toward one of the main gates to the town, the Menin Gate at the eastern edge of Ypres, where they will meet the Menin Road. *AWM*

Gallipoli commemoration medal be forwarded to her. Gibson had died at age sixty-five in a Sydney repatriation hospital in 1954.[275]

From Broodseinde to Passchendaele: 4-12 October

Although still muddy, the Ypres battlefield during September had been more readily traversable. Plumer's "bite and hold" approach had seen real, albeit expensive progress in the September battles. This all ended with the return of the rains. Any attempts by Haig to continue the fight to gain the heights would now be tempered by the weather. Yet Haig appears not to have taken this into account. Convinced as he was of the impending collapse of the German army, his desire to drive through Passchendaele to the Channel ports saw him insist on a forced pace of advances. Plumer had only been capable of such success with fine weather and adequate artillery. With the rains, the capacity to bring up that artillery in its entirety was forsaken, but the determined advance of the troops was ordered.[276] The outcome was one that saw the earlier successful battles overshadowed by failure. Germany and her army did not collapse and the Belgian ports remained under German control.[277]

With the Gheluvelt plateau secured, the Australian I and II Anzac Corps then attacked the next section of the crescent-shaped ridge. Although called "Broodseinde" after a very small hamlet on the east side of the ridge, the battle was more about advancing along that ridge. Capturing the heights around here would give the British a clear view of the ultimate objective on that ridge, Passchendaele.

As Bean and Edmonds would record in their official histories, the Broodseinde attacks were a spectacular success. That made three successful attacks in a row since 20 September: Menin Road, Polygon Wood, and on 4 October, Broodseinde. Then the rains returned.

The Cloth Hall and the adjacent cathedral at Ypres in 2008, completely rebuilt to their former glory. At the end of the war, the British wanted to preserve the place as an untouched memorial ruin to those who served and died in the Ypres sector. *Author's collection*

Chapter Fifteen

Passchendaele

Dating Passchendaele

For this account, the action at Poelcappelle on 9 October is included with the events of Passchendaele. This reflects its treatment in both the British and Australian official histories and particularly the Australian Medical History. British official historian Edmonds gives it scant attention; just over a dozen pages, with nearly half of these devoted to the dominant factor, the weather. Bean's account in volume IV of the Australian official history gives Poelcappelle a mention in the index, but no heading in the text. Bean concentrates on the weather for eight pages under the heading "The conditions, October 5-12th." Indeed, Bean places the events at Poelcappelle squarely within those of Passchendaele. Chapter XXI is headed, "The Plan breaks Down, Passchendaele I – October 9th."[278] Further, Bean's treatment of what were later officially titled "First" Passchendaele (12 October) and "Second" Passchendaele (26 October to 10 November) confers more continuity on the whole period. He dates Passchendaele as commencing 9 October (thereby including Poelcappelle) and includes the events of Second Passchendaele. This approach takes little account of the British official dates given clearly in Edmonds' volumes dealing with 1917; rather, it reflects the greater Australian involvement in First Passchendaele.

The Fighting for Passchendaele

The rains returned the same afternoon Broodseinde was secured and persisted. The resulting ground conditions meant that fewer guns could be brought up for the proposed advance of 9 October. The same situation existed 12 October; there was simply too much mud and too little time. The shortage of guns was hoped to be remedied by a greater rate of fire from those that were brought up. This failed because the pack animals that were required to bring up the extra shells faced the same insurmountable conditions.[279] In the absence of adequate artillery and shells, both Godley and Monash come in for criticism from Bean in the official history for their attempts to quicken the advance of the infantry:

> It had been agreed that 100 yards in 8 minutes would be the proper pace for the infantry's progress throughout the attack of October 12. The 3rd Division would now have to advance the first 500 yards at twice that speed. If Generals Monash and Godley had had experience of the Somme, it is unlikely that they would have agreed to this arrangement. Had Godley really known the conditions of October 9th – the thinness of the barrage, the complete absence of smoke

screen, the ineffectiveness of bombardment, the exhaustion of the troops – how could he have hoped for success.[280]

Just as in August, the October fighting failed to make significant gains. The Australians were short on artillery support and physically exhausted from trying to maneuver through the rain, mud, and freezing temperatures. Under such conditions, leaders can be seen to lose touch with the battlefield's realities. This problem existed within the four battalions comprising 6 Brigade. Much of the information in Bean's personal diaries remained there, never to see the light of day in his subsequent official history. Bean's immense amount of research material for the period is also contained in a series of folders, within one of which is this unpublished account of crisis in command. It is marked "No. 1. Confidential. Historical Note" and deals with Gen. John Paton's command of 6 Brigade's four battalions (the 21st, 22nd, 23rd, and 24th) at Poelcappelle. It was almost certainly written in October 1917:

> It is well known that the battalions of the 6th Brigade were not at all enthusiastic about having General Paton sent to them as the successor to General Gellibrand. The Brigade has greatly deteriorated since he went to it and Norman [Brigade Staff Captain] tells me that there are a larger number of applications for the Flying Corps and for the Indian Army from officers of the 6th Brigade than from any other Brigade in the AIF
> The first battle which Paton fought with his Brigade was the Battle [Poelcappelle] of October 9th ….. The actual conduct of the action of the Brigade during this fight was controlled by the four [batallions']Commanding officers who all arranged to occupy the same dugout. They took the whole management of the fight into their hands, merely communicating with the Brigadier and the Brigade Major by telephone ….. They used to send direct instructions to Norman ….. he would bring the supplies up to them, and the four of them through this action acted in place of the Brigadier. It was an extraordinary development and entirely due to the want of confidence which they had in General Paton.[281]

Paton returned to Australia in August 1918.

Despite the atrocious conditions, the failures to advance at Poelcappelle on 9 October and the so-called First Passchendaele of 12 October, Haig pressed his forces on, convinced of an imminent collapse in German morale. Those senior commanders and staff in a position to see otherwise—Plumer, Gough, Harington, Birdwood, and Godley in particular—either could not convince Haig otherwise or did not raise objection. Haig remained unmoved by an intelligence report on the matter and was more than prepared to censure intelligence reports that conflicted with his own views, even to the point of questioning their veracity on the basis of the writer's religion. On 15 October, Haig would write:

> It is stated in a note by the DMI [Director of Military Intelligence] War Office dated 1 October (WP49) 'The moral of the troops in the field gives no cause for anxiety to the German High Command'. I cannot think why the War Office Intelligence Department gives such a wrong picture of the situation except that

> General Macdonogh (DMI) is a Roman Catholic and is unconsciously influenced by information which doubtless reaches him from tainted (i.e. Catholic) sources.[282]

On 18 October, Haig used the Canadians to make progress where the Australians had not, with a final assault on Passchendaele. By 10 November, Passchendaele and its ridge were taken. The Australians had provided some support on the Canadians' southern flank. By 14 November, they had been withdrawn from the line.

This is a brief outline of events; there are plenty of detailed descriptions of the battles.[283] We return to the eyewitness accounts of the Australians, starting with Charles Bean's private reservations about the continual push toward Passchendaele. On 9 October, Bean confided to his diary:

> I believe that the official attitude is that Passchendaele Ridge is so important that tomorrow's attack is worth making whether it succeeds or fails; also Harington [of Plumer's 2nd Army staff] having fixed a day for the attack intensely dislikes going back on it, especially once the troops are in position. I must say I suspect that they are making a great bloody experiment – a huge gamble and more than that; a deliberate attempt to see how it works. I think they are playing on the morale of their troops. Harington said that the top of the Ridge was sandy and as "dry as a bone". I feel, and most of the correspondents feel, awfully anxious about tomorrow. They [the command] don't know the fight there was for the last ridge [Broodseinde], these major generals back there, they don't know how nearly the Broodseinde crest held us up. They don't realise how much and desperately hard it will be to fight down such opposition in the mud ….. Every step means dragging one foot out of the mud and you can't nip around craters, as in Thursday's fighting, when you want to outflank the opposition.[284]

The reference to Thursday is to Broodseinde on 4 October. Bean then observes what he interprets as the unfolding shift from careful advance to wishful thinking;

> I thought the principle was to be "hit, hit, hit, whenever the weather is suitable." If so, it is thrown over at the first temptation.[285]

To the troops, there was always that bit further to go. Of Passchendaele, Lt. Henry Neaves of the 45th Battalion wrote:

> When we went into this sector there was considerable discussion as to how long it would be before we had the Bosche on the run and it was frequently said that when one more ridge was captured we would be able to dominate the German positions for miles. One or two ridges were captured but after each capture there was still the same tale "only one more ridge."[286]

Australian Capt. Eric Dark—a doctor attached to the British army's 9th Field Ambulance— was at Passchendaele with the British troops on 16 October. He led eleven squads of bearers and established a dressing station under the cover of a pillbox. They had been warned of the likelihood of a German gas attack. Sentries were posted to raise the alarm while the medical staff concentrated on treating the constant stream of wounded coming into the post. Presently, those sentries raised the gas alarm and masks were donned. What follows is a lengthy but valuable account of the unassuming dedication of medical staff, the clinical, almost detached observations of a doctor, the problematic condition of undertaking detailed work while wearing a gas mask, and the effects of gas on the human body. They are somewhere near the Ravebeek Valley, about a mile southeast of Passchendaele. The "Thomas splint" refers to an immobilizing splint used by the medical staff on fractured limbs:

> Wounded constantly came in, walking cases and stretcher cases that the bearers brought from the forward area. No other M.O. was with me so I was fully occupied with dressings. Just before dawn a heavy shell got a direct hit on one of the block houses, blowing it in and seriously wounding two infantrymen. When I got there with my corporal, Sachs by name, and stretcher bearers, I found that both men had compound fractures of the femurs [thighs].
>
> We had our gas masks on, as the all clear had not yet sounded, and set about trying to fix the men up. In the conditions, with the men lying on the floor that was littered with smashed concrete, the air thick with dust of the explosion, and our sight constantly blurred by fogged eye-pieces, it seemed impossible ever to get the wounds dressed and the fractures properly put up on Thomas splints. After fumbling about for some time I made a decision and told Sachs "Look Corporal we are getting nowhere; you and I will take off our masks so that we can do the job properly." He made no demur and worked well and dextrously to help me get the men fixed and away.
>
> It was a horrible night and by dawn, 32 of my 44 bearers were casualties, mostly gassed, ultimately 16 of them died, including Sachs, a good man, whom probably my order killed.[287]

At dawn, Dark went back to the advanced dressing station. He returned to his forward post with extra stretcher bearers and set about tending more of the wounded. Around midday on 17 October, his party was relieved. By then, the gassing of the previous night had taken its effect on Capt.Dark. The relief medical team:

> Found me nearly blind from intense irritation and swelling of the cornea, and constantly vomiting. The gas had been a mixture of mustard and phosgene. He put me on a stretcher where I felt horribly exposed, hoisted on the shoulders of the four bearers.

It was late afternoon by the time Dark was left at a Casualty Clearing Station. What sight he had was gone altogether by the next morning:

> I was quite blind for four or five days; also I had a violent bronchopneumonia, spitting up quarts of thin blood-stained serous muck. They gave me quarts of what they told me was sodium hyperchlorite, which was supposed to be helpful ..... They kept me at the C.C.S. for ten days, in which time I lost 20 pounds.

Dark was repatriated to England and sent to a convalescent home:

> While there a grateful [British] army gave me 6 months leave, without salary, but with permission to go home, if I paid my fares both ways. As soon as the leave came I asked to be discharged: the major simply asked if I was fit, and when I said yes, he promptly discharged me without any examination – the slovenly bastard.

Dark did indeed return to Australia on leave. He then returned to serve in the British army at a hospital in Macedonia. He survived the influenza epidemic and the war. During the Second World War, he enlisted in 1942 at the age of fifty-three. He died in 1987 at age ninety-eight.

Lt. William Fisher of the 42nd Battalion records an excellent account of the conditions in which the Australians were fighting for the Passchendaele Ridge. In his diary on 24 October 1917 he writes his experiences of the last two weeks. The dead and wounded he refers to were British troops from the battalions they had been sent to relieve:

> For the past fifteen days we've been through the hardest and most trying time the battalion has ever experienced. About 7/10/17 [7 October] we got word to proceed to Passchendaele – or rather to the line just before it. It was not quite known exactly where the line was ….. I went over and down the slope - which was littered with dead, both theirs and ours. I got to one pill box to find it just a mass of dead, and so I passed on carefully to the one ahead. Here I found about fifty men alive ….. Never have I seen men so broken and demoralized. They were huddled up close behind the [pill] box in the last stages of exhaustion and fear. Fritz had been sniping them off all day and had accounted for 57 that day – the dead and dying lay in piles. The wounded were numerous – unattended and weak, they groaned and moaned all over the place, and their comrades took no notice. Some had been there four days already – their wounds were festering – they had no food and their damned Headquarters seemingly cared not a whit for them. It was ghastly. Finally the company came up – the men done after a fearful struggle through the mud and shell holes ….. I spent the rest of the night in a shell hole – up to my knees in mud and with the rain teeming down. For two days we stayed like that.[288]

A withdrawal of some 1,000 yards was ordered, during which the Australians were heavily shelled with explosives and gas:

> The men were falling out in numbers owing to utter exhaustion, illness, and casualties, so the morning of the next day the battalion numbered a mere handful at seventy-four! ….. The next day we were ordered to retake the line – and then our units sunk to the lowest pitch ….. the men were utterly done ….. That night my two runners were killed as they sat beside me, and casualties were numerous again. He [the German artillery] blew me out of my shellhole thrice, so I shifted to an abandoned pillbox. There were 24 wounded men inside – two dead Huns on the floor and six outside, in various stages of decomposition. The stench was dreadful ….. When day broke I looked over the position. Over forty dead lay within twenty yards of where I stood and the whole valley was full of them.

However, one doesn't worry about that, and I slept and ate with two dead Huns on the floor under my feet and six outside the door. I wished they wouldn't smell so much, that was all. One Hun was amusing. He was sitting up against the wall and all his head was gone save the bare skull – it was clean inside as an egg – just the skull inside and his hair outside ….. I feel about eighty years old now.

Fisher was killed near Corbie in April 1918.
At about the same time, Pvt. John Bartley of the 30th Battalion was also on the battlefield:

It rained, and when the 60th Battalion was due to come along as a relief, it was found that they could only arrive in small batches, for many of them became bogged in the mud, and this delayed the men going out ….. Mud was everywhere, and to make matters worse the troops were carrying full pack. No puttees were worn. Sandbags were used in their place, and these dropped on the men's boots and collected a good deal of heavy mud ….. It was truly a second Somme. Now and then men would roll completely over in the mud, and hardly had strength enough to rise up again on account of the pack. Duckboards were blown out in places, and two companies ("D" and "B") met at a swamp, and both companies had to wade through this together. Each man had to wade waist deep through the bog in order to reach the duckboards on the other side.[289]

Bartley was wounded in the thigh in April 1918, but recovered and returned to the fighting in August 1918.
It continued into November. Of the 3rd Battalion that went into the Zonnebeke area on 5 November, Cpl. Leonard Jones observed:

November in Flanders. Half the Battalion had got into Zonnebeke Lake coming out [on being relieved]. They were at the end of their tether and did not look like men at all. On to Wallon Capel [a rear rest area]. Half the Battalion had to go by train, so bad were their feet.[290]

Later that month, the 3rd Battalion returned to a relatively quiet part of the line well south of Passchendaele. As Jones recorded, the troops were nevertheless suffering:

Fritz got a few with rifle grenades and shells in front. Although it was a "quiet" part and winter with snow, rain and biting winds, the boys had a rotten time out on patrol at night. The whole area was a repetition of Flers.

Charles Bean wrote in his diary of the state of affairs of the Australian divisions. His first concern was numbers: the divisions were all under strength. He was certain that after any offensive in the spring of 1918 there would be:

….. no more reinforcements after a Spring [1918] offensive – probably five full divisions to start it with and only three afterwards. This would mean a certain break up of one division at the end of the [Spring 1918] offensive – possibly two, unless recruiting improves. Recruiting can only improve by conscription or by some special effort ..... it is conscription or the break-up of a division.[291]

His second concern—and one to which he had previously sought to exert some influence—was about the British and Australian commanders. He saw too many British officers holding staff positions that Australians could ably fill. On this matter he felt that:

General Birdwood's hand will have to be forced to get that staff. He is too loyal to his old [British] friends to turn them out.

He then turns his observations to the command positions, including that of the commander of a future corps on the Western Front made up solely of Australians. As already noted, Bean was no admirer of Monash, in whom he saw ungentlemanly and self-serving ambition:

But Monash for an Australian commander in chief one cannot have. He is not the man. The purity and absence of jealousy or political intrigue in Birdwood's administration is worth anything. There is no "eye-wash," bluff and humbug and insincerity in it; and there is in Monash's. White would do, but not Monash.

Bean strongly admired Brudenal White. He also admired Gellibrand. Unlike the overly ambitious Monash, Bean viewed them both as self-effacing, diligent, and more intent on service than ribbons:

Gellibrand, a thousand times too proud to push his own barrow – a man who would rather pick crusts out of the gutter than go begging and claiming a step in promotion – all the force knows that he is the best man we have ..... Gellibrand is the one man, White barred [equally capable] who would be fitter to command the AIF than General Birdwood himself.

No such statements are to be found in the official history.

Bean saw himself as a correspondent and future historian more than a journalist. His view of one of Australia's most influential publications, *The Bulletin*, reveals this. *The Bulletin* was founded in 1880 and lasted until 2008. From the outset it was a champion of protectionism. It was also anti-monarchical and did much to create, promote, and praise the image of the off-hand, casual, but capable Australian male, in itself something of a straw man construct. Its masthead at the time was "Australia for the White Man." In a diary entry of 9 November 1917 toward the end of Passchendaele, Bean took issue with its style of reportage of the AIF. He obviously saw pleasure craft as a sign of wealth. Heron is the commanding officer of the 41st Battalion:

Heron, like Morshead [33rd Battalion], is an educated man. His father has a motor boat and is therefore probably pretty well off. It is curious how this type of man appeals to Australians more than the type the Bulletin would give you as the typical Australian – the punctilious type more than the slack type.

There were doubtless Australian soldiers of the relaxed, irreverent, tall, rangy bushman type on the Western Front, men who upset senior officers and squinted across the line with a casual indifference. The sharper characteristics of the Australian troops more likely sprang from the fact that they had migrated to or were born in a new country. The subsequent construction of the Aussie Digger heritage owes at least as much to the imagined Australia as to the real Australia.

The End of Third Ypres

By December, the offensive had ground to a halt. It was too cold and muddy to press on beyond the Passchendaele ridge system. The Australians were effectively replaced by the Canadians in the final assault on Passchendaele. While it had been secured, Passchendaele was not really the ultimate object of the offensive: that had been Roulers, Bruges, and the Belgian coastal ports, all of which remained in German hands. The Australian battalions retired southwest of Ypres in the Hazebrouck area. Winter had set in.

Thomas Cleary of the 2nd Pioneers Battalion found more warm clothing in mid-December as the cold weather set in:

> I got a nearly new tunic, leather vest and balaclava from the C.C.S. [Casualty Clearing Station] – clothing discarded by wounded: must try there again for hat and puttees.[292]

In early December, the Australians were required to vote a second time in a referendum on conscription [the drafting of soldiers into the force]. As and when possible, the soldiers on the Western Front voted during the first two weeks of December. Leicester Johnson of the 20th Battalion observed:

> Tuesday 11/12/1917. Intensely cold again today. Went for a short route march in drill order this morning to warm us up a bit, finishing the morning with a few games. Polling commenced today on the Australian Compulsion Referendum. I am very much afraid that as far as the soldiers' vote on this side is concerned, NO will have a tremendous majority, as from what I hear wherever I go amongst the soldiers, I would estimate fully 90% are voting against Compulsion ….. I have had some great arguments on this question in the hut, only two of us voting YES. We have the mob (about 20) against us.[293]

The referendum saw conscription voted down for the second time. Australian soldiers remained volunteers throughout the war.

Christmas 1917

Thomas Cleary, 2nd Pioneers Battalion:

> Xmas Day. Cold windy and wet today. Dinner. Rabbit stew and small piece of pudding.
>
> Boxing Day.Steenwerck. Had dinner with Anzac Coves [a group of soldiers that informally created a performing troop for the benefit of other Australian soldiers. They charged for their performances] Best feed I have had for two years. Rum, wine and beer, also poultry and pudding. Everything has been snow covered since Xmas Day.

A small section of the vast cemetery at Tyne Cott, near Passchendaele. The remains of a German fortified pill box seem incongruous. There are several such pillboxes at the cemetery. The graves are set out around them. *Author's collection*

Verdi Schwinghammer, 42nd Battalion:

We were given a tin of fruit and a tin of preserved sausages (one tin between two of us) for Christmas dinner. My pal and I were hungry so we opened ours for breakfast and ate half, putting the remainder in the tins on the ledge of the dugout, covering them with a board with a stone on it. The rats were very bad in the trenches. We were off duty so went to sleep for two hours in our dugout. On waking up and going to get our dinner we found that the rats had knocked off the covering while we were asleep and had eaten everything. So we had dry biscuits for our dinner.[294]

Apcar de Vine, 4th Battalion:

25.12.17. The forage parties returned during the early hours of the morning with 17 fowls and 7 sacks of potatoes, also a case of rum taken from a rum dump. Each man has also put 1 franc into a fund and I have bought plenty of oranges, apples, nuts, etc. After giving the officers 2 fowls for their dinner we made ourselves very warm and happy for the rest of the day and night with plenty of rum.[295]

The Cost

The Australians had been in Flanders since July. Between July and December 1917, their casualties amounted to 82,083. Of these 10,947 were dead. Of the 71,206 wounded, a staggering 39,871 men had been removed from the battlefield as non-battle casualties caused by the cold, wet, muddy, freezing conditions. Shell shock and respiratory ailments, trench foot, and frostbite were the main causes. Most of the dead and battle-wounded are accounted for in September and October: 47,320. This period included Menin Road, Polygon Wood, Broodseinde, Poelcappelle, and First Passchendaele.[296]

Chapter Sixteen

The Situation During Winter 1917-1918

The State of the AIF

By October, the AIF was a diminished force. Replacements had dwindled to a point where nearly all battalions were now under strength. Those who remained were suffering the setbacks of Poelcapelle (9 October) and two attempts on Passchendaele (12 October and 26 October to 10 November). They were cold, undernourished, mostly exhausted, always tired, and morale was waning. As observed in the *Australian Army Medical Services History*:

> The Battles of Poelcappelle (October 9th and First Passchendaele (October 12th) were pushed through to their bitter failure in a desperate effort to achieve a break-through in the north before the winter.[297]

The Creation of the Australian Corps

For some time, the Australian government had wanted its divisions on the Western Front brought together. As of 1 November 1917, I Anzac Corps was renamed the Australian Corps. The 3rd Division—the only Australian division in the cosmopolitan II Anzac—was then withdrawn from II Anzac and attached to the new Australian Corps. The remaining divisions in that corps were reassigned and II Anzac ceased to exist. From May 1918, the Australian Corps was commanded by John Monash.

Whilst this suited the government's ideal of an all-Australian force, it also reflected a serious shortage of replacements. The losses during the second half of 1917 were appalling. The five divisions were some 18,000 men below strength.

So parlous was the situation that in November 1917, the 4th Division was withdrawn to the Boulogne area as a sort of reserve depot force while the other four divisions (1st, 2nd, 3rd, and 5th) were sent to rest in a quiet sector behind Messines. The 4th Division had been hard tried during 1916 and 1917, and by now was the weakest. It had some brief rest and was returned to the line at Péronne in December, after a successful German counterattack to the British advance at Cambrai in November.

In fact, the Australians had been running out of men since 1916. Pozières, Mouquet Farm, and then Bullecourt and Passchendaele had taken their toll. Those who survived were weary of the fighting, the mutilation, the filthy conditions, and the deaths. In the absence of a draft and in the face of dwindling recruitment numbers in Australia, the new corps looked to three sources for replacements. The first was the small pool of trained Australian reinforcements in England. These were quickly absorbed by late October and had themselves contributed to the casualty lists at Passchendaele. The second source was reinforcements in training in England, along with convalescents who were becoming fit for return to the lines. These two groups were estimated at 28,000 men. The third source was the wounded and sick still in hospital. It was estimated a further 7,000 could be found among them. This made for a grand total of 35,000 replacements to be allocated during the winter. Some of these were lost during the relatively minor 1917-1918 winter campaigning. By 1 March 1918, the new Australian Corps remained 8,000 men below full establishment.[298] For those in Australia, the war was portrayed as an ongoing task and to all intents, a manageable one.[299]

All armies have their share of malingerers, shirkers, and deserters. All armies also have a natural friction between the front line soldiers on the one hand and base men and the military police on the other. The Australian divisions were no exception. The desertion rate among Australians was the highest on the Western Front. The refusal of the Australian government to allow the death penalty to be used led to more desertions. The hardest prison could be no worse than the horrors of the battlefield. Desertion increased during the winter months.[300]

Germany, Russia, and Italy

The static trench warfare that so quickly developed after the opening maneuvers of mid-1914 had now ended at Third Ypres. Although bogged down in the mud of Passchendaele at the end of 1917, the fighting had nevertheless been for strongpoints and pillboxes more than taking a series of trenches. The Allies had always taken to the offensive in this war, but now, with a bigger German army massing on the Western Front, the rationale had shifted to defense. That bigger German army was a direct result of the Russian withdrawal from the war.

During November, the Russians had withdrawn from the fighting in the east. By December, Lenin and the Bolsheviks were in power and a cease-fire concluded with Germany. On 10 December the Russians, along with the Romanians, signed an armistice with the Central Powers. This immediately released thirty-five German divisions for the Western and Italian fronts. Three German divisions were sent to the Italian front, where on 24 October, an Austro-German force broke the Second Italian Army at Caporetto. Haig was required to release six British divisions to that Italian front. The French also diverted six divisions to Italy; a move necessitating the disbandment of three French divisions to make up the numbers.

The German army had developed new artillery and storm troop tactics toward the end of 1917 that were successfully tested at Riga, Caporetto, and on the Western Front. The Battle of Cambrai (20 November to 7 December 1917) saw a tank-led British assault initially break the Hindenburg Line, only to have the advances repulsed by these new German tactics. The German divisions on the Western Front were subsequently organized and trained in these new tactics over the winter. Against this were signs of systemic resource problems; the Allied naval blockade was beginning to take its full effect. Germans were starving at home. Oil, petrol, and other raw materials were in such short supply that any future German offensives would of necessity be short-lived. If the Germans were to make such a grand offensive, their leaders knew it would be their last.

Britain and France

Any prospect of an Allied spring offensive was now replaced by preparations for what was obvious: an impending, major German offensive on the Western Front. The French had already suffered severe morale problems during 1917. The diversion of some of their forces to the Italian Front left them with only 100 divisions on the Western Front, all of them under strength.

So it was for the British. Haig had requested 334,000 reinforcements over winter and only received 174,000 by the New Year.[301] During the winter of 1917-1918, morale in the British Forces had declined and desertions were on the rise.[302] In early 1918, most BEF divisions were under strength; their divisions were reduced from twelve to nine battalions. There is evidence suggesting that the British had more than enough trained officers and men held back in Britain to replenish their divisions. As much as Lloyd-George wanted victory, he also wanted to continue control over Haig's ongoing propensity for adventurous offensives.

The question arises as to why Haig was not replaced. He very nearly was, and he spent Christmas in the expectation that he would be dismissed. His survival appears to lie somewhere between the reportage in the press crediting Haig with victories during 1916 and 1917, his connections with the Royal Family, and a fear that public confidence would be shaken if such an apparently successful leader was stood down.[303] By the end of 1917, Haig was certainly the subject of a more virulent press and his favor with the public was at an all-time low.[304]

The Americans and the Western Front

Apart from their newfound numerical superiority on the Western Front after the collapse of the Russian war effort, there was another reason to assume the Germans would launch a major offensive in the spring of 1918. It was known to both sides that the growing presence of American troops on the Western Front would soon swell to a force that would change the situation in favor of the Allies.

The American forces have often been held to have joined the war too late and committed their forces to battle too slowly. The United States had been materially helping the Allies since 1915 and had declared war on Germany on 6 April 1917. Without the arrival of the Americans on the Western Front, the events of 1918 would have played out much less favorably.

However, there was strong disagreement over how they should be used. Although the British finally agreed to the formation of an independent Australian Corps and an independent Canadian Corps, they remained intent on absorbing the Americans into their own divisions as they became available, rather than treat them as a separate army in the field. The Americans' understandable insistence to maintain a separate army delayed their entry.[305] This is yet another "history war" and will not be dealt with in this account of the Australians on the Western Front. Gen. John Pershing—the commander of the American forces—did have 130,000 troops in France by December 1917, but he was not going to deploy them without at least a further twelve weeks' field training.

German Preparations for 1918

The Germans were well aware of the forthcoming impact of the American reinforcements. The decision to launch an offensive was made on 11 November 1917 by the German staff; they then told the field generals, who complied. This was a military staff decision from a German war machine that operated far more independently of its government than was the case with the Allies. The Kaiser was not involved. "Germany" had handed over governance to the military.

The German High Command had a number of standing attack plans and more were being developed. One was for an attack in the Ypres sector: *George*. Some other plans concentrated on the south around Verdun: *Castor* and *Pollux*. There was *Mars*—aimed to take Arras—and *Michael*, which aimed to break through the British line where it met the French near St. Quentin.

It was Operation *Michael*, or at least a variation of it, that was chosen as the main attack plan. In its amended form, *Michael* was to be launched on a wider front than just the St. Quentin area. Now it would extend from La Fère, south of St. Quentin, to near Arras in the north. Here the ground would be driest, the Allies could be split, and the British chased up to the Channel. Although the battle developed differently, the original intention was for the Germans to break through, then turn right (north) and roll-up the British. These were the same places that were so heavily fought over in 1916 and 1917.

There is a similarity between the Schlieffen Plan of August 1914 and *Kaiserschlacht* of March 1918: they both rather hopefully relied on a quick victory before a greater Allied response could be mounted. Both plans assumed a territorial reach beyond their logistical capacity.

One prominent British war correspondent named Philip Gibbs was at St. Quentin in March. He had already incurred the wrath of the censors and had been arrested and sent back to England. Now he was back during March 1918:

> I looked about for trench systems, support lines, and did not see them, and wondered what our defence would be if the enemy attacked there in great strength. Our Army seemed wonderfully thinned out. There were few to be seen in our outpost line or reserve. It was all strangely quiet. Alarmingly quiet.[306]

The British and Dominion forces had not fought a defensive battle for over two years.

Chapter Seventeen

KAISERSCHLACHT

Die Kaiserschlacht ("The Imperial Battle") commenced at 4:40 a.m. on 21 March 1918. A number of offensives were planned, only some of which were commenced and then often in a revised form. We will look at only two of these: the main one code-named Operation *Michael* and a subsidiary operation farther north in Flanders code-named *Georgette*. The rationale for *Michael* lay in Gen. Ludendorff's assumption that the war—in terms of a complete German victory—was now lost. Now, it was about gaining as much territory as possible to bargain with at the inevitable peace negotiations, as it was a wistful attempt to reoccupy France and push the British into the Channel.

It involved a direct assault on St. Quentin but quickly developed into a much broader front. Around 10,000 German artillery and mortar pieces poured fire into a forty-three mile long front extending west to an area of 150 square miles. By ten o'clock that morning, the Germans had fired 1,160,000 shells, both chemical and explosive. At Bapaume, Péronne, and Flesquières, there were at least 3,000 mustard gas casualties. Around 700 German aircraft, many equipped for bombing and strafing, were used both on the troops in the lines and in the transportation centers beyond. After five hours of bombardment, the British yielded ground.[307]

A comparison of this German offensive with the Allied one nearly two years earlier in July 1916 reveals how successfully *Kaiserschlacht* was conducted. By the end of that first day, the Germans had taken ninety-eight and a half square miles and forty-six ruined villages. Compare this with the British and French efforts on the Somme in 1916: ninety-eight square miles and forty-six villages in 140 days for over half a million casualties. In the first ten hours of 21 March, German casualties numbered around 35,000. Of these, it is estimated 10,852 were killed, 28,778 were wounded, and 300 were prisoners. The British casualties for 21 March 1918 totaled 38,512. A comparison with the German figures emphasizes the surprise with which the British were taken: 7,512 dead, 10,000 wounded, and a staggering 21,000 taken prisoner.[308]

Whether the Germans really wanted to take Paris before rolling-up the British to the Channel remains unclear, but the attacks developed a distinct direction toward Paris. Operation *Michael* officially lasted until 5 April. The whole German offensive in the direction of Paris—both north and south of the Somme—ground to a halt on 17 July.

Before this halt in mid-July, bitter fighting took place from late March, both in the north (Ypres, Hazebrouck, and Armentières) and in the south (the Somme area). With some 117,000 troops in France, the Australians constituted just over ten percent of the British and Dominion frontline troops on the Western Front.[309]

Except at Messines in the north, the Australians were not in force on the front line on 21 March. They were quickly called south to the Somme area as the offensive developed. With the fall of Bapaume on 25 March, the Australian 3rd and 4th Divisions prepared for an imminent departure to the south.[310] The other three divisions (the 1st, 2nd, and 5th) were also sent to the Somme area.

In the North

As operation *Michael* began to peter out, Ludendorff launched Operation *Georgette* in the Flanders area on 9 April. It was aimed squarely at that section of the line held by the Portuguese division that was part of the British First Army. The Germans demolished the defenses there and overran them. The Portuguese fled. As Bean writes:

> The Portuguese melted – why they should have been expected to fight so formidable an enemy in a cause of which they knew little is a question on which military and political leaders might well have pondered. They fled almost to the coast.[311]

Armentières was abandoned as the German forces swept on, occupying the old 1917 Australian lines at Messines. By 11 April, the Germans were only five miles east of Hazebrouck; its capture would clear the German advance to the Channel ports.

Many Australians experienced something of a round trip during early April 1918. Sent from the Ypres sector in the north to the Somme in the south, they were promptly returned to the north. Arthur Kilgour of the 1st Field Ambulance—based near Ypres—was one of those who endured the round trip from Flanders to the Somme and back again in quick order. He wrote in his diary:

> March 27 1918. It is hard to credit that the Hun should be on the Somme district again. Most probably we will be back there again. After saying goodbye to the Somme last August we little dreamt that we would be back there again after all the terrible and bloody battles fought there. Oh! It is hard to have to return to the Somme for the Somme is indeed to the Australians Australia's graveyard.[312]

By 7 April Kilgour had reached Amiens, which was by now under heavy artillery bombardment:

> Amiens is the Hun's objective but thank God up to the present he has failed in his attempt. Amiens is one of the finest cities in France and just at present it is threatened with complete destruction. God grant that it doesn't go the way of Ypres, Bapaume, Albert, etc.

Then, on 12 April, Kilgour's field ambulance section was suddenly assembled at Amiens station. Fifteen hours later they were deposited back in the Ypres sector. Another new German offensive—*Georgette*, in the north—saw to their return. The defenses were being stretched thin as the German offensives mounted.

Another soldier who experienced the 1st Division's hasty return to Flanders was Sgt. Apcar de Vine of the 4th Battalion. Having completed some leave in London, he was hurried back across the Channel on 26 March. On 2 April he departed for the Somme, arriving outside Amiens on 6 April. On 11 April he was on his way back north, writing in his diary:

We do not know where we are going but we expect to be sent back to the North, from where we have received the very bad news that Fritz made a big advance against the Portuguese front and is still advancing with great success over a very wide front, threatening to gain the Channel ports.[313]

Late in the evening of 12 April, the 4th Battalion detrained at Hazebrouck behind Ypres and immediately marched to Strazeele some four miles east, then another four miles farther east and south of Meteren. By now, it was the early hours of 13 April. De Vine wrote in his diary:

The church and many of the houses are burning very fiercely all night ….. we pass many refugees ….. Scattered bands of English Tommies are running about in a panic stricken state, not knowing where they are or where they are going. They are apparently relieving themselves from the outpost line without waiting for us to come up to them, nobody seems to be in charge and every man does as he likes ….. Many hundreds of these Tommies are collected during the night and are now temporarily attached to us.

By noon the next day they had dug in. There had been no food, water, or sleep for the Australians for forty-eight hours. There followed days of continuous attacks, skirmishes, and plenty of entrenching in bitterly cold conditions of frost and snow. On 21 April, de Vine removed his boots to inspect his feet; it was the first time he had them off in nine days and nights. After being relieved by the 5th Battalion on 22 April, they returned to the rear of the line next to the village of Caestre. He wrote:

23.4.18. Today we had a general wash and brush up. Visited Caestre in the evening. There is not a single civilian left in the village ….. The village has been completely looted, dozens of barrels of beer and thousands of bottles of wine, champagne etc lying about. 4th Battalion are having a good time. Barrels of beer are being rolled and wheeled to the camp, others are opened in the streets where everybody has as much as they want ….. Many of the boys have got into the houses and put on civilian clothes over their khaki.

By 28 April they were back in the front line, enduring the bitter cold, heavy German shelling, and gunfire until relieved on 10 May by the 15th Battalion of the West Yorkshire Regiment. They continued in and out of the line in the area. By late August, they were back on the Somme at Morcourt, on the Somme River, just northeast of Villers-Bretonneux.

All battalions of the 1st Division played a significant part in stopping, then driving back the Germans before Hazebrouck. Only at the start of August would the 1st Division return to the Somme to join the rest of the Australian Corps. Sunday, 4 August, was the fourth anniversary of Britain's entry into the war. After a church service, the British Second Army commander, Sir Herbert Plumer, approached those 1st Division officers present;

….. and said that it was not his practice to pay compliments or to bestow praise, especially with the war still unended; but he would like to thank them before the 1st Division left him – it was well known that they would be leaving immediately for the south – that there was no other division, certainly in his army, and, he thought, probably none in the whole army, which had done so much to break down the German morale as the 1st Australian Division.[314]

In the South

On 25 March, Bapaume—the town the Australians had fought so hard to take in 1916—fell to the advancing Germans. Over the following days, 4 Brigade (of the 4th Division) held out at Hébuterne against the Germans. Sgt. Christopher Sandilands of the 16th Battalion wrote some pithy observations on death, incompetent Australian officers, and equally incompetent Australian soldiers in his diary at Hébuterne:

> 7 April. The trenches are in a bad state. Cleaned out the slush and repaired broken parapets. In doing so unearthed Private Jones of Swan Hill of the Trench mortars, he was killed in action yesterday and was buried by the shell that broke the parapet. His mates came looking for him just as we got him clear and they buried him in the shell hole in the parapet we were preparing.[315]

The majority were buried on the spot like this poor fellow and the location noted or marked. Many others were lost, their scattered remains simply part of the soil. The neat rows of plots in the Commonwealth War Graves Cemeteries that dot the Western Front are the original burial sites for only a tiny proportion of the men killed. Many remained unburied, or their remains were located in trench sites and shell holes after hostilities. The cemeteries seen today are the result of their re-interment after the war. Those of whom no trace could be found have their names inscribed on the walls of the missing. The vast panels at such places as the Menin Gate are a chilling reminder of how many have no known grave. Sandilands continues his diary entries:

> 8 April. Raining all night, up to our hips in mud and slush, the sides of the trenches are falling in. No place for men to take shelter. No sleep since coming into the front line. Our officer has not been near us to give me a little rest, we only see him once or twice a day when he is on his way to and from Coy HQ from his dugout.

They were relieved by the 14th Battalion the next evening:

> Moving out of the new sap, one of my men got stuck in the mud. Sent my platoon on. A Corporal in charge then went back to dig the man out. He [the man stuck in the mud] is a waster and will not try to get out. After an hour and a half work I managed to get him out, then had to find out where my Company was quartered ….. Am dead beat.

A month later, Sandilands was seriously wounded in the thigh and hand by a shell.

Meanwhile, the other two brigades of that division (12 and 13) were being assembled outside Albert, but it was too late. The German forces had by then occupied Pozières, Mouquet Farm, Thiepval, and Albert itself. By the end of March, it was nevertheless obvious to Ludendorff that the overall offensive was failing. What he did next was the purest expression of the Germanic concept of "total victory through absolute destruction."

He also launched a diversionary offensive (*Georgette*) in Flanders, but settled on the main goal of capturing Amiens and hopefully Paris. All this was to be undertaken with the knowledge that any chance of real victory was lost and in the absence of German army resources to sustain the attacks in both the north and the south.

The British forces had borne the brunt of the German offensive on the Somme. The Australians arrived to find confusion and retreat. Pvt. David Whinfield of the 60th Battalion at Ypres had assumed the duties of stretcher bearer. He is another example of a soldier who, for his own reasons, actively sought this role. It was just as dangerous as front line combat, more so in many instances. Here is his diary entry for 30 March 1918. They have arrived east of Amiens, at the town of Corbie:

> Tommies still going backwards with broken up tales.Poor Corbie, its poor people. What a terrible loss to them. Today control of the town by police had not taken place and the troops did whatever they choose. I was in many dozens of places and found that the people had bolted, stampeded for some reason or other, meals left half eaten, a blacksmith left in the middle of a job, valuables were left behind, even money had been forgotten in the great panic. Our chaps looked at it that Fritz would get what we didn't ….. there was much shameful waste. Looking for things in drawers and throwing the stuff onto the floor to be trampled on.[316]

In a letter home to his parents, Lt. John Ridley of the 53rd Battalion wrote of another town, Aubigny, just outside Corbie:

> I will long remember the sight of that village – absolutely plundered, houses ransacked, clothes and furniture in all directions, civilians gone, meals half eaten left on the tables. A state of things existed in several villages which I was to see later.[317]

There are many accounts of such "ratting" in the diaries of the Australians who found themselves in various deserted towns and villages at the front. At times the situation—particularly if alcohol was nearby—could draw men into dangerous places. This recollection from Lieutenant Henry Neaves of the 45th Battalion:

> Villers-Bretonneux was subjected to much shelling and the Bosche put over a lot of gas shells. Most of the cellars had good stocks of wine in, and many of the men used to go into the village and get bottles of this drink. The consequence was that many of them became intoxicated ….. The French on our right used to visit the village frequently and they could be seen leaving with bags of bottles across their shoulders. Our own chaps of course were not slow in getting in for their "cut."[318]

Neaves may not have taken from the cellars, but he did take from the soldiers. One night, while riding on a limber near the town, he witnessed a group of drunken Australians arguing to such an extent that he was able to relieve them of a sack full of wine bottles without them noticing. It was subsequently consumed by the officers.

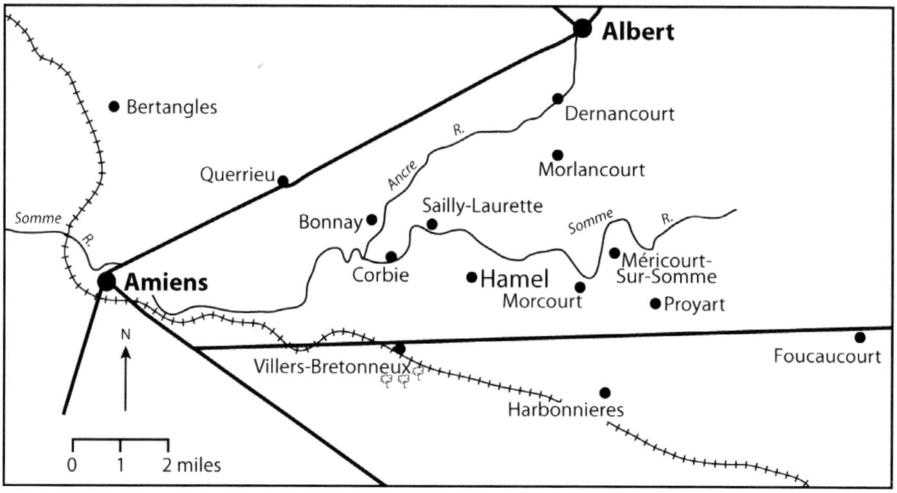

Villers-Bretonneux, Area of Operations, 1918

Equally frequent are accounts of disorganization amongst the retreating British forces. The 60th Battalion was soon placed slightly north of Corbie, at Bonnay. Whinfield wrote in his diary of the broader situation he learned from battalion news sheets:

> I saw the 28th and 31st [March] papers. It says the rush is checked but thinks that another is being got ready for Amiens and we are guarding it. The poor Tommies don't know who is to blame, officers, heads [higher commanders] or men but it is the first two – such fools, no initiative – they must be led or nothing is done. They didn't fight here it seems but just saw Jerry massing and walked away back. Our fellows stopped the rot here.

At about the same time, Pvt. John Bartley with the 50th Battalion was to the south of the Somme, in the woods just outside the village of Gentelles:

> The wood was very thick. Several villages lay handy, and Fritz was busy dropping shells into them. In this wood was found what Fritz had left of a Tommy regiment – the Sherwood Foresters. Their greeting was "Jerry's a-coming", although Fritz was four kilometres away in front. It is a fact that, while these men spent a couple of nights in this wood, yet they had made no attempt to make any kind of shelter. The first thing the Aussies did was dig in.[319]

The Australians were less than impressed with the rush of British soldiers they encountered as they themselves moved forward.

On 4 April, after British forces had fled the defenses in disorder, the Germans captured Le Hamel. This village lies about three miles northwest of Villers-Bretonneux. The next day, the Australians were overwhelmed at Dernancourt. Situated outside the already

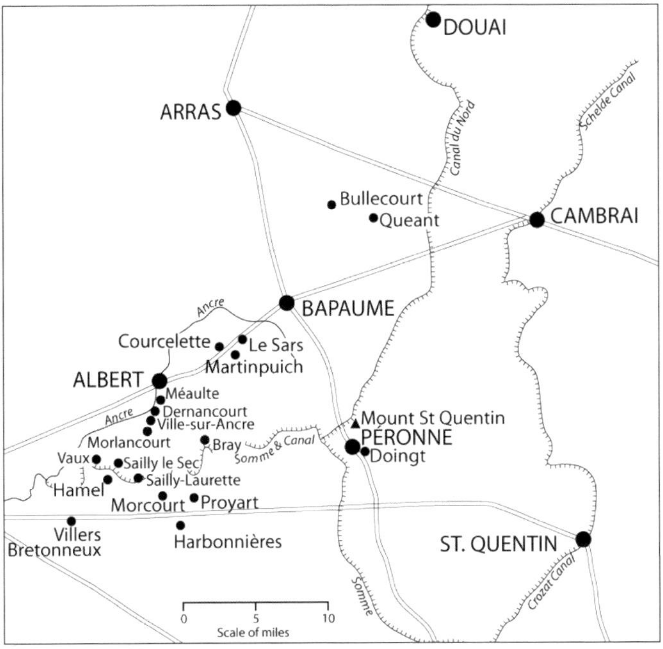

Péronne Area, August-October 1918

captured town of Albert, it lies well northwest of Le Hamel.[320] The front in the south was becoming fluid. Soldiers in retreat were met by reinforcements coming in the opposite direction at several places. Around Dernancourt, the Australians took 1,100 casualties alone. By now, the town of Villers-Bretonneux was well and truly in the front line.

Villers-Bretonneux

It was obvious the town would be the axis of a major battle; it stood in the path of any advance on Amiens. By 5 April, Operation *Michael* had officially ended, but the Germans still sought to take Amiens *via* Villers-Bretonneux. They took up positions close to Villers-Bretonneux and with their artillery pounded the area. This was accompanied by constant aerial attacks and extensive use of mustard gas.

Most troops in the area—Australian and British, as well as the French just to the south—were exposed to gas. In the vital moments between realization of a mustard gas attack and donning masks many were exposed. In some areas, the masks simply failed to offer protection as the gas drenched the soldiers' clothing. Official lists of gas "casualties" record those incapacitated or killed. They do not account for the widespread postwar debilitation of those who were regularly exposed to gas but withstood its immediate effects. References abound in the diaries and memoirs to multiple exposures to "a touch of gas."

At this point, there developed a fair amount of push and shove between the British and Australian commanders. Claims of British incompetence met accusations of Australian willfulness. These matters have been dealt with ably elsewhere.[321] A notable British casualty was Gough, in whom Haig found a convenient scapegoat. In the British Fifth Army, Gough was replaced by Rawlinson and the Army itself was renumbered the Fourth, presumably because Rawlinson's command of the Fourth Army on the Somme in 1916 resonated with future hopes.

At 6:00 a.m. on 24 April, the Germans struck at Villers-Bretonneux. The British troops occupying the town retreated as German troops supported by tanks approached. To the south of the town, three British tanks engaged their German counterparts in the first tank battle. By noon and after a failed British counterattack, the Germans held all of the town and parts to its north and south.

Despite British attempts to put two Australian brigades immediately into the line to retake Villers-Bretonneux, their commanders rejected the request in a heated exchange with their British counterparts; they wanted a night attack. The British acquiesced. At 10:00 p.m., the Australians commenced a two mile long advance. This was nevertheless a hurriedly organized affair. The British troops who that day lost the town then failed in an attempted counterattack came under sharp criticism. Sgt. Jon Keeley of the 51st Battalion:

> It was I think about 9 a.m. on April 24th and being behind the line the 51stBn was on parade. Runners were noticed making towards the Company Commanders and I will always remember the first words spoken by a member of my platoon and they were, "Hullo, where have the bloody Poms run now?" ….. We were just formed up moved off in fighting order kit and during the march the C.O. called Company Commanders forward and they in their turn explained what was to be done to the men during the ten minute rest each hour. I don't think that an action was fought during the whole period of the War with so little preparation.[322]

Fifteen Brigade under Brig. Gen. Harold "Pompey" Elliott (he had commanded this brigade at Fromelles) attacked to the north of the town. Thirteen Brigade under English-born Maj. Gen. Sir (Thomas) William Glasgow attacked to the south of the town. Their intentions were to by-pass the center, meet beyond it, and then mop-up any remaining enemy positions.

There are a number of accounts of the battle of 24/25 April from members of the 51st Battalion. It was part of the southern advance and appears to have suffered the worst of any battalion on either side of the town. English-born Cpl. Edward Steadman was with the 51st Battalion. They were part of the 13 Brigade advance to the south of the town. His reference to "Anzac Eve" shows just how significant that day had become to Australians by its third anniversary:

> Fritz came over with his bombing planes, he dropped several bombs and killed quite a few of our mob. Shortly after five o'clock we were about to have our tea, when we got orders to pack as we were going to do a hop over, we were told that we would have tea on the march ….. We had to be there by ten o'clock to line the tape ready to hop over. We did not get there until ten past ten and Fritz was waiting for us coming. We had only just got as far as our eighteen pounder guns when we met the Tommies coming back in droves ….. We had not gone more than 200 yards past our own guns when we were met with a terrible bombardment ….. we had no time to line the tape. The barrage and machine gun fire they were putting over was terrible. They were in Monument Wood [on the southern outskirts of Villers-Bretonneux] and we were cutting it off advancing

on each side of it. When we had got over about 100 yards of ground we came to barbed wire entanglements. The slaughter at that spot was awful.[323]

The retreating British mentioned by Steadman were the remnants of their earlier daylight counterattack. The 51st Battalion encircled Monument Wood at the southern outskirts of the town and eliminated the German positions at terrible cost to both sides. Early in the morning of 25 April, Steadman was sent with a party back over the battlefield to bring up food rations:

You can guess what a slaughter house is like, but I never saw anything like it in my life and I would never like to see it again ….. quite a lot of us could not eat after seeing such an awful sight on the battle field.

The 51st Battalion was almost wiped out. Steadman recalls perhaps 200 men at roll call later that day. Here is another account from 51st Battalion soldier Pvt. John Mulqueeny, part of C Company. They had reached the outskirts of the town on 24 April, and later that night were told they were to immediately go into the attack:

Captain Harburn of C Company addressed his men and told us what was expected from us in a speech that was rather amusing. He told us we were going over the top that night. He said the monument [Monument Wood] was our objective and that nothing was to stop us from getting there, that was our goal ("gail" he pronounced it and caused a twitter). In his own words he said kill every bloody German you see, we don't want any prisoners and God Bless you ….. He was one of the very few officers who got through the Villers-Bretonneux stunt ….. Fritz killed his brother Jack at Passchendaele and he had a grievance. He practically had charge of the Brigade or seemed to during the final stages of the battle. He evidently stood on someone's corns higher up for he got rapped over the knuckles later on and his splendid efforts did not receive the recognition which we all know he was entitled to.[324]

Mulqueeny survived the advance, only to be severely wounded later that day:

Further along a sunken road was a lone German machine gun, and to those of us in the open he caused no end of trouble. He got Sergeant Dagnell of our platoon in the arm and shoulder. He was able to walk out. The same fellow from his hidden post got me a few minutes later. Twice he hit me with a bullet on the right arm just above the elbow and the arm was useless. Then he got me on the right knee with a bullet and it is still there. That stopped me from walking ….. The 51st Battalion went into that stunt over 900 strong. Somewhere about 160 answered the roll-call in the morning.

The story for the 52nd Battalion is the same: on parade in the morning just before lunch, then ordered into the line with minimal preparation and advice received during the march up. One of them was Welsh-born Alfred Nicholas, a miner and now a sergeant in the second wave of the attack. They quickly filled the front line spaces made in the lines of the 51st Battalion. His recollections of the evening of 24/25 April:

> The front line was thinning out, and we gradually got in line with them [the 51st Battalion]. When we had advanced about two thousand yards the line stopped. I cannot give any reason for it. I only had about half a dozen men from other companies and battalions. I immediately endeavoured to get in touch with some of our officers but could not locate any. In walking along the line inquiring if there were any Australian officers about, I was halted by a young English officer wearing a gas mask. He asked me who I was at the same time covering me with a revolver. He asked me if the smoke that was coming from some German shells fired to the rear of us was gas. My reply was, "If this is gas I would have been dead long ago." He then ordered his party of about two or three dozen men from some of the Midland Counties regiment to take off their gas masks. I could get no information from him regarding our position. I travelled further south, and after going a little distance noticed a crowd retiring ..... and found it was the same English officer taking his men to some comfortable dugouts further back. I ordered them back, to the front line, which they obeyed.[325]

Immediately after this Nicholas was shot in the arm and retired to the rear lines. Although seemingly disorganized and distressed, not all British soldiers fled. Pvt. William Turner saw the British stand their ground:

> During the whole day of the 25th an 18-pounder manned by Tommies and on the right flank of the 56th shelled the Fritz machine-gun positions with shrapnel at point blank range, about 400 yards ..... The gun crew had a charmed existence as Fritz tried all day to blow it out with his guns, but as far as we could see there were no casualties on the gun and it certainly was effective right to the close of the day.[326]

The Australians had been at the forefront of the retaking of Villers-Bretonneux. The place has assumed mythic status in the memory of the Australians on the Western Front. It is the place where Australians celebrate overcoming odds the British could not. It was not quite like this. The British forces had fought on unequal terms, and they too were present when the Australians retook Villers-Bretonneux. The notion that the Australians saved the town and stemmed the German advance on Amiens tends to characterize the annual Anzac Day celebrations held in the town by the French and the Australians. While this meets commemorative needs, it somewhat underestimates the British effort, just as Gen. Monash overemphasized his role in leading the Australians to a victory of his design.[327] It also relegates far more deadly Australian actions such as Pozières, Mouquet Farm, and Bullecourt to lesser places in the memory of the war. Perhaps the date of the action (24/25 April) has won it an easy and accessible recognition.

April to July 1918

Whilst the war on the Western Front continued unabated during May and June, the period marks something of a hiatus for the Australian Corps and is reflected in the official history. Relative to other periods, it is a more indirect and abbreviated account, though there were some significant developments worth noting.

The Australians engaged in trench raiding and line straightening more than outright offensives. Although the art of trench raiding was one at which the Australians excelled, the frequency and daring with which they continued earned their efforts the sobriquet "peaceful penetration." This appears to have sprung from an ironic use of this term that had once been used to describe the means by which the Germans sought to gain economic hegemony on the continent and in the dominions before 1914.

Apart from this rather private warfare, there were other developments. The French endured a major offensive on the Aisne when the German army struck on 27 May. The Germans got to within fifty miles of Paris before their offensive faltered. By June this new German salient, which had extended along the Marne, was reduced by French and British counterattacks.

During May, the Americans began arriving in force. By the end of the month, there were 106,000 American troops in France. Another 41,000 arrived in June, 54,000 in July, 61,000 in August, and 71,000 in September. This made for a total of 330,000 fresh, untried, but eager troops. While they saw limited action, they fought bravely. They also often fought naively, much as the Australians had done on the Dardanelles as a fresh force in 1915. Whether given their due credit or not, there is no doubt the arrival of the Americans in such large numbers changed the course of the war. The very thought of their impending arrival had pressed the German High Command into the March Offensive. Their subsequent and growing presence would have been viewed as catastrophic by the German command.

Leadership of the Australian Corps changed when Sir William Birdwood left to command a re-formed British 5th Army. It was Haig's wish that Birdwood take this new position and it was also Haig who backed Monash as the first Australian to command the Australian Corps. There was intrigue in this move. Many, including Bean, felt Brudenell White should have been selected. The matter was resolved when Monash took command and the departing Birdwood took Brudenell White with him as his new chief of general staff.

The Cost

Total Australian casualties for the period April to July 1918 stand at 22,454. Most but not all of these casualties were incurred at Hazebrouck in the north and in the south at Dernancourt, Le Hamel, and Villers-Bretonneux. The casualties for the previous quarter (January to March 1918) were 6,366; they indicate a much lower level of activity. The combined casualties for the first half of 1918 therefore stand at 28,820. Of these, 5,770 were killed or died of wounds or gas. A further 22,591 were wounded, shell-shocked, and gassed. There were also 459 prisoners of war.[328] For the remaining nineteen weeks of war on the Western Front, the death and injury tolls would be even worse.

Chapter Eighteen

To the End: The Last Nineteen Weeks

Four significant actions are covered in this chapter. The first is the attack on Hamel on 4 July. It saw the first commitment of American troops alongside the Australians. The second involves almost simultaneous events farther north, along the Dernancourt – Morlancourt sector. This is often treated as less significant than Hamel. The oversight is rectified here. The third is the so-called Amiens Offensive of 8 August. The Australians have received disproportionate credit in this offensive. They alone did not "save the war" in that attack. They participated with other forces in what was later termed by Ludendorff as "the black day of the German army."[329] The fourth is the breaking of the Hindenburg line in September. Again, this was not solely the action of Australian soldiers. They had, however, gained a fierce reputation.

Hamel

Hamel is just south of the Somme River, about three miles northeast of Villers-Bretonneux. Monash was keen to use the Australians in a straightening of the line north of that town. The Australians had been pushed out of Hamel twelve weeks earlier. Initially, Monash had dismissed the idea of taking Hamel; it seemed too costly. His mind was changed after viewing a demonstration of the new British Mark V tanks. They were faster, more maneuverable, and more reliable. He was offered sixty of the tanks and ten companies of Americans from the 33rd Division to take Hamel in conjunction with the Australians. The attack was set for a propitious day, 4 July.

Something went very wrong the day before. Pershing ordered the American 33rd Division out of the battle. In his diary Charles Bean wrote that he:

> Saw the Americans companies coming out – those that the order had reached. They were most depressed. It is said that there are probably a fair number of Americans who will refuse to hear the order.[330]

At 3:10 a.m., the attack commenced with four companies of the Americans ready, eager, and still in the line. Monash had carefully planned an attack that employed an infantry advance with a preliminary barrage, tanks, and considerable air support. It was a success, but a costly one. The Australians took 1,200 casualties and the Americans 176. Along with the town they captured an extensive amount of artillery and 1,600 German prisoners.[331] Bean was present and wrote in his diary:

> The wounded were coming down, Americans and Australians mixed. They mix perfectly – get on as well as the Australians and New Zealanders. One American whom we spoke to seemed a little doubtful as to how his particular lot had done. He seemed to me to think that they had muddled a bit. He said "If we had had a few more weeks of shellfire we might have been more used to it ….. Their attitude was that they were a bit bewildered when the barrage came down. Until then I didn't realise that these Americans had some of them been only four weeks in France ….. they had never heard a shell before that morning.[332]

In that case, it is surprising the Americans had acquitted themselves so well. Pershing's reluctance to place his untried troops in the line is well known. However, since at least April, the Americans had been detached as observers to front line units to experience just such conditions and to familiarize themselves with battle conditions. These more experienced troops did not seem to be present in any force. Those troops with only four weeks in France should never have been committed to an attack such as this.

The Australians and Americans got on well. Arthur Kilgour would confide to his diary:

> The Yanks are mixing up a lot with us. Indeed it is good to see the spirit of comradeship which exists between the Americans and the Australians ….. The Yanks who are attached to our unit are teaching all the boys baseball and our boys are getting baseball mad.[333]

The Battle for Hamel was significant, but not the sole action on 4 July. It was but part of a continuing build-up of pressure on the German positions. The Germans were themselves exhausted after their March offensives and many parts of their line were thinly held. Monash received much credit for the successful attack on Hamel. It was a model of careful planning and coordination.

The Dernancourt – Morlancourt Sector

While the battle for Hamel looms large in Australian collective memory, equally aggressive but less remembered attacks were being made by the Australians north of the Somme in the Dernancourt – Morlancourt sector. This sector is a good four miles north of Hamel, on the Ancre River. Sgt. George Elms of the 60th Battalion records the action. Elms is on that northern Dernancourt – Morlancourt line at a village that stands between the two named Ville-sur-Ancre. His preference for being in the first wave is based on experience with the intense bombardment the second line receives from the Germans during attacks:

> On July 3rd we got word that the 59th were doing a hop over early in the morning and we were to follow them if needed and you can bet we wanted to lead for it was always safer nearer to Fritz. We just took fighting order and left our blankets and overcoats, etc for it was warm and there were dugouts in his line. We had a "hop out" trench [a sap leading from the front trench] dug in no-man's-land and had to keep a patrol out while the 59th got into position and then went back to wait for the music and the inevitable counter bombardment ….. The music started a bit before daylight ….. the wounded and prisoners started coming in and we

> knew we would be wanted and just on daylight we hopped over and went across to Fritz's line and were lucky as we got to within thirty yards of his line before he saw us and put a machine gun on us and didn't we scuttle and got in with the 59th and built fire steps as we reckoned on a counter attack.[334]

A German counterattack materialized at the Morlancourt end of the sector and although fierce was a failure; Elms terms it in Australian slang as "a complete gutzer." By late that afternoon, the remnants of the 59th and 60th Battalions still in the front line were desperately low on ammunition and water. Elms again:

> That night I had to send six men down to the 58th on the river and spend the rest of the time thieving and getting (same thing in the army) rations, water and ammunition and got some of our things we left behind.

By then Elms was in charge of the platoon. The commanding officer had been either killed or wounded; Elms only provides the Australian generic term for incapacitation ("knocked"). The fighting continued into the next day. The afternoon of 5 July, the German shelling intensified on their part of the line:

> When "Wooruff," I felt hot and cold heavy things hit me all over and the parapet all came down and I was reckoning it wasn't so bad to die after all, when I saw daylight, my mate who was alongside me had wiped the dirt off my face and said, "Poor old George" .....he and another mate helped me out as I was buried ..... and we off up the trench about fifty yards and up the sap to the old front line and there we dressed one another after lighting a cigarette and off to the Aid Post and we got dressed (six of us with that shell) and went by ambulance and stretcher to Franvilliers. I could not hear anything much ..... I was so bad in the head.

Franvilliers was six miles behind the line. Elms' casualty form shows he suffered severe injuries to the head, left arm, and shoulder. He was repatriated to England and did not fight again.

Whilst men such as Elms had made part of the way back to the Aid Post alone, others were receiving the attention of the stretcher bearers on the battlefield. It has already been noted that stretcher bearing was a dangerous occupation. Stretcher bearer William Turner was witness to the awful events in the Morlancourt sector during that July. He records a number of incidents. In this one, a shell has made a direct hit on a stretcher party:

> Three bearers and the casualty were dead in a heap and we made a search for the fourth bearer thinking that we might be able to help him. We found him dead 30 yards or so away. The whole of his chest-wall was blown away and the stumps of his ribs and his organs were exposed. In a superhuman effort he had attempted to reach a Vickers [machine gun] post which was on the rise ahead.[335]

Troops were still encountering heavy shelling well behind the lines. There really was no safe place. The dry July conditions broke and returned the area to slush. Pvt. David Whinfield—also of the 60th Battalion—was with a party of reinforcements that had reached a post somewhere east of Bonnay, about four miles behind the front line of the Dernancourt – Morlancourt sector's front line. His diary entries:

> Thursday 18th July. It was breaking day before we reached reserves and broad daylight by the time we got to second reserves. The sap was so slushy and slippery with several thunder showers ….. We missed supper last night and by the time we laboured along to bunk and breakfast every man was looking and feeling pretty washy on it.
>
> Friday 19th July. We have Captain Robertson over us and he earns whole hearted hate from all. His going away from Bretonneux was doubtful and he does his best to make everyone's life miserable. This morning we are dishevelled and he had a snap parade and in the remnants of the company we had 33 and he dealt out a reprimand to every individual. Mine was for muddy boots.[336]

Bastardry was alive and well in the AIF. So too was compassion, and Australians freely grieved over their dead friends. Somewhere behind the lines on 27 July, Whinfield sought out the graves of four lost friends:

> Don Fraser and I went and had a look at Carl Ryan's grave ….. Bob Catto, Bill Moore and Phillips and Carl are buried together in nowhere, but it gives a splendid view of Corbie church and the Somme Valley towards Laurette. A shell had lobbed alongside blowing the crosses to bits. We tidied the graves putting a strong enclosure around, logs around the mounds and generally made them cared for.

Six days later, Whinfield confided to his diary:

> The Yanks are interesting to talk with. Everyone is intelligent. They are so easy to approach. We have mutual admiration.

And on 27 July:

> Had yarns with several Yanks. They and the Aussies hit it off well. Every man is a pleasure to talk with.

Such observations are made in many diaries. Clearly the Australians and Americans got on well, more so than with the English and certainly more so than with the Portuguese. It was for the New Zealanders, Canadians, Americans and, perhaps above all, the Scots that the Australians held the highest regard. The Scots had as fierce a reputation as the Australians. Such mutual admiration appears to be grounded in a sense of independence and a shared view of the English.

These front line actions continued throughout July and the carnage mounted. Amidst such terrible loss, it was nevertheless possible for those troops being rested from the

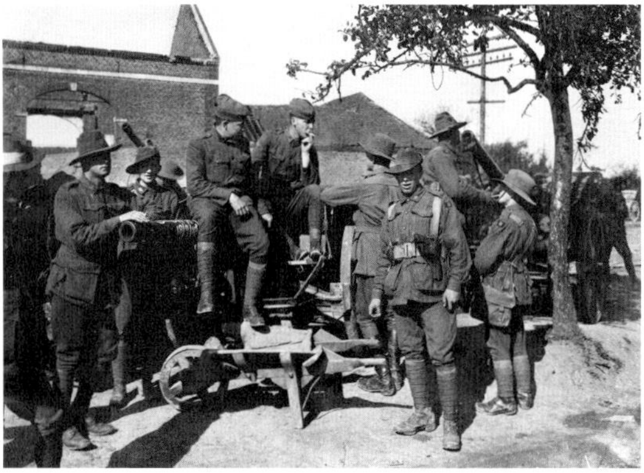

Shortly after the Battle for Hamel on 4 July. Two American soldiers sit on a captured German artillery piece in the company of Australian soldiers. *AWM*

line to experience recreation and sport. Lt. Henry Neaves of the 45th Battalion was one who enjoyed the spectacle of a Race Day at Allonville behind the lines:

> The attendance was very large, all nationalities and countries were represented – English, Scotch, French, American, Belgian, Canadian, New Zealand etc. This meeting was held within eight miles of the firing line and our balloons and those of Fritz could be seen plainly from the grounds. During the progress of the races a Fritz aeroplane came over our lines and brought down one of our balloons in flames. The chaps in their parachutes could be seen with the naked eye from the racecourse ..... An unfortunate incident occurred in the first race when two horses collided and both riders were killed. The riders were Captain Kemmis who organised the meeting and Lieutenant Smith. I think that these races constituted the best day's sport that the men had had in France and everyone went home after thoroughly enjoying himself.[337]

Neaves himself would be wounded just over two weeks later, on the first day of the offensive of 8 August. Morlancourt and Dernancourt would not be captured until 10 August.

The 8 August Offensive

Popularly known as the Battle of Amiens by the Australians, it is also known to the French as the Third Battle of Picardy.[338] In his official history, Charles Bean does not devote a chapter heading using that name. Rather, he addresses the actions in two consecutive chapters: chapter XIII, "The Origin of 'August 8th'"; and chapter XIV, "Der Schwarze Tag."[339] In Edmonds' British official history, the much greater British and French contribution is reflected in the title of the relevant volume: "8th August – 26th September: the Franco-British Offensive." Edmonds devotes the first eight chapters to the Battle for Amiens, by which term the British identify it.[340]

These titles confer on the so-called Battle of Amiens a separate identity. This tends to bely the existing continuity of a broader push toward and through the German lines, particularly around the Somme River, that had commenced in early April. This offensive theme goes back at least to Villers-Bretonneux. Further manifestations of the growing impetus of an offensive are found—amongst many other places—at Hamel, Dernancourt, and Morlancourt. What happened on 8 August was as much if not more a culmination of efforts begun over four months earlier. What was evident to all over the following four days was the collapse of the German army.

Nor was the Battle of Amiens fought for Amiens. That town had been saved when the German's Operation *Michael* disintegrated in front of Villers-Bretonneux, well east of Amiens. Indeed, the start line for the so-called Battle of Amiens was proximate to villages some ten miles east of that city.

The Australian Corps under Monash was south of the Somme River. Their start line ran roughly south-southwest from Sailly-Laurette on the Somme River to a point about a mile beyond Villers-Bretonneux, on a railway line running roughly east. The final objective—the blue line—ran south from Méricourt-sur-Somme in the north to Harbonnières in the south. To the north of this rough square was British III Corps and to its south was the Canadian Corps.

The attack commenced at 4:20 a.m. In the Australian Corps sector, the 4th and 5th Divisions went first. According to Monash's plan, they would be leapfrogged later by the 2nd and 3rd Divisions. For the time being, the 1st Division would remain as reserve. Monash's plan was brilliant and complex. In a new variation, the 2nd and 3rd would in turn be leapfrogged by the 4th and 5th Divisions. Monash had thoroughly briefed his officers and each had specific instructions. All had initial barrages laid on and subsequent tank and air support. Modified carrier tanks would bring supplies more reliably to the advanced line.

There was certainly strong German resistance, but it was overcome. There was also wholesale surrender by sections of the German forces, particularly in the north of the sector around Morcourt. The Australians suffered 2,000 casualties. They took their objectives and collected nearly 7,300 prisoners and substantial numbers of artillery pieces and materiel. Immediately to their south, the Canadians took 6,000 prisoners.[341]

An account of the evening of 7/8 August from Pvt. Geoffrey Rose, a signaller and runner with the 30th Battalion:

> At 1.30 a.m. on 8th August we fell in and marched ..... Tanks, looking tremendous in the dark, rumbled along beside us, their engines making a loud humming noise. I wondered how it was that Fritz didn't notice them ..... bombing planes cruised up and down German lines to drown the noise ..... I sat on the step of a dugout waiting. We were all feeling a bit nervy ..... We got a sip of rum and that knocked the nerves out of us ..... At 4.20 a.m. to the tick the barrage opened. I never expect to hear the like again ..... At 5.15 a.m. we hopped over the top and formed up on our tape, behind our tanks. I was only just out of the trench when a shell landed on my left. I felt a hell of a kick in my side, but at the same moment I saw Brisbane – a stretcher bearer, who was just getting out of the trench – fall back, calling out and holding his eye. I saw that he had been hit and forgot my little affair. Sgt. Major McKinnon was by me, and said "What have you done to your 'ammo'?" I looked at my side pouches and discovered that two clips had been completely spoilt and my pouches cut open. There was also a hole in the telephone case that I was carrying. The piece of

Warfusée, east of Villers-Bretonneux, 8 August 1918, the signature date for the Battle of Amiens. Lieutenant Rupert Frederick Downes addresses his Platoon from B Company, 29th Battalion, during a rest before the advance to Harbonnières, the battalion's second objective. The battalion was raised in Victoria. This particular photograph is accompanied by a detailed record of the subjects and is something of a story of Australians, British Australians, and the collision of civilian life with war. From left to right: 5085 Sergeant (Sgt) William Patrick O'Brien; 4271 Private (Pte) James Cryer; 4103 Pte Charles Alfred Olive; 677 Lance Corporal (L Cpl) Louis Price MM; 5095 Pte Harry James Phillips; 4733 Pte Horace Joseph Buckley; 509 L Cpl Alexander Bethuen Craven; 5088 Pte Patrick O'Grady; 5057 Pte Timothy Leyden; 5116 Pte Edward Thomlinson; 5014 Pte Herbert Davidson; 6827 Pte Horace John Towers; 4349 L Cpl Thomas John Barrett Pope; 2568 Pte John Leslie Gordon Arlow; 3207 L Cpl John Bird; 560 Pte Frederick George Hall (front of line); and Lieutenant R. F. A. Downes (right). O'Brien was killed in action on 9 August 1918. Cryer was born at Bury, Lancashire, and was a farmer when he enlisted at Armidale, New South Wales. Olive, of Lara, Victoria, was initially rejected before enlisting in September 1916. He was killed in action near Bellicourt on 30 September 1918. Price of Maryborough, Victoria, was an original member of B Company. He was awarded the Military Medal for bravery in Belgium in 1917. Phillips, a packer in civilian life and the youngest in the platoon at nineteen years of age, was wounded on 29 August 1918, returning to Australia in December 1918. Buckley, a clerk of Kyneton, Victoria, was given to frequent periods of absenteeism. He was wounded in action on 9 August 1918. Craven, a laborer of Ballarat, Victoria, served three years with the battalion. O'Grady of Galway, Ireland, was employed as a miller in Melbourne, Victoria. Leyden of Trentham, Victoria, a railway employee in civilian life, was gassed on 27 August 1918. Thomlinson, a driver of Stawell, Victoria, and the oldest member of the platoon at forty four years of age, had been taken on strength with the battalion on 6 June 1918. Davidson was a leather worker from Brunswick, Victoria. Towers was a farm laborer of Cootamundra, New South Wales. He was admitted to the Abbeville Hospital on 9 November 1918, suffering pneumonia. He died there on 11 November 1918, the day the war ended. Pope, born at Westbury-on-Tyne, Gloucestershire, was a farmer in Sydney, New South Wales. He was wounded in action on 30 September 1918. Arlow of Warrnambool, Victoria, a blacksmith in civilian life, was killed in action near Bellicourt on 30 September 1918. Bird was a carpenter from South Melbourne, Victoria. Hall, an iron moulder of South Melbourne, Victoria, was an original member of B Company. He was wounded in action twice. Downes, of Camden, New South Wales, was an orchardist prior to enlistment. He sailed as a second lieutenant and was promoted to lieutenant in May 1917. He was awarded the Military Cross for "conspicuous gallantry and devotion to duty" at Morlancourt in July 1918 and, like most of his men, was transferred to the 32nd Battalion with the reorganization of battalions that took place later in 1918. *AWM*

shell had gone through the telephone case and had been stopped by the cartridges. I pulled out the piece of shell and kept it as a souvenir.[342]

An early morning mist made orderly progress much more difficult:

> We now found that we had advanced too fast and were up with the attacking battalions, instead of one hour's march behind them. We were in isolated groups of men – all going the same way through the fog, but as far as battalions were concerned, inextricably mixed.

Here again are the same problems that beset any advancing force: lack of communication and disorientation. Without voice control, the best prepared plans fell to chance and circumstance. Later that morning, Rose saw a soldier fall to German machine gun fire:

> He gave a couple of kicks and lay still. The [stretcher] bearers looked at him and left him for dead. Great was our surprise some time later, to see him return to the Battalion alive and well. I don't know how he managed it.

The Australians had taken most of their final objectives by the end of the first day. Three days later, after successfully taking and consolidating Harbonnières, the 30th Battalion was relieved and returned behind the lines to rest. There they encountered a fool of an officer, the kind who was known as a "goat":

> We pulled into a farmhouse near Villers-Bretonneux for dinner. Major Bilton (the goat) and his Company came in after us. He insisted on his men marching to attention before they halted. The rest of the Battalion bleated at him to show their opinion of him, and the C.O. had a few hard words with him about annoying the boys.

Only in the AIF would such a scene unfold.

What the events of 8 August did reveal was the collapse of German morale. This, more than the place or time of battle, was the defining theme. The day may have been "a black day" for the German army, but a German *dénouement* was really there for those German commanders who wished to look well before their March Offensive. The Australians had been at the center of the offensive and no doubt their fighting prowess was a major factor in the success. They did not, however, "win the war." Monash saw himself as central to the success.

Monash was quick to bring his achievements to public notice. In 1919, he published *The Australian Victories in France in 1918.* It has been described by one authoritative source as "propaganda, but not far off the truth."[343] Of particular note was Monash's description of his apparent orchestration of what became known as the Battle of Amiens in August 1918. The Australians performed bravely and were at the center of the advance, but were by no means the sole participants. Seventeen years after the war Bean, in his capacity as official historian, corresponded with Brudenell White on the subject. In June 1935 White wrote to Bean, suggesting an entirely different source for the planning of the Battle of Amiens:

> Whilst we were at Bertangles, and only a comparatively short time before we relinquished the Corps, General Rawlinson came down to us with Archie Montgomery his Chief of Staff and said he had an important and confidential matter to discuss ..... We therefore shut ourselves in General Birdwood's office and Rawlinson expounded to us a plan then in the Commander in Chief's [Haig] mind for a big offensive ..... the Canadians would probably be on our right. What I prepared is of no importance however. The important point is that the plan for the August offensive was the Commander in Chief's and Rawlinson's. This is beyond question. When John Monash's book came out Montgomery wrote to me saying that Rawlinson and he were – what is the right word? – not annoyed and not offended but perhaps "quite surprised" that Monash had asserted that the plan was of his own devising ..... it was Haig who really conceived it and prepared for it.[344]

August into September

The Americans were also involved farther south. Their rapid deployment had seen quantities of American supplies discarded in the rush. Thomas Cleary—the man who had dressed himself through the previous winter by arguing with quartermasters and liberating items from Aid Posts —was impressed:

> A number of the Yankee units are leaving here for the south. Like most other new troops they have woke up to the fact that it is impossible to carry their full equipment and are dumping stuff everywhere. I salvaged a new shirt and a lovely pair of boots beautifully finished inside with the seams and rough side of the leather outside. They are only half the weight of our boots.[345]

The advance toward Péronne continued during the remainder of August. It was slow, bloody, but gradual progress. Geoffrey Rose provides us with insight into the nature of men, war, fear, death, and gas around the village of Foucaucourt. These extracts from his memoirs, including a further note on the previously mentioned "goat," Maj. Bilton:

> August 27th. I had a dead Scotty and a dead Aussie, both about three days gone, for company. They were nearly black and very much blown up. Someone had got away with the Scotty's kilt, leaving him half naked ..... We found another old trench and went up it, shortly coming on to the Fritz who had been giving all the trouble. He had been shot through the neck by one of our men. He had tried to bandage himself up, but without effect, and was lying back looking exceedingly dead and white. I got his pocket book but there was nothing much in it. I took his pay book as a souvenir, but threw it away again, as I thought I might get captured and it would not look too well.
>
> August 28th. While I am thinking of it – during the next two days advancing, Major Bilton was posted as missing. He was eventually discovered in one of these dugouts. He said that he thought he could direct his Company best from there. I'm afraid that cold feet were his failing.[346]

They advanced farther east to Villers-Carbonnel, a few hundred yards from the Somme Canal and just south of Péronne:

> On 29th August about 5.30 a.m. the 31st Battalion came through us and began to advance ….. Fritz had got across the canal all right, and seemed as if he thought he had gone far enough. After a while he started shelling, mostly with light stuff, and had us ducking up and down the trenches. He also fired mustard gas at us. I got a couple of light splashes on my hand.

Within hours these had turned into large, angry blisters. Mustard gas would remain in liquid form for days and contact with small, unnoticed portions much later would result in injury:

> August 31st. Another gas blister had formed on my left hand, so I showed it to the A.M.C. They let the stuff out of it and I had no further trouble.

By 3 September, the Australians were in Péronne. Heavy street fighting—something none had before experienced on the Western Front—took its toll. To the northern end of the town stands Mont St. Quentin. It rises about 350 feet above the point where the Somme River abruptly turns southward as a canal. Extensive, boggy marshes to each side of the canal make this difficult territory to traverse and the taking of Mont St. Quentin again cost the Australians dearly. Here, Monash's skills at battles of maneuver and rapid change of tactics were on display. He was more than just a set-piece battle general.

To the End

From there the Germans fell back to their last resort, the Hindenburg Line. From 5 September, they were pursued by the British, Americans, and Australians. Just in front of the Hindenburg Line stood a series of outposts known as the Hindenburg Outpost Line. In the area where the Australians operated, the Hindenburg Outpost Line ran from just east of Bellicourt in the north down to Bellenglise in the south. All this was some twelve miles east of Péronne and Mont St. Quentin.

An anxious Australian government led by a very anxious Prime Minister William Hughes knew that for most of 1918, the Australian Corps was under strength and totally lacking sufficient reserves. At this time the Australian Corps, save for the 4th Division, were resting out of the line. Hughes reportedly advised Monash in late September that he wanted all Australians out of the line by the middle of October.[347] This Monash did, but only after using the 4th Division in support of the Americans to stretch even farther east and take Montrebrehain, over four miles farther east again past the Hindenburg Line. Then it was all over for the Australians. The Germans sued for peace and signed an armistice three weeks later on 11 November 1918.

11 November

On this day, Pvt. Arthur Kilgour of the 2nd Battalion wrote in his diary:

> Great excitement prevails in the camp today. Word has just come through that Germany has signed the Armistice. Can it really be true? It is hard to realise that war is no more. An end to our suffering. God be praised.[348]

Pvt. Thomas Cleary of the 2nd Pioneers wrote:

> 11.11.18. The day of days. We had two victories today. We won the War and defeated the 5th Field Company at Soccer.[349]

Although written four days before, stretcher bearer Private David Whinfield—recently transferred to Australian Headquarters in London after nearly two years on the Western Front—reflected on the ambiguity of being both an Australian and a British subject:

> Thursday 7th November. Well we are in a strange land. In a land of our own but not of it.

The Cost

During the last nineteen weeks of the war (1 July to 11 November) on the Western Front, the Australians suffered 31,535 casualties. This exceeds the total for the first twenty-six weeks of 1918. Nearly all of these casualties were incurred between the beginning of July and the end of September: a thirteen-week period of slaughter. In those last nineteen weeks 6,417 were killed or died of wounds or gas. A further 20,460 were wounded. No Australian Army has since exceeded such losses.[350]

Chapter Nineteen

REMEMBERING

A notable historian has observed that any work of history tends toward autobiographical confession.[351] All works on the Great War carry some infusion of the author's own values and views. This book is no exception. It openly admits an admiration for Australians in the worst of conditions: war on the Western Front.

Casualties by Numbers

The AIF incurred a total of 53,850 deaths from battle during the Great War.[352] The theaters in Egypt and Palestine claimed 987. Gallipoli claimed 7,818. The Western Front took 45,044.[353]

The death toll on the Western Front (45,044) can be refined to battle deaths, a slightly lower figure of 44,764.[354]

The *Official Medical History* gives three sources for Australian arrivals on the Western Front. Between 1916 and 1918, 96,503 arrived from Australia via Egypt. Another 152,296 came as new reinforcements from the United Kingdom. A further 56,787 are then listed as "recovered from U.K." This represents wounded and ill who were repatriated to the UK and once deemed fit for further service, were returned to the battlefields. A fourth minor category can be added: the 657 servicemen who by some means were in the UK and served in France between 1914 and the end of 1915. This makes for a grand total of 305,586 servicemen. Obviously, this figure includes some double counting with the inclusion of the "recovered" servicemen.

If the number of recovered is removed, a more realistic total of 248,799 is arrived at; a quarter of a million men, nearly all of them serving as front line soldiers. Of these, 44,764 were killed, or 18% of the total. Wounded, including shell shocked, gassed sufficiently for hospitalization and prisoners of war came to 134,697, or 54% of the arrivals. Total Australian casualties on the Western Front—killed, wounded, prisoners of war, shell shocked, and gassed—therefore comes to 179,461. That is 72% of those who served on the Western Front.[355]

Reflecting on the Great War

Just what was the Western Front? A physical terrain? A moral landscape? A playground for uncaring commanders? A place of loss or redemption? A battlefield? A late twentieth – early twenty-first-century theme park for tourists? A life-sized war gaming table for the competing egos and world views of military historians? It was and remains perhaps all of these things, and more.

What of the Anzac Legend? It is the collective memory of these disastrous events that are completely out of the ordinary and now beyond living memory. These events have been reshaped to fit the quite often disparate purposes and states of mind of the present population at the present time, whenever that may be: the 1920s, the 1930s, or now.

The harnessing and manipulation of the past into legendary terms warrants balance and perhaps counterpoise with the real thoughts of those who were there. It is the purpose of this book.

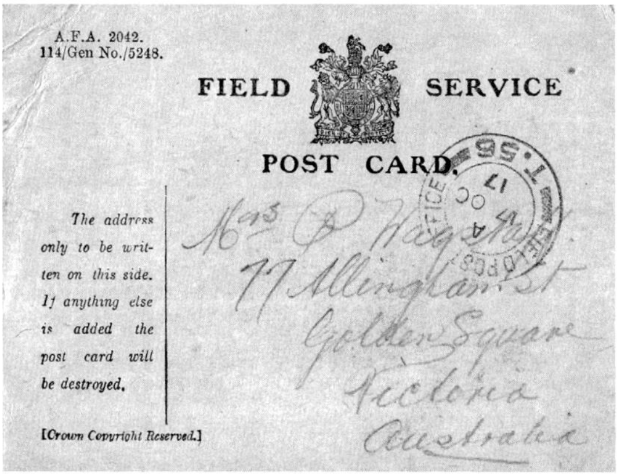
A.F.A. 2042.
114/Gen No./5248.

FIELD SERVICE

POST CARD.

The address only to be written on this side. If anything else is added the post card will be destroyed.

[Crown Copyright Reserved.]

Mrs P Wagstaff
77 Allingham St
Golden Square
Victoria
Australia

Capt. Percy Wagstaff was a mining engineer who arrived in France with the 2nd Australian Tunnelling Company at the end of August 1916. He regularly corresponded with his wife by letter, but also took every opportunity to use the Army Field Service Post Card system. Contrary to the strict instructions printed on the form, he has managed to write substantially more than is permitted in the "received" section. *Author's collection*

Capt. Eric Dark, an Australian who by late 1914 had found his way into the British Army as a doctor. He served with the 9th Field Ambulance attached to the British Guards Division. In this portrait he holds the rank of lieutenant. He returned to Australia and became a medical practitioner. He reenlisted for the Second World War. *New South Wales State Library Archives*

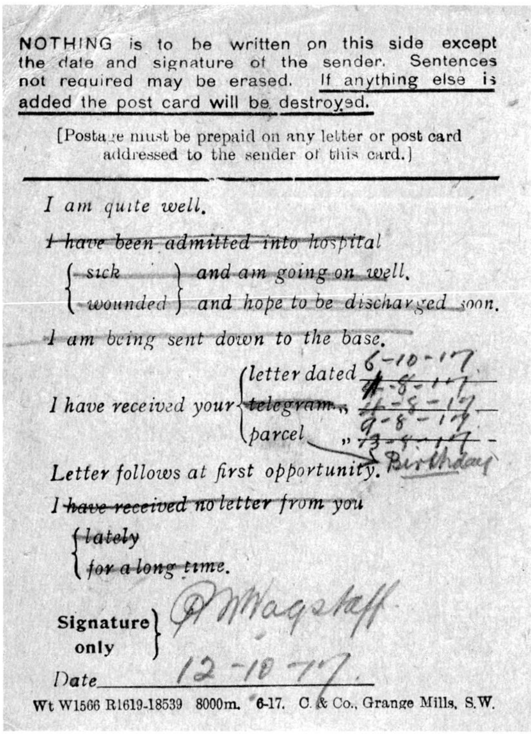
NOTHING is to be written on this side except the date and signature of the sender. Sentences not required may be erased. If anything else is added the post card will be destroyed.

[Postage must be prepaid on any letter or post card addressed to the sender of this card.]

I am quite well.

~~I have been admitted into hospital~~

~~sick~~ ~~and am going on well.~~

~~wounded~~ ~~and hope to be discharged soon.~~

~~I am being sent down to the base.~~

I have received your letter dated 6-10-17, ~~4-8-17~~; ~~telegram~~ " 4-8-17; parcel " 9-8-17, ~~13-8-17~~

Letter follows at first opportunity. Birthday

I ~~have received no letter from you~~

~~lately~~

~~for a long time.~~

Signature only: P Wagstaff

Date 12-10-17

Wt W1566 R1619-18539 8000m. 6-17. C. & Co., Grange Mills, S.W.

A going-away family portrait, typical of the hundreds of thousands of such prints commercial studios made. The background scene is a canvas prop depicting neatly arranged bell tents and is common to many such images. George Swanton of the 24th Battalion sits with his wife and their newborn daughter. George's brother John was killed on Gallipoli. George himself died of wounds at Pozières on 28 July 1916. The author interviewed the daughter in the picture (Joan Swanton) in December 2009, when she was ninety-four. She too has since died. Her enduring observation of the Great War was, "it certainly cleaned the men out of this house." *Author's collection*

Sergeant William Banks, 46th Battalion. Banks enlisted in 1915 and served at Pozières and later at Flers, where he was withdrawn from the line, suffering shell shock, trench feet, and the effects of gassing in November 1916. He did not recover fully and was repatriated to Australia in 1917. The war turned this personable man of thirty-seven years into a physical and mental wreck. He became surly, unapproachable, and endured bouts of debilitating rashes and boils. He drank heavily and died in 1950. *Author's collection*

Endnotes

Chapter 1:

1. On the development of German military culture, its subsequent approach to civilians as objects of military necessity, and the separation of German military culture from national political norms, see Hull, *Absolute Destruction*, especially chapters 2-7.
2. Nicolson, *The First World War: Europe 1914-1918*, 3ff.
3. For a deeper discussion see Tuchman, *The Proud Tower: A Portrait of the World before The War, 1890-1914.*

Chapter 2:

4. Census of the Commonwealth of Australia, 1911.
5. Ibid.
6. Commonwealth Department of the Parliamentary Library Reseacrh Note no. 23, 200-01.
7. See Andrews, *The Anzac Illusion*, p. 7.
8. Only 160,000 convicts (men and women) were transported to Australia from 1788 until the system petered out in 1868. Free migrants had been flowing into the country from the early 1790s. Australian Government Department of Foreign Affairs and Trade www.dfat.gov.au/aib/history. On just when Australia actually became an independent nation, see Hudson and Sharp, p. 138. Technically, it may have been as late as 1942 or even 1945.
9. On the concepts of "race" and "Australian race," and the fear of Japanese expansion after Britain had withdrawn most of her naval fleet after the signing of the 1902 Anglo-Japanese treaty, see Gammage, 2-3.
10. *Oxford Companion to Australian Military History* (hereafter *OCAMH*), p. 47.
11. *OCAMH,* 155-156.
12. Gammage, 3.
13. AWM38, 3DRL606 Diaries.
14. A. B. Patterson. "The Arrival of the New South Wales Troops in South Africa" in Gerster and Pierce (eds). *On the Warpath*, pp. 31-36.
15. For a discussion on the prior existence of an Australian national character, be it real or imagined, see Beaumont, *Australia's War*, chapter 6, especially 149-150.
16. Carlyon. *The Great War*, 774.
17. AWM38, 3DRL606 Folders.
18. Bean, *Anzac*, vi.
19. AWM4, Class 23 Infantry.
20. Bean, *Anza*c, 48.

Chapter 3:

21. For a firsthand account of the complete chaos of the retreat of the British Expeditionary Force and the French Fifth Army through their fortuitous if unwitting deformation of the intended right wing of the German Schlieffen Plan, see Edward Spear's *Liaison, 1914: a narrative of the Great Retreat.*
22. See Simkins et al.. *The First World War: the War to End All Wars*, pp. 194-206 for a concise account of the complex maneuverings of the Germans and the Russians to the end of 1914.
23. Haythornthwaite. *Gallipoli, 1915*, 10, 37.
24. Bean. *The Official History of Australia in the War of 1914-1918.* 12 volumes. [hereafter *OH*], vol. 1, 171-173.
25. Bean, *Anza*c, 68-74.

26. Simkins et al., 291-301. See also Fleming. *The Australian Army in World War I*, 10-13. This recent reading of the events varies from Bean's more contemporary account of matters cited in the previous footnote.
27. Simkins, 295-296.
28. Bean, *OH*, vol.1, viii-ix.
29. Bean, *OH*, vol.1, xxii-xxiii.
30. De Vine. Diary, AWM 1DRL/0240.
31. James. Diary, State Library of Victoria, MS9611.
32. Cited in Gammage, *The Broken Years: Australian Soldiers in the Great War*, 109.
33. Jones, *Memoir*.
34. To "crime" someone was to place them on a charge. As a corporal, Jones had the power to do this over a trooper. To be "crimed" was to be placed on a charge. Being crimed was a common occurrence. Having the matter proceeded with or taken to any extreme conclusion appears to have been less frequent.
35. Young ed., *Hail and Farewell: letters from two brothers killed in France in 1916*, 56.
36. Cited in Gammage, 112.
37. Three recent examples of the Bean-as-legend-maker argument may be found in Ball, "Re-Reading Bean's Last Paragraph," *Australian Historical Studies*, vol. 122, 2003, 231-247; Lee, "Greeks and Moderns: the Search for Culture in the *Official History of Australia in the War of 1914-1918*," *Australian Literary Studies*, vol. 23, 2007, 106-120; and Londey, "A Possession for Ever: Charles Bean, the Ancient Greeks and Military Commemoration in Australia," *Australian Journal of Politics and History*, vol. 53, 2007, 344-359.
38. Cited in Gammage, 110.
39. Dennis et al.. *The Oxford Companion to Australian Military History* [hereafter *OCAMH*], 232.
40. Simkins, *The First World War*, 300.
41 http://www.awm.gov.au/encyclopedia/gallipoli. The casualty figures are still subject to variation. The *Australian Army Medical History* gives slightly different numbers. These are used in chapter 20.

Chapter 4:

42. Bean, *OH*, vol. lll, 33-42.
43. Jones, Diary,
44. Spears, *Liaison 1914*, 36.
45. The Prince of Wales was Edward, son of George V, who later became British royalty's short reigning King before abdicating in favor of his feelings toward American socialite Wallis Simpson. "Birdie" is an affectionate name for one of the few British commanders the Australians held in high regard, Gen. Sir William Birdwood. He was at Gallipoli in command of the Anzac forces and later commanded I Anzac Corps on the Western Front.
46. Each battalion was identifiable by a two-tone color cloth badge of various shapes, making for considerable permutation. The original 3rd Battalion wore a horizontally aligned rectangle of brown on green. For the new battalion, these colors and shape were kept but worn vertically. Such subtle changes were practised wherever possible in the "doubling" and doubtless gave continuity to the change.
47. The origin of the appellation "King Billy" is confused. What is known is that at least one, possibly several, male aborigines during the mid-to-late-nineteenth century were accorded or claimed the appellation. In colloquial parlance through to the 1940s, to be a "king billy" was to be something of a pretender to high status.
48. Hammond, Diary.
49. The diarist was with 54th Battalion, which along with the 53, 55, and 56 comprised 14 Bde. Ironically, it was the 5th Division that saw action on the Western Front first (at Fromelles), although it was the last of the Australian and Anzac divisions to leave Egypt.
50. Stanley, *Bad Characters: Sex, Crime, Mutiny, Murder and the Australian Imperial Force*, 37ff.
51. An account of these incidents may be found in *OCAMH*, 585.
52. Cited in Gammage, 131.

53. One AIF division (3rd) did bypass Egypt. Assembly began in Australia in March 1916. This division was sent directly to England in July 1916. After intensive training it crossed to France in December 1916.
54. Bean, *Anzac*, 194. The British may well have worried more for the health of their own. Australian troops had been thoroughly vaccinated and inoculated. Such procedures were not compulsory in the British army in France. The only cases of typhus received at an Australian hospital in Marseilles established for just such an eventuality came from the British divisions returning from Egypt.
55. Hammond, Diary,
56. Bean, *OH*, vol. III, 87-93.
57. "Glasso" refers to a product applied not to the eyes, but rather to the glass eyepieces of the mask section of the small box respirator then in use. The product came in the form of a paste enclosed in a lead squeeze tube. It was to be applied to the outsides of the lenses to counteract the corrosive effects of the gas. Its formal description is "Glasso Anti-dimming Composition." Troops were exposed to tear gas—commonly referred to as "Tear"—during training in the sector. This training is noted in the battalion war diary for the entry dated 8 July, where the following reference is made to this deliberate exposure for training purposes, ". . . also the effect of Tear Shells. This test inspired the men with great confidence . . . it might be more often applied with good results."

Chapter 5:

58. It took the Germans longer than planned to reduce the Belgian forts at Liége. From then on, the Schlieffen plan was showing its weaknesses. See Tuchman, *August 1914*, ch. 11.
59. For an excellent summary of the Schlieffen Plan, the French Pan XVII, and the immediate consequences, see Sewell Tyng's *The Campaign of the Marne, 1914*, chapters 1-3.
60. Gary Sheffield, *The Somme*, 9.
61. On this see Horne and Kramer, "War Between Soldiers and Enemy Civilians, 1914-1915," in Chickering and Förster (eds). *Great War, Total War: Combat and Mobilization on the Western Front, 1914-1918*, 153-168.
62. For a fuller discussion of these events and substantial bibliographic support, see Hull, *Absolute Destruction*.
63. The retreat of French and British forces and their heroic stalling engagements as they were driven back to the Marne are given very detailed treatment in Spears, *Liaison: 1914*. Spears provides a unique insight into the frictions within the French command during the retreat. A very readable account of the battle in early September that led to the end of maneuver and the commencement of entrenchment is given by Tyng, *The Campaign of the Marne: 1914*.
64. Beckett, *The Great War*, 223.
65. For an account of the events of 1915—particularly the disappointments at Loos—see Neillands, *The Death of Glory: the Western Front, 1915*. [hereafter, *1915*].
66. Spears, *Liaison: 1914*, 288.
67. Neillands, *1915,* 258.
68. For an account of the role of artillery see Strong and Marble, *Artillery in the Great War.*
69. See Doughty, *Pyrrhic Victory: French Strategy and Operations in the Great War*, 261. Also Afflerbach, "Planning Total War? Falkenhayn and the Battle of Verdun, 1916," in Chickering and Förster (eds), *Great War, Total War: Combat and Mobilization on the Western Front, 1914-1918*, 113-131, especially 122.
70. Boraston, (ed) *Sir Douglas Haig's Despatches*, London, 1920. Cited in Greenhalgh, "Why the British Were on the Somme in 1916," *War in History*, vol. 6, no. 2, 147-173.
71. Haig saw it as a victory. Some historians agree. See Sheffield, *The Somme*. Philpott, *Bloody Victory: the Sacrifice on the Somme and the Making of the Twentieth Century*. Others are less convinced: see in particular

Harris, *Douglas Haig and the First World War* [hereafter, *Haig*]. Also see Prior and Wilson, *The Somme*. Others argue it was a German victory, see Sheldon, *The German Army on the Somme, 1914-1916*. For the depths of sentiment the matter arouses, see the exchange between William Philpott and Elizabeth Greenhalgh in Greenhalgh, "Why the British Were on the Somme in 1916," *War in History*, vol. 6, no. 2, 1999, 147-173. Philpott, "Why the British Were Really on the Somme: A Reply to Elizabeth Greenhalgh," *War in History*, vol. 9, no. 4, 2002, 446-471. And Greenhalgh, "Flames over the Somme: A Retort to William Philpott," *War in History*, vol. 10, no. 3, 335-342.

72. Edmonds, *British official history*, vol. I. 17, 73.
73. Harris, *Haig*, 213.
74. Greenhalgh, 170-171.
75. For a detailed description of the German defenses and their depth, see Prior and Wilson, *The Somme*, 335-41.
76. Harris, 232.

Chapter 6:

77. Bean, *Anzac*, 197-199.
78. Sheffield and Bourne, *Douglas Haig*, 186.
79. AWM, War Diaries 1/29/4 Part 1. May 1916.
80. Pederson, *Anzacs on the Western Front* [hereafter, *Anzacs*], 5.
81. Bean, *OH*, vol. III, 346
82. Letter, Elliott to Bean, 17 August 1926, AWM38 3DRL606/243A/1
83. Bean, *OH*, vol. III, 328-353
84. Hammond, Diary,
85. AWM38 3DRL606/243A/1
86. Hammond, Diary,
87. Letter, Donnan to the Director of the Australian War Memorial, 7 March 1934, AWM38 3DRL606/243A/1
88. AWM38 3DRL606/52/1
89. *Australian Dictionary of Biography* adb. anu. edu/biography (hereafter *ADB*).
90. AWM38 3DRL606/52/1.
91. Bean, *Anzac to Amiens*, 236. In *OH*, vol. III, 447, Bean's summation is more guarded, but still pointed.

Chapter 7:

92. Bean, *O*H, vol. III.
93 Bean, Diary, AWM383DRL606/52/1. See also Letter, Bean to Monteath, 25 November 1926 in AWM38DRL606/244/1.
94. Beckett, *The Great War: 1914-1918*, 225.
95. Prior and Wilson, *The Somme*, 112.
96. Keech, *Pozieres*, 30.
97. Gliddon, *Somme 1916: a Battlefield Companion*, 373.
98. Prior and Wilson, *The Somme*, 121.
99. Bean, *Anzac to Amiens*, 237-238.
100. *OCAMH*, 563
101. War Diaries: 3rd Battalion, July 1916 AWM423/20/17 and 1st Brigade, July 1916 AWM423/1/12.
102. Annette Kellerman (1886-1975) was an Australian professional high diver, swimmer, and vaudeville and film star famous for scandalous one-piece bathing suits. To the Australian soldiers marching through Albert, the precariously leaning statue of the Virgin Mary atop the bomb-damaged basilica was somewhat irreverently known by this name.
103. Jones, Diary,
104. Quartermaster Sergeant.
105. Jones, Diary,
106. Jones, Diary,
107. Bean, Diary, AWM383DRL606/54/1.
108. Jones, Diary,
109. AWM38DRL606/244/1.
110. National Archives of Australia [hereafter, *NAA*] Series B2445. Gordon, J. H. G.
111. Letter, Powell to Rimoldi, 10 August 1916, AWM383DRL606/244/1
112. Letter, Barbour to Browne, 24 November 1916, AWM383DRL606/244/1
113. Bean, Diary, AWM383DRL606/54/1.
114. Young and Gammage (eds). *Hail and Farewell: Letters From Two Brothers Killed in France in 1916*, 146-148.
115. Bean, Diary, AWM383DRL606/54/1
116. Bean, Diary, AWM383DRL606/54/1
117. Bean, Diary, AWM383DRL606/54/1.
118. AWM38DRL606/244/1

119. Bean, *Letters from France*, 1917, 68-69.
120. Bean, *OH*, vol. III, 614-617.
121. Bean, OH, vol. III, 615.
122. Beckett, *The Great War*, 92.
123. Bean, *OH*, vol. III, 724.
124. Harris, *Douglas Haig and the First World War* (hereafter, *Haig*); see chapter nine for a recent, thorough analysis of the situation, especially 210-213.
125. Ibid., 211.
126. Travers, *The Killing Ground: the British Army, the Western Front & the Emergence of Modern War, 1900-1918* [hereafter, *The Killing Ground*], 153.
127. Haig, Diary, 197.
128. Haig, Diary, 214.
129. Haig, Diary, 202.
130. Prior and Wilson, *The Somme*, ch. 14; Bean, *OH*, vol. III, ch. 19, especially 647-650; Charlton. *Pozieres: Australians on the Somme, 1916*, ch. 11, 192-194; Travers, *The Killing Ground,* ch. 7, 152-153 and 176-179.
131. Bean, *OH*, 647-649.
132. Letter, Haig's Chief of General Staff to Generals Rawlinson and Gough, 3 August 1916. Cited in Bean, *OH*, vol. III, 547-648.
133. Letter, White to Bean, 1 May 1928, AWM3DRL606/244/1.
134. Haig, Diary, 208-211.
135. Letter, AWM383DRL606/244/1.

Chapter 8:

136. RAAF Point Cook Archives.
137. Bean, *OH*, vol. III, chapters 21-23.
138. Bean, *OH*, vol. III, 726-727.
139. Letter, Wanliss to Bean, 23 August 1925, AWM38DRL606/245/1.
140. Bean subsequently made use of these versions with further editing in the official history and at the same time encouraged Rule to have them published as a separate book, a matter in which Bean and Wanliss appear to have used their influence.
141. AWM38DRL606/245/1.
142. AWM38DRL606/245/1.
143. Sheffield, *The Somme*, 101.
144. Bean, *OH*, vol. III, 862ff.
145. http://www.awm.gov.au/wartime/36/article.asp
146. Pederson, *Anzacs*, 19.
147. Bean, *OH*, vol. III, 863ff.
148. Bean, *OH*, vol. III, 871.
149. Bean, *Anzac to Amiens*, 264-265.
150. Bean, Diary.
151. Letter, Leane to Bean, 7 June 1923, AWM38DRL606/244/1.
152. Rule, Diary, AWM38DRL606/245/1.

Chapter 9:

153. Neaves, Diary, AWM2DRL/0752.
154. Pederson, *Anzacs*, 73-89.
155. Haig, In Sheffield, Diary [hereafter, Haig, Diary], 225.
156. Bean, *Anzac*, 266-267.
157. Pederson, *Anzacs*, 91.
158. Jones, Diary.
159. Neaves, Diary, AWM2DRL/0752.
160. Bartley. Diary, 30 November 1916, AWM383DRL606/246/1.
161. Rule. Diary, AWM383DRL606/245/1.
162. Jones, Diary,
163. Edmonds. Diary, AWM383DRL606/246/1.
164. Rule. Diary, AWM383DRL606/245/1.
165. War Diary, 4th Infantry Battalion, November 1916, AWM423/21/21.
166. War Diary, 4th Infantry Battalion, November 1916, AWM423/21/21
167. Jones, Diary.
168. Jones, Diary.
169. De Vine, Diary, AWM383DRL606/246/1.
170. Ibid.
171. Haig, Diary, 225.
172. For a discussion of this see Prior and Wilson, *The Somme*, 221-223. Also see Brown, *The Imperial War Museum Book of the Somme*, 209.
173. Cited in Harris, 268.
174. Elliot, Diary, AWM3DRL606/246/1.
175. Harris, 268.
176. Bean, *OH*, vol. III, xvi. For a more detailed description, see Harris, *Haig*, 274.
177. Haig, Diary, 271.

Chapter 10:

178. AWM383DRL606/245/1. Again, this

original, unblemished, and unedited account from Rule's diary transcript seems a preferable source to the moderated version that made up his subsequent book, *Jacka's Mob*.

179. Jones, Diary.
180. Neillands, *Attrition*, 297-307.
181. Harris, 279-297.
182. Pederson, 105.

Chapter 11:

183. Bean, Diary, 3DRL606/75/1.
184. Williams, *An ANZAC on the Western Front: The Personal Reflections of an Australian Infantryman from 1916 to 1918*. First published in 1933 as *The Gallant Company: An Australian Soldier's Story of 1915-18*, 78.
185. War Diary, 56th Infantry Battalion, AWM4 Sub-class 23/73. March 1917.
186. Williams, 88.
187. Bean, Diary, 3DRL606/75/1.
188. Spears, *Prelude to Victory* [hereafter, *Prelude*], 604.
189. See Bean, *Anzac*, chapter XIX and Pederson, 135-139 for abbreviated accounts. For the usual, intricately detailed account of events, both on the taking of the outpost villages and for the opening of First Bullecourt, see Bean's *OH*, vol. IV, chs. VIII and IX. See Harris, *Haig* for an analysis of the political maneuvering that nearly saw Lloyd George have Haig sacked prior to Arras (ch. 11) and the preparations of Haig and Nivelle for the Battle itself and its outcomes, including Nivelle's sacking and Haig's rehabilitation (ch. 12). For a more concise encapsulation, see Graham Keech, *Bullecourt*.
190. Bean, Diary, 3DRL606/75/1.
191. Letter, White to Bean, 13 December 1929, AWM 3DRL606/247/1.
192. Bean, *OH*, vol. IV, 285-286.
193. Bean, *OH*, vol. IV, 289-293.
194. Gallwey, Diary, AWM383DRL606/247/1.
195. Ibid.
196. War Diary, 4th Infantry Brigade, AWM23/4/19.
197. War Diary, 12th Infantry Brigade, AWM23/12/14.
198. Lt. Col. H. K. Denham, C.O., 46th Battalion AIF "Report re Operation of April 11th 1917," dated 19 April 1917, War Diary, 12th Infantry Brigade, AWM23/12/14, appendix 11.
199. Lt. Col. Raymond L. Leane, Commanding 48th Battalion, "Report on Operations of TANKS April 11th 1917," dated 19 April 1917, War Diary, 12th Infantry Brigade, AWM23/12/14, appendix 11.
200. Bean, *OH*, vol. IV, 351.
201. Spears, Prelude, 605.
202. Letter, Arnold (48th Bn) to Bean, 1 January 1922, AWM3DRL606/247/1.
203. Butler, *The Australian Army Medical Services in the War of 1914-1918* [the *Australian Official Medical History of the Great War*, hereafter, *AAMSOH*], vol. II, 156.
204. *AAMSOH*, vol. II, 145.
205. Johnson, narrative, AWM2DRL/537.
206. Keech, *Bullecourt*, 119.
207. Harris, 324-327.
208. Bean, *OH*, vol. IV, 541-545.
209. Harris, pp. 316-318.
210. *AAMSOH*, vol. II, 156.

Chapter 12:

211. Doughty, 354.
212. A detailed account of the French mutiny and its causes is found in Doughty, ch. 7.
213. See Doughty, ch. 8 for a full account of the subsequent strategy of "healing" for the rest of 1917.
214. For a concise account of Plumer see Peter Simkin's biography in Beckett and Corvi (eds) *Haig's Generals*, 141-163.
215. Travers, *The Killing Ground*, 203. See chapters 8 and 9 for a detailed analysis of how the British official history was written.
216. *BOH 1917*, vol. II. See p. xix for the acknowledgment of Bean's work. The differences in the interpretation of events are nevertheless considerable. Compare with Bean, *OH*, vol. IV.
217. Harris, 298-300.

218. Harris, ch. 13, provides a clear and detailed account of this period.
219. On the significance of this reshaping of the battlefield by natural means see Beckett, *The Making of the First World War*, 1-30.
220. Bean, *OH*, vol. IV, 556.
221. The British and Australian official histories include references to these mining operations. A very detailed and superbly illustrated account has been written by Barton et al., *Beneath Flanders Fields: the Tunnellers' War, 1914-1918*.
222. Oldham, *Ypres: Messines Ridge*, 56.
223. Harris, 342-343. In the *BOH 1917*, vol. II, Edmonds gives a higher shell total of 3,561,530.
224. Bean, *OH*, vol. IV, 557-558.
225. Oldham, 80.
226. See Oldham, p. 45 for a clear map and concise tabulations on each mine's start and completion dates, explosive capacity, depth, and gallery length.
227. Grieve's progress may be charted closely on British Ordnance Survey Trench Map 28. S. W. 4.
228. Grieve, *Personal Account*, AWM3DRL606/248/1.
229. Fisher, Diary, AWM3DRL606/248/1.
230. Fisher refers to the company being reduced to fifty-eight men. The normal establishment was between at least 100 to 150.
231. Dark, *Memoir*.
232. Neaves, *Memoir*, AWM2DRL/0752.
233. Bean, Diary, AWM3DRL606/81/1.
234. Turner, *Messines 1917: The Zenith of Siege Warfare*, 53. This book provides a clear and accessible account, accompanied with excellent illustrations and maps. The actions of the three participating Corps are covered.
235. *AAMSOH*, vol. II, 180.
236. Doughty, 148-151.
237. Beckett, *Great War*, 236.
238. For example, see Haythornthwaite, *The World War 1 Source Book*, 90-92. Also *AAMSOH*, vol. III, chapter 1.

Chapter 13:

239. See British historian Chris Baker's site *The Long, Long Trail: The British Army in the Great War, 1914-1918* for information on the sequence of the battles. It is recommended as a reliable source of information on those who fought and where and when, as well as some commentary on various aspects of the Western Front. It has an understandable British emphasis, but includes considerable reference to the Commonwealth forces. See www.1914-1918.net.
240. See Bean, *OH*, vol. IV and Edmonds, *BOH 1917*, vol. II.
241. These three phases are employed in *AAMSOH*, vol. II, 184-186.
242. Bean, *OH*, vol. IV, chs. XVIII, XIX, and XX.
243. *AAMSOH*, 184ff.
244. Haig, Diary, 298.
245. This period is perhaps more confusing because of its treatment in the official histories. Bean explains little. He has less to say because the Australians were not initially involved.
246. Bean, *OH*, vol. IV, 698-697.
247. Harris, ch. 14. In this lengthy chapter may be found a clear account of the politics of the preparation for Third Ypres and the subsequent outcomes.
248. Bean, *OH*, vol. IV, 683-695.
249. Haig, Diary, 307.
250. Rawlinson, Staff Paper, Cited in Bean, *OH*, vol. IV, 726.
251. Murdoch had lost to Bean to be the official correspondent, but had since established himself in London as the editor of the London cable service for the Melbourne *Sun* and *Herald* newspapers. He had been at Gallipoli and had acted as courier for a letter to the then British prime minister, Herbert Asquith, from another journalist, the Englishman Ellis Ashmead-Bartlett. Word had got out and Murdoch had been arrested at Marseilles while delivering the letter. These were matters of censorship. Bean, Ashmead-Bartlett, Gibbs, and Murdoch believed that the British High Command—whether on Gallipoli or on

the Western Front—was over-controlling. In France in July 1917, Bean had met up with Murdoch and Gibbs and effectively conspired to formally complain to the subsequent British prime minister Lloyd George about Gough, censorship, and a raft of other grievances. It was less a plot than a discontent. Gibbs initially urged Bean to see Lloyd George.

252. Letter, Bean to Lloyd George, 15 July 1917, AWM3DRL606/82/1.
253. Haig, Diary, 319.
254. The commencement of Third Ypres, the disproportionate losses incurred, the impact of the rain during August, and the return of Plumer to command of a vital section of the front are well covered in Prior and Wilson, *Passchendaele*, chs. 9 and 10. See also Bean, *OH*, vol. IV, 721-733.

Chapter 14:

255. *AAMSOH*, vol. II, 184.
256. Jones, Diary.
257. Ryder, Diary, AWM2DRL/48.
258. Lt. George Vaughan, *Report on Operations of 20/21st September, A Company. 12th Battalion*, in AWM3DRL606/249/1.
259. AWM3DRL606/249/1.
260. Edwards, *Memoir*, AWM3DRL606/249/1.
261. When a trench is dug, the spoil is mainly mounted to its front, the parapet. Spoil laid to the rear of a trench is the parados. The soil of both the parapet and the parados may be set in sandbags or simply thrown into a mound.
262. See Edmonds, *BOH*, 1917, vol. 2, 280, fn. 1.
263. The actions of the British are discussed in Edmonds, 1917, vol. 2, chapter XV. Those of the Australians are covered in usual minute detail in Bean, vol. IV, chapter XIX, especially 813-832. See also Prior and Wilson, *Passchendaele*, for their cast on events from an Australian perspective. Their criticism—not entirely unjustified —of Haig's command assumes unrelenting proportions. For an equally critical account of Haig's command employing more reasoned arguments, see Harris, *Haig*, 366-388.
264. Whinfield, Diary. "Machonicies" is a reference to Maconochies' tinned meat and vegetable stew, widely used as a standard ration on the Western Front.
265. For a valuable, counterbalancing insight into Australian attitudes toward authority, British responses to Australian soldiers, and the unsavory behavior of some in the AIF, see Peter Stanley, *Bad Characters: Sex, Crime, Mutiny and Murder and the Australian Imperial Force*.
266. Gullett to Tivey, *Unofficial Narrative Summary. Attack on Polygon Wood by 29th Bn. AIF on Sept. 26th, 1917*, AWM3DRL606/249/1.
267. NAA, Sidney Gullett, Service Records, NAB2455.
268. Ibid.
269. Kilgour, Diary, AWM2DRL/42.
270. Johnson, Diary, AWM2DRL/537.
271. Neaves, Diary, AWM2DRL/0752.
272. Cleary, Diary, AWM3DRL/2578 (File 419/20/6).
273. Johnson. Diary, AWM2DRL/537.
274. Gibson. Diary, AWMPR01354.
275. The letter is included in Gibson's Service Records at the National Archives.
276. A detailed account of how Haig came to these conclusions and won support for them in London is given in Prior and Wilson, *Passchendaele*, 138-155.

Chapter 15:

277. Harris. *Haig*, 379-382.
278. Edmonds, *BOH*, 1917, vol. 2, 323-337. Bean, *OH*, vol. IV chapter XXI. Bean's chapter heading makes the position clear, "The Plan Breaks Down. Passchcendaele I, October 9th." Bean's subsequent chapter XXII includes in its title "Passchendaele II." However, these are not intended as specific chapters dealing with the First and Second Passchendaele battles. It is in chapter XXII, pp. 902-909 that Bean includes the section "The conditions, October 5-12th."
279. Bean, *OH*, vol. IV, 902-906.

280. Ibid, 907.
281. Bean, *Folder*, AWM3DRL606/354/1.
282. Haig, Diary, 336-337. It seems extremely unlikely that not one of these people did not make some effort to temper Haig's obsession with the advance or counter his conviction that German morale was about to collapse. Prior and Wilson in *Passchendaele* insist they did not. This itself seems unlikely, given that Macdonogh did.
283. For a concise summary see Bean, *Anzac*, 368-373. The fullest in-depth analysis is in Bean, *OH*, vol. IV, chapters XX, XXI, and XXII. See also Edmonds, *BOH*, 1917, vol. 2, 303-319, then chapter XVII.
284. Bean, Diary, AWM3DRL606/89/1.
285. Bean, Diary, AWM3DRL606/89/1.
286. Neaves, Diary, AWM2DRL/0752.
287. Dark, *Memoir*.
288. Fisher, Diary, AWM3DRL606/254/1.
289. Bartley, Diary, AWM3DRL606/254/1.
290. Jones, Diary.
291. Bean, Diary, AWM3DRL606/91/1.
292. Cleary, Diary, AWM3DRL/2578.
293. Johnson, Diary, AWM2DRL/537.
294. Schwinghammer, Diary, AWM2DRL/234.
295. De Vine, Diary, AWM3DRL/606/250/1.
296. *AAMSOH*, vol. II, 243.
297. *AAMSOH*, vol. II, 232.
298. Bean, OH, vol. IV, 1-3.
299. *From the Australian Front: Christmas 1917*.
300. For an account of these matters see Stanley.
301. Simkins et al., *The First World War*, 137-139.
302. Harris, *Haig*, 418.
303. Middlebrook, *The Kaiser's Battle*, ch. 1.
304. For a detailed account of this period, see Harris, *Haig*, 409-437.
305. Bean, *OH*, 60-61.
306. Gibbs, *Realities of War*, 403. As well as being one of five British official war correspondents on the Western Front, Philip Gibbs also wrote several accounts in book form after the war. In these he sought redress for the heavy censorship imposed on the press. His *Realities of War*, published in 1920, is an early (if not the first) critical assessment of the British GHQ and Haig. More criticism was to come in a subsequent book, *Now It Can Be Told*, also published in 1920.

Chapter 17:

307. For a concise account of *Kaiserschlacht*, see Gray, *Kaiserschlacht 1918: The Final German Offensive*. See p. 35 for the gas casualties figure.
308. The source for these often-quoted figures is Middlebrook's *The Kaiser's Battle: 21 March 1918: the First Day of the German Spring Offensive*. Although dealing primarily with the first day, this remarkably detailed work includes a lengthy analysis of the aftermath. See especially chapters 13 and 14. See pp. 308-309 for the figures for areas taken and p. 322 for the summation of casualties.
309. Bean, *Anzac*, 404.
310. Pederson, 289.
311. Bean, *Anzac to Amiens*, 427. For the most detailed account of the actions of the 1st Division in the north see Bean, *OH*, chapter XI.
312. Kilgour, Diary.
313. De Vine, Diary, AWM3DRL/606/250/1.
314. Bean, *Historical Note*, AWM3DRL606/252/1.
315. Sandilands, Diary, AWM PRO1350.
316. Whinfield, Diary.
317. Ridley, Letter, undated. Extracted from *Resumé of Experiences on the Western Front from February 1918 to September 1918*, AWM3DRL606/273/1.
318. Neaves, Diary, AWM2DRL/0752.
319. Bartley, Diary, AWM3DRL606/273/1.
320. Pederson, 327.
321. Pederson, 305-309, 328-330. Bean, *OH*, vol. VI, chapter X. Harris, 455-467, 473-476.
322. Letter, Keeley to Bean, 24 June 1935, AWM3DRL606/273/1.
323. Letter, Steadman to Bean, 18 June 1935, AWM3DRL606/273/1.
324. Letter, Mulqueeny to Bean, 23 June 1935, AWM3DRL606/273/1. Mulqueeny died

a few months after writing this letter.
325. Letter, Nicholas to Bean, n. d. circa June 1935, AWM3DRL606/273/1.
326. Letter, Turner to Bean, 17 August 1927, AWM3DRL606/273/1.
327. *OCAMH*, 237.
328. *AAMSOH*, vol. III, 912.

Chapter 18:
329. Pederson, 379.
330. Bean, Diary, AWM3DRL606/116/1.
331. Pederson, 366.
332. Bean, Diary, AWM3DRL606/116/1.
333. Kilgour, Diary, AWM2DRL/42.
334. Elms, Diary.
335. Turner, Diary, AWM3DRL606/273/1.
336. Whinfield, Diary.
337. Neaves, Diary, AWM2DRL/0752.
338. See the Australian War Memorial literature and their website http://www.awm.gov.au.
339. Bean, *OH*, vol. VI.
340. Edmonds, *BOH*, *Military Operations: France and Belgium, 1918*. Volume IV.
341. The figures are drawn from Pederson, 383. For a concise and clear account of the whole battle and all its participants, see McCluskey, *Amiens 1918: the Black Day of the German Army*.
342. Rose, Memoir, AWMMSS1128.
343. *Australian Dictionary of Biography*, vol. 10.
344. Letter, White to Bean, 27 June 1935, AWM3DRL606/253/1.
345. Cleary, Diary, AWM3DRL2578.
346. Rose, Diary.
347. Pederson, 487.
348. Kilgour, Diary, AWM2DRL/42.
349. Cleary, Diary, AWM3DRL2578.
350. *AASMOH*, vol. III, 912.

Chapter 19:
351. Schama, *The Embarrassment of Riches: an Interpretation of Dutch Culture in the Golden Age*, xiii.
352. *AAMSOH*, vol. III, 900, Table no. 30.
353. *AAMSOH*, vol. III, 900.
354. Ibid., 909, Table no. 38.
355. Ibid., 912.

Bibliography

Archives

Australian War Memorial, Canberra

War Diaries

Corps

AWM4 Sub-class 1/29 – General Staff, Headquarters, 1st Anzac Corps

AWM Sub-class 1/32 – General Staff, Headquarters, 2nd Anzac Corps

Brigade

AWM Sub-class 23/1 – 1st Infantry Brigade

AWM Sub-class 23/3 – 3rd Infantry Brigade

AWM Sub-class 23/4 – 4th Infantry Brigade

AWM Sub-class 23/12 – 12th Infantry Brigade

Battalion

AWM Sub-class 23/19 – 2nd Infantry Battalion

AWM Sub-class 23/20 – 3rd Infantry Battalion

AWM Sub-class 23/31 – 14th Infantry Battalion

AWM Sub-class 23/37 – 20th Infantry Battalion

AWM Sub-class 23/41 – 24th Infantry Battalion

AWM Sub-class 23/48 – 31st Infantry Battalion

AWM Sub-class 23/54 – 37th Infantry Battalion

AWM Sub-class 23/59 – 42nd Infantry Battalion

AWM Sub-class 23/62 – 45th Infantry Battalion

AWM Sub-class 23/63 – 46th Infantry Battalion

AWM Sub-class 23/65 – 48th Infantry Battalion

AWM Sub-class 23/71 – 54th Infantry Battalion

AWM Sub-class 23/72 – 55th Infantry Battalion

Records of C.E.W. Bean

Diaries

AWM38 3DRL606/52/1 – July 1916

AWM383DRL606/54/1 – July-August 1916

AWM383DRL606/55/1 – August 1916

AWM383DRL606/56/1 – August 1916

AWM383DRL606/57/1 – August-September 1916

AWM383DRL606/58/1 – September 1916

AWM383DRL606/72/1 – February-March 1917

AWM383DRL606/75/1 – March-April 1917

AWM383DRL606/77/1 – April-May 1917

AWM383DRL606/81/1 – June 1917

AWM383DRL606/82/1 – July 1917

AWM383DRL606/83/1 – July-August 1917

AWM383DRL606/84/1 – August 1917

AWM383DRL606/89/1 – September-October 1917

AWM383DRL606/91/1 – October 1917

AWM383DRL606/92/1 – October-November 1917

AWM383DRL606/93/1 – November 1917

AWM383DRL606/116/1 – June-September 1918

Folders

AWM38 3DRL606/237/1 – October 1914-1918
AWM38 3DRL606/243A/1 – 1916-1934
AWM38 3DRL606/244/1 – 1916-1933
AWM38 3DRL606/245/1 – 1915-1925
AWM38 3DRL606/246/1 – 1916-1929
AWM38 3DRL606/247/1 – 1917-1933
AWM38 3DRL606/248/1 – 1917-1931
AWM38 3DRL606/249/1 – 1917-1932
AWM38 3DRL606/250/1 – 1917-1937
AWM38 3DRL606/252/1 – 1918-1935
AWM38 3DRL606/254/1 – 1917-1933
AWM38 3DRL606/260/1 – 1916-1930
AWM38 3DRL606/271/1 – 1917-1938
AWM38 3DRL606/272/1 – 1917-1932
AWM38 3DRL606/273/1 – 1918-1937
AWM38 3DRL606/274/1 – 1918-1941

Notebooks

AWM38 3DRL606/165/1 – May-September 1917
AWM38 3DRL606/169/1 – September-October 1917
AWM38 3DRL606/178/1 – 1915-1917
Various photographs.

National Archives of Australia

Various individual service records.

State Library of Victoria, Melbourne

Various diaries.
Census of the Commonwealth of Australia, 1911.

Michell Library, Sydney

Dark. *Memoir*. Mitchell Library. Manuscript Section. State Library of New South Wales. Dark Papers, MLMSS5049, Item 1, Box 1 (1).

Royal Australian Air Force Museum, Point Cook

Diary of Henry Hammond.
Various photographs

Websites

http://www.awm.gov.au
http://www.1914-1918.net
http://www.adb.anu.edu/biography
http://www.dfat.gov.au/aib/history

Official Histories

Bean, C.E.W. *Official History of Australia in the War, 1914-1918* (Sydney: Angus and Robertson, 2nd ed., revised, 12 vols.,1937).

Edmonds, James E. *History of the Great War: Military Operations: France and Belgium* (London, Imperial War Museum: 13 vols., 1938).

Official Publications

Bean, C.E.W. *Anzac to Amiens: A Shorter History of the Australian Fighting Services in the First World War* (Canberra: Australian War Memorial, 1948).

From the Australian Front, Christmas 1917 (London, Cassell: 1917).

Unpublished Firsthand Accounts, Letters, Diaries, and Memoirs

Banks, William
Cleary, Thomas
Dark, Eric
De Vine, Apcar
Donnan, Sidney
Elms, George
Gibson, Donald
Hammond, Henry
James, William
Johnson, Leicester
Jones, Leonard

Kilgour, Arthur
Neaves, Henry
Newton, Leslie
Rose, Geoffrey
Ryder, William
Sandilands, Christopher
Schwinghammer, Verdi
Swanton, George
Wagstaff, Percy
Whinfield, David

Published Firsthand Accounts, Diaries and Memoirs

Johnson, Carl and Andrews Barnes. *Jacka's Mob: A Narrative of the Great War by John Edgar Rule* (Prahran: Military Melbourne: 1999). First published as Edgar Rule. *Jacka's Mob,* Sydney: Angus and Robertson: 1933

Williams, Harold R. *An ANZAC on the Western Front: The Personal Reflections of an Australian Infantryman from 1916 to 1918* (Barnsley: Pen and Sword, 2012) First published as *The Gallant Company: An Australian Soldier's Story of 1915-18*, Sydney, Angus and Robertson: 1933.

Young, Margaret, and Bill Gammage (eds). *Hail and Farewell: Letters from Two Brothers Killed in France in 1916, Alec and Goldy Raws* (Kenthurst: Kangaroo Press, 1995)

Published Works

Afflerbach, Holger, "Planning Total War? Falkenhayn and the Battle of Verdun, 1916" in Roger Chickering and Stig Förster (eds), *Great War, Total War; Combat and Mobilisation on the Western Front, 1914-1918* (Cambridge, Cambridge University Press: 2000) pp. 113-131, esp. p. 122.

Andrews, E.M., *The Anzac Illusion: Anglo-Australian Relations during World War I* (Cambridge, Cambridge University Press: 1993)

Badsey, Stephen, *The Franco-Prussian War: 1870-1871* (Oxford: Osprey, 2003)

Ball, Martin, "Re-Reading Bean's Last Paragraph," *Australian Historical Studies*, vol. 122, 2003, pp. 231-247.

Banks, Arthur, *A Military Atlas of the First World War* (Barnsley, Leo Cooper: 1997)

Barton, Peter, Peter Doyle, and John Vandewalle. *Beneath Flanders Fields: The Tunnellers' War, 1914-1918* (Montreal, McGill-Queen's University Press: 2004)

Barton, Peter, *The Somme: A New Panoramic Perspective* (London, Constable: 2006)

Barton, Peter, *Passchendaele: Unseen Panoramas of the Third Battle of Ypres* (London, Constable: 2007)

Barton, Peter, with Jeremy Banning, *The Battlefields of the First World War: The Unseen Panoramas of the Western Front* (London, Constable: 2008)

Barton, Peter, with Jeremy Banning, *Arras: The Spring 1917 Offensive in Panoramas including Vimy Ridge and Bullecourt* (London, Constable: 2010)

Beaumont, Joan, *Australia's War: 1914-18* (St Leonards, Allen and Unwin: 1995)

Beckett, Ian F.W., *The Great War 1914-1918* (Harlow, Pearson: 2001)

Beckett, Ian F.W., *Ypres: The First Battle, 1914* (Harlow: Pearson, 2004)

Beckett, Ian F.W., and Steven J. Corvi (eds), *Haig's Generals* (Barnsley, Pen and Sword: 2006)

Beckett, Ian F.W., *The Making of the First World War* (New Haven, Yale University Press: 2012)

Boff, Jonathan, *Winning and Losing on the Western Front: The British Third Army and the Defeat of Germany in 1918* (Cambridge, Cambridge University Press: 2012)

Bond, Brian ed., *'Look to Your Front': Studies in the First World War by the*

Commission for Military History (Staplehurst, Spellmount: 1999)
Bridger, Geoff, *The Great War Handbook: A Guide for Family Historians and Students of the Conflict* (Barnsley, Pen and Sword: 2009)
Brown, Malcolm, *The Somme* (London, Pan Macmillan: 2002)
Carlyon, Les, *The Great War* (Sydney, Macmillan: 2006)
Charlton, Peter, *Pozieres: Australians on the Somme, 1916* (London, Leo Cooper: 1986)
Chickering, Roger, and Stig Föster, *Great War, Total War: Combat and Nobilisation on the Western Front: 1914-1918* (Cambridge, Cambridge University Press: 2000)
Doughty, Robert A., *Pyrrhic Victory: French Strategy and Operations in the Great War* (Cambridge, Harvard University Press: 2005)
Duffy, Christopher, *Through German Eyes: The British and the Somme, 1916* (Weidenfeld and Nicolson, London: 2006)
Fleming, Robert, *The Australian Army in World War I* (Oxford: Osprey, 2012)
Fussell, Paul, *The Great War and Modern Memory: The Illustrated Edition* (Sterling, New York: 2009. First published 1974)
Gammage, Bill, *The Broken Years: Australian Soldiers in the Great War* (Carlton: Melbourne University Press, 2010)
Gerster, Robert, and Peter Pierce (eds.), *On the Warpath: An Anthology of Australian Military Travel* (Melbourne: Melbourne University Press: 2004)
Gibbs, Philip, *The Battles of the Somme* (Toronto, McClelland, Goodchild, and Stewart: 1917)
Gibbs, Philip, *Realities of War* (London, Heinemann: 1920)
Gibbs, Philip, *Now It Can Be Told* (New York, Harper and Brothers: 1920)
Gliddon, Gerald, *Somme, 1916: A Battlefield Companion* (Phoenix Mill, Sutton: 2006)
Gray, Randal, *Kaiserschlacht 1918: The Final German Offensive* (Oxford, Osprey: 1991)
Greenhalgh, Elizabeth, "Why the British were on the Somme in 1916," *War and History*, vol. 6, no. 2, 1999, pp. 147-173.
Greenhalgh, Elizabeth, "Flames Over the Somme: a Retort to William Philpott," *War and History*, vol. 10, no. 3, 2002, pp. 335-342.
Greenhalgh, Elizabeth, *Victory through Coalition: Britain and France during the First World War* (Cambridge, Cambridge University Press: 2005)
Harris, J.P., *Douglas Haig and the First World War* (Cambridge, Cambridge University Press: 2008)
Haythornthwaite, Philip J., *Gallipoli 1915: Frontal Assault on Turkey* (Oxford: Osprey, 1991)
Haythornthwaite, Philip J., *The World War One Source Book* (London, Cassell: 1996)
Horne, John, and Alan Kramer, "War Between Soldiers and Enemy Civilians" in Roger Chickering and Stig Förster (eds). *Great War, Total War; Combat and Mobilisation on the Western Front, 1914-1918* (Cambridge, Cambridge University Press: 2000) pp. 153-168.
Hull, Isabel V., *Absolute Destruction: Military Culture and the Practices of War in Imperial Germany* (Ithaca: Cornell University Press, 2005)
Keech, Graham, *Pozières* (Barnsley, Leo Cooper: 1998)
Keech, Graham, *Bullecourt* (Barnsley, Leo Cooper: 1999)
Lee, Christopher, "Greeks and Moderns: the Search for Culture in the *Official*

History of Australia in the War of 1914-1918," *Australian Literary Studies*, vol. 23, 2007, pp. 106-120.

Lomas, David, *First Ypres: The Graveyard of the Old Contemptibles* (Oxford: Osprey, 1994)

Londey, Peter, "A Possession for Ever: Charles Bean, the Ancient Greeks and Military Commemoration in Australia," *Australian Journal of Politics and History*, vol.53, 2007, pp. 344-359.

Macdonald, Lyn, *Somme*. (London, Michael Joseph: 1983)

MacDonald, Lyn, *1914* (London, Michael Joseph: 1987)

MacMillan, Margaret, *Paris 1919: Six Months that Changed the World* (New York, Random House: 2002)

McCluskey, Alistair, *Amiens 1918: The Black Day of the German Army* (Oxford, Osprey: 2008)

Middlebrook, Martin, *The Kaiser's Battle. 21 March 1918: The First Day of the German Spring Offensive* (London, Penguin: 1983)

Muller, Julius W. ed., *Two thousand Questions and Answers About the War* (New York, The Review of Reviews Company: 1918)

Neillands, Robin, *Attrition: The Great War on the Western Front, 1916* (London, Robson: 2001)

Neillands, Robin, *The Death of Glory: the Western Front, 1915* [hereafter, *1915*] (Great Britain, John Murray: 2006)

Nicolson, Colin, *The First World War: Europe, 1914-1918* (London: Pearson, 2001)

Oldham, Peter, *Messines Ridge* (Barnsley, Pen and Sword: 2012)

Pederson, Peter, *Anzacs on the Western Front* (Milton, John Wiley and Sons: 2012)

Philpott, William, "Why the British were Really on the Somme, a Reply to Elizabeth Greenhalgh," *War and History*, vol. 6, no. 2, 1999, pp. 147-173.

Philpott, William, *Bloody Victory: The Sacrifice on the Somme and the Making of the Twentieth Century* (London, Little, Brown: 2009)

Prior, Robin, and Trevor Wilson, *Passchendaeke: The Untold Story* (New Haven, Yale University Press: 1996)

Prior, Robin, and Trevor Wilson, *The Somme* (New Haven, Yale University Press: 2005)

Schama, Simon, *The Embarrassment of Riches: An Interpretation of Dutch Culture in the Golden Age* (New York, Random House: 1987)

Sheffield, Garry, *The Somme* (London, Cassell: 2003)

Sheffield, Gary, and John Bourne (eds.), *Douglas Haig: War Diaries and Letters, 1914-1918* (London, Weidenfeld and Nicolson: 2005)

Sheldon, Jack, *The German Army on the Somme, 1914-1916* (Barnsley, Pen and Sword: 2007)

Simkins, Peter, Geoffrey Jukes, and Michael Hickey, *The First World War: The War to end All Wars* (Oxford: Osprey Publishing, 2003)

Spears, Edward, *Liaison 1914: A Narrative of the Great Retreat* (New York: Stein and Day, 1968. First published 1930)

Spears, Edwaed, *Prelude to Victory* London, Jonathan Cape: 1939)

Stanley, Peter, *Bad Characters: Sex, Crime, Mutiny, Murder and the Australian Imperial Force* (Millers Point: Murdoch Books: 2010)

Strong, Paul, and Sanders Marble, *Artillery in the Great War* (Barnsley, Pen and Sword: 2011)

Travers, Tim, *The Killing Ground: The British Army, The Western Front and the Emergence of Modern War, 1900-1918* (Barnsley, Pen and Sword: 2009. First published 1987)

Travers, Tim, *How the War Was Won: Command and Technology in the British Army on the Western Front, 1917-1918* (London, Routledge: 1992)

Tuchman, Barbara W., *The Proud Tower: A Portrait of the World Before the War, 1890-1914* (New York, Ballantine: nd. First published by Macmillan, 1966)

Turner, Alexander, *Messines 1917: The Zenith of Siege Warfare* (Oxford, Osprey: 2010)

Tuchman, Barbara, *August 1914* (London: Pan Macmillan, 1994)

Tyng, Sewell, *The Campaign of the Marne,1914* (Yardley: Westholme Publishing, 2007. First published 1935)

Young, Margaret, and Bill Gammage (eds.), *Hail and Farewell: Letters from Two Brothers Killed in France in 1916* (Kenthurst, Kangaroo Press: 1995)

Index

Mouquet Fm
Ovillers Courcelette Rd
To Bapaume
Windmill
Neuer Ganter Weg
Gierich Weg
Ganter Weg
Tom's Cut
Cemetery
Lines
O.
G.
Trench
Pozières
Valley
To Ovillers